MARKETS, CHOICE AND EQUITY IN EDUCATION

Sharon Gewirtz, Stephen J. Ball
and Richard Bowe

Open University Press
Buckingham · Philadelphia

Open University Press
Celtic Court
22 Ballmoor
Buckingham
MK18 1XW

and

1900 Frost Road, Suite 101
Bristol, PA 19007, USA

First Published 1995

A catalogue record of this book is available from the British Library

ISBN   0 335 19369 2 (pb)   0 335 19370 6 (hb)

Library of Congress Cataloging-in-Publication Data
  Gewirtz, Sharon, 1964–
    Markets, choice, and equity in education/by Sharon Gewirtz, Stephen J.
  Ball, and Richard Bowe.
       p.   cm.
    Includes bibliographical references and index.
    ISBN 0-335-19370-6 (hb). – ISBN 0-335-19369-2 (pb)
    1. School choice – Great Britain – Case studies.   2. Education – Great
  Britain – Marketing – Case studies.   3. Education – Economic aspects –
  Great Britain – Case studies.   4. Politics and education – Great Britain – Case
  studies.   I. Ball. Stephen J.   II. Bowe, Richard.   III. Title.
  LB1027.9.G48   1995
  371'.01–dc20   95-14758
                                                                CIP

Typeset by Type Study, Scarborough
Printed and bound in Great Britain by
Biddles Ltd, Guildford and King's Lynn

Ed 97/2   14.99

MARKETS, CHOICE AND EQUITY
IN EDUCATION

CONTENTS

LIST OF TABLES

ACKNOWLEDGEMENTS

The research upon which this book is based was funded by the ESRC (award no. 232858). The conduct of the fieldwork, the analysis of the data and the development and writing up of our analysis have variously relied upon and benefited from the cooperation, support, critical insights, comments and hard work of a number of people. Those people in our case-study schools and LEAs who were so helpful (except for 'Mr Grumpy') and the parents who gave time for interviews cannot be named for obvious reasons but we are keenly aware of our debts to them and in the case of the schools at least we hope that our various attempts at feeding back our analysis have been useful. Others can be named: we are grateful to Liz Cawdron for her high quality transcription of tapes, to Rachel Darby for help with interviewing, to Julie Maguire for transferring postcode data onto disks, to Alan Edis for his patient work with census and postcode data, to BSc Students Chitra DaSilva and Sophia Graves who were attached to the project and interviewed parents, and to Julie Pearce for secretarial support. Our thinking about the research has been stimulated and supported by colleagues at King's and in the Parental Choice and Market Forces Seminars. In particular, we want to mention Christine Barry, Jo Boaler, Jane Broadbent, Stephen Crump, Roger Dale, Miriam David, Chiz Dubé, Tony Edwards, John Fitz, Deborah Gewirtz, Flynn Gewirtz-O'Reilly, Caroline Gill, David Halpin, Hans Knip, Hugh Lauder, Meg Maguire, Richard McLaughlin, Sally Power, David Squires' computer, Carrie Supple, Rien van der Vegt, Carole Vincent, Tony Warnes, Anne West, Geoff Whitty and Dylan Wiliam. We are especially grateful to Alan Cribb for his encouragement and wisdom.

RESEARCHING EDUCATION MARKETS

Introduction

The market solution (to just about anything) currently holds politicians around the world in its thrall. We should not be surprised by this, for the market provides politicians with all the benefits of being seen to act decisively and very few of the problems of being blamed when things go wrong – because, so the theory goes, the market is a mechanism which produces its own order. Responsibility is devolved to the individual consumer and the aggregate of consumer choices provides the discipline, of accountability and demand, that the producer cannot escape. The energetic and careful are rewarded and the slothful and ignorant are punished. If things go wrong, then misguided consumers or tardy producers are to blame, not politicians. The market appears to be a hands-off policy. If we have faith in the market and its order, we also know (that is, are supposed to believe) that things will turn out all right in the end, even if there is a degree of creative destruction along the way. The forces of the market will out, the good will survive, the weak will go to the wall, and everyone will be better off than before (if not equally well off – an absence of inequality in the marketplace means an absence of striving and competition).

Schools in England[1] are now set within the whole paraphernalia of a market system, albeit a market which is strongly politically regulated – a planned (Saltman and von Otter, 1992) or quasi-market (Le Grand and Bartlett, 1993). The framework of market discipline is set by parental choice, open enrolment, devolved budgets and formula funding. School budgets are now overwhelmingly determined by student numbers. This framework was established by the provisions of the Education Reform Act 1988[2] and given reinforcement by the 1993 Act. Open enrolment was a commitment in the Conservative Party's 1987 General Election manifesto, which spelled out the basic political thinking behind the idea of an education market.

> Schools will be required to enrol up to the school's agreed physical capacity instead of artificially restricting pupil numbers, as can happen today. Popular schools, which have earned parental support by offering good education, will then be able to expand beyond present physical numbers. These steps will compel schools to respond to the views of parents.

The education market (like all markets) is intended to be driven by self-interest: first, the self-interest of parents, as consumers, choosing schools that will provide maximum advantage to their children; second, the self interest of schools or their senior managers, as producers, in making policy decisions that are based upon ensuring that their institutions thrive, or at least survive, in the marketplace. The demand for school places is inelastic, that is, the number of potential students is fixed. Where there are surplus school places, the result is meant to be competition, emulation and rivalry: survival can only be ensured by attracting consumers away from other schools.

The development and adoption of the market solution to 'problems' of cost, control and performance in public-sector areas of collective consumption by the Conservative Party draws upon a number of specific sources and influences both theoretical and political (see Ball, 1990, for a full discussion). The market solution represents a paradigm shift in the *economics* of education policy and indeed of social policy generally. It also carries with it a weighty *political* agenda: first, the deconstruction of the principles of collective responsibility embedded, however weakly, in the welfare state after the Second World War; second, the replacement of professional control with managerial control; and third, the diminution of the roles and powers of the local state and the concomitant diminution of local democracy. Since the passing of the 1988 Act, the local provision of educational services is no longer meant to be planned in relation to 'need' by local education authorities (LEAs) but is left to family choices and management decision-making. These are the bases of the 'natural' order, the 'hidden hand' of market forces, although in practice the school market is not entirely unplanned nor entirely natural. It is focused, framed and influenced by the political objectives of the Conservative Government. The Government retains control of, and imposes, a system of performance indicators upon the education market, through, for example, national tests and the publication of league tables. These are intended to provide the system of information and knowledge which is so important in any market, in allowing consumers to make the 'best' choices. But they also orient the provision of education towards certain goals and purposes.

Aims and scope of this book

The new framework for schooling outlined above is the background to, and focus of, the study reported here. Whilst the 1988 Act and ensuing legislation has spawned a fair amount of research activity, much of this has been conducted at a fairly abstract and theoretical level. Most of the empirical research is piecemeal and tends to be very specifically focused, either on particular actors in the market, such as parents (e.g. (David *et al.*, 1994) and governors (Deem *et al.*, 1994), or on particular elements of the market mechanism, for example, local management (Levačić, 1992), grant-maintained (GM) schools (Fitz *et al.*, 1993) and City Technology Colleges (CTCs) (Whitty *et al.*, 1993), or on the market's implications for particular constituencies, for instance ethnic minorities (Troyna *et al.*, 1993) and children with special needs (Lee, 1992; Vincent *et al.*, 1993). Other work has looked at the relationship between parental choice and school 'responsiveness' (e.g. Woods, 1993). Yet another body of research has looked at the impact of parental choice on the distribution of educational resources (e.g. Adler *et al.*,. 1989; Willms and Echols, 1992). On the whole, studies which are of direct relevance to the analysis of the education market tend to be focused on *either* parental choice, *or* school responses, *or* the distributional outcomes of choice and competition. Table 1.1 offers a simple overview of the differences in focus, methods and analysis in each case. The design and aim of our study is founded upon the linking together of these three elements of the market. Only by relating choice, response and distributional outcomes together in particular local market settings will be it begin to be possible to understand, evaluate and theorize the education market as a social, economic and political phenomenon. We present a set of concepts and analytical frameworks which, we believe, provide some useful starting points for a theory of education markets.

It is our basic contention that there is no one general education market in operation in England. Education markets are localized and need to be analysed and understood in terms of a set of complex dynamics which mediate and contextualize the impact and effects of the Government's policy. These dynamics can be identified and one of our concerns is to

Table 1.1   Research in the education marketplace

	Choice	*Response*	*Distribution*
Focus	Listing of parents' criteria	School strategies in the marketplace	Who 'chooses' and the impact of choice on school recruitment patterns
Methods	Questionnaires and structured interviews	Questionnaires, interviews, and case studies	Statistical analysis of 'choice-making', appeals, etc. and recruitment profiles
Analysis	Artefactual empiricism	Descriptive empiricism	Social arithmetic

articulate a model for the analysis of local markets. Also, importantly, we argue that certain general trends, patterns and changes are evident across local markets (where there is competition between schools) – in particular, trends related to school organization and provision, and patterns of advantage and disadvantage, as related to social class.

In part, we intend to contribute to a better understanding of the market solution as a *global* phenomenon. It is increasingly commonplace in the sociology of education in the UK to observe similar market-oriented shifts in educational and social policy in other countries. For the most part, attempts to make sense of such policy initiatives are focused upon the nation as the key unit of interest. Thus, 'explanations' for the growth of market-orientated welfare provision are strongly informed by the identification of similar characteristics within nation-states (Dale, 1994) (for example, the rise of the New Right, the crisis of the fiscal state, the pressures of demographic change – a growing elderly/dependent population – or the introduction of new production and management techniques) and/or a sharing of policy initiatives between states (Halpin and Troyna 1995). Nonetheless, as Dale and Ozga (1993) have pointed out, there are considerable differences in how governments have used the market form. This applies both to the extent of the use of the market form, the purposes it is intended to serve and the precise market mechanisms that governments put into place via legislation (Bowe, 1995). There are also differences and similarities in the ways in which markets have been established in different areas of social policy. In England, for example, health, community care and social services, housing and the criminal justice system are all being restructured alongside education. All these examples involve the replacement of near monopolistic forms of generic state provision with competitive individual ones: they all involve the devolution of budgets to the level of institutional provision (hospitals, GP surgeries, schools, social service departments, housing associations etc.); they all involve the insertion of the social psychology and culture of competition into the daily practice of service delivery; and virtually all have been accompanied by the advocacy of, or requirement for, techniques of entrepreneurial management. However, the market structures and mechanisms are in each case very different (Saltman and von Otter, 1992; Le Grand and Bartlett, 1993). In particular, none of these other social markets allows for quite the same degree of direct consumer choice as do the parental choice provisions of the Education Reform Act 1988. The information systems, transaction costs and pseudo-price mechanisms are very different in each case. Furthermore, there are a whole range of intricate variations in the operation of markets within and across nation-states that reflect the struggles and negotiations people make as they live and work around and within 'lived markets'. An understanding of how public-sector markets work involves devoting careful attention to the similarities and differences within and between markets and within and between nation-states. Here we aim, in part, at facilitating such an analysis by providing a detailed account of the workings and effects of three overlapping local education markets in one English city – London. A similar position to our own is adopted by Lauder *et al.* (1994) who, using a mix of qualitative and quantitative methods, are researching a 'lived market' in Greencity, New Zealand. They have argued that (1994: 1):

> markets need to be studied in context because the outcomes generated by educational markets will be determined by both the formal properties of the market and informal arrangements within that market. Formal properties of a market are typically established by legislation. Informal arrangements within a market are created by the actors, in this case especially schools, who seek to change or modify the nature of the competition which confronts them.

Analysis of the interaction between the formal and informal properties of markets in specific local contexts is essential if we are to identify and begin to make sense of global commonalities *and* variations in the operation and effects of public-sector markets.

Demand, supply and distribution

Three interrelated points of focus will be discussed. The first concerns the so-called demand side of the market relation (the consumers), the second the supply side (the producers) and the third the implications of markets for patterns of distribution of educational opportunity.

The consumers

In Chapter 2 we will consider how families, and more specifically parents, engage with the market and how they make their choices. Our methodological and analytical approach to parental choice of school is based, in part, upon a dissatisfaction with the existing research. We have argued elsewhere (Bowe *et al.*, 1994) that a great deal of the early research on parental choice is 'captured by the discourse' of the market (for example, Boulton and Coldron, 1989; Hunter, 1989; Coldron and Boulton, 1991; Thomas and Dennison, 1991; West and Varlaam, 1991). That is, the concerns, methods of data collection, techniques of analysis and representation of conclusions in this research are sociologically and politically naive. Briefly, the research shows a central interest in either how far a market-led system will actually result in parental choice being 'driven' by examination results (which some Conservative politicians believe will result in a raising of standards) or they aim to help schools to market themselves or become more responsive to parents' interests. Thus, the researchers concentrate upon identifying parents' different 'reasons for choice' and their respective importance or priority. This single-mindedness in locating factors of choice and listing their importance in effect organizes the possibilities of response from parents. The research outcomes are an artefact of technique. What might be termed the 'factor/list approach' actually imposes an *a priori* view of the nature of choice upon the research setting and other possible accounts of the process of choice are excluded. The empirical emphasis is exclusively on the content rather than the processes of choice. Nonetheless, a view of process is implicit. The view that factors and reasons form the basis for human behaviour bears a strong resemblance to the assumptions that underlie economists' abstract accounts of market behaviour (especially the individual rational calculus of classical economics). These are assumptions which also informed the Government's thinking in relation to the 1988 Act: that is, that 'responsible' choosers will undertake a rational, logical approach, listing factors in a hierarchical fashion to derive criteria for choice which can then be set against a sample of schools. The factor/list approach fails to capture the messy, multidimensional, intuitive and seemingly irrational or non-rational elements of choice. Matters of compromise, mind-changing and vicissitude are replaced by simple certainties. The approach also rests on the assumption that each factor of choice is discrete and unambiguous (for both the researcher and the researched). However, 'reasons' such as examination results, discipline, uniform and the child's happiness are ambiguous. Their precise meaning is contextually specific but most of the research to date has failed to recognize this. Most worryingly, the adding up of individual responses to make a list of typical responses, lifts individuals out of their everyday lives, their routines, their concerns and loses the particularities of the way in which they construct the activity of choice-making within their own social milieu. The resultant listings, emerging from the process of analysis, are in fact researchers' reconstructions and recontextualizations of 'the parent'; they represent aggregated versions of the parent. Social patterns and discontinuities in choosing are obscured. Choice is thus desocialized and depoliticized. (For a more detailed discussion of these issues, see Bowe *et al.*, 1994.)

Our intention is to move decisively away from these techniques and attempt to escape from, and address, the ideology of choice, thereby 'unleashing critique' (Thomas, 1991). In our analysis of parental choice in Chapter 2 we will take the 'mundane' processes of school choice to be part of a larger canvas of contemporary politics and explore the extent to which choice interrupts or exacerbates established patterns of inequity in education. A second type of parental choice research has already started to do this. Work done in Scotland (Adler *et al.* 1989; Echols *et al.*, 1990; Willms and Echols, 1992; Echols and Willms, 1993), in England (Edwards *et al.*, 1989; Woods, 1992), and in the USA by Moore and Davenport (1990) has begun to point to some relationships between choice-making and social class. Although more sociologically sensitive than the first body of work, these latter studies offer little more than some general indications of the implication of social class in patterns of choice and opportunity. They are descriptive and speculative rather than explanatory and tend to be theoretically bland. In various ways, these studies gesture towards the significance of cultural resources or 'educational inheritance', as ways of understanding class differences. However, these gestures remain weakly articulated and poorly grounded in research data. Lareau (1989: 179) makes a crucial point about the use of such arguments.

> Demonstrating that people possess highly valued cultural resources is only part of the story. It fails to reveal which cultural resources individuals use when and with what effect or, put differently, how cultural resources are transformed into cultural capital. What is needed is a more contextually based analysis of the stages of cultural transformation in the educational process.

We suggest that the analysis of choice of school provides one critical point where cultural resources are 'cashed in', and we will attempt in Chapter 2 to begin to do just what Lareau suggests: to examine how, in the specific case of school choice, cultural resources are used and with what effects.

The producers

Our second point of focus is on the supply side of the market relation. Here we are concerned to understand how both LEAs and schools are responding to the market framework established by the 1988 Act. Chapter 3 describes the three local markets which provide the empirical focus of our study, exploring the nature of competitive relationships in the three authorities and the market 'situations' of particular schools. We isolate factors within 'lived markets' – such as LEA policies, local histories and social geographies – and demonstrate how they combine in particular ways to mediate and distort the disciplinary framework established by legislation.

Chapters 4, 5 and 6 explore the impact of the market on the culture and values of schooling through an analysis of management roles and styles (Chapter 4), school semiologies (Chapter 5) and internal practices (Chapter 6). Again, our focus and approach differs somewhat from much of the existing research. Both public and academic debate around schooling in the marketplace has tended to have been dominated by two discourses. The first discourse is concerned with the relationship between 'freedom of choice', 'diversity' of provision and devolved management, on the one hand, and 'standards', 'effectiveness', 'efficiency' and 'responsiveness' on the other (Chubb and Moe, 1990; Woods 1992, 1993). The second discourse focuses on patterns of distribution of educational opportunity, and on patterns of differentiation and segregation in provision (for example, in England – Edwards and Whitty, 1992; in Scotland – Adler et al., 1989; Echols et al., 1990; in the USA – Chenoweth, 1987; Levin, 1990; Moore and Davenport, 1990; Hershkoff and Cohen, 1992; and in Israel – Goldring and Shapira, 1993). Research rooted within both of these discourses (some research straddles the two, for example Espinola, 1992) tends to have been either speculative or mainly quantitative and has been virtually exclusively concerned with extrinsic rather than intrinsic forms of evaluation (Cribb, 1995); that is, issues of 'input' and 'output' are the objects of analysis rather than the values, processes, practices, languages and relationships which constitute education provision. This is of concern, as market forces, as we will see, have serious implications for 'what goes on inside the school gates' (Power 1992). Work by Hatcher (1994) and Ozga (1995) has begun to consider the impact of the market on the internal processes of schooling, focusing specifically on the management of teachers, but their analyses have yet to be sufficiently empirically grounded. In Chapters 4, 5 and 6 we want to begin to fill the gaps left by existing research through a qualitative analysis of key developments occurring inside the 'black box' of English schooling. We will draw heavily upon the 'distributional' discourse identified above and will also shed some light on issues of concern to those operating within the hegemonic 'responsiveness' discourse, but essentially we want to locate our analysis within a third (if overlapping) discourse which emphasizes the changing *culture* of schooling. In particular, we will focus on the processes, practices, languages, relationships, institutional identities and values which are evolving in response to the new policy environment.

The distributional effects of markets

One of the key arguments deployed in favour of markets in education is that educational systems which have choice and competition as their organizing principles are more equitable than those which are bureaucratically planned and controlled. Indeed education markets have been advocated on the grounds of equity by left-wing academics and politicians as well as by those on the right. Thus, running through our analysis is a concern to explore the consequences of education markets for equity in the provision of schooling, and in Chapter 7 we attempt to weave together the main threads of our analysis in order to evaluate the claim that certain kinds of education markets are likely to effect a more equitable distribution of educational resources than planned provision. Equity is, of course, a contested concept and there appear to be two competing definitions implicit in the arguments advanced in favour of choice in education. Broadly speaking, the arguments of those on the right seem to be predicated on a desert-based definition of equity and those on the left appear to be using a needs-based definition. In our conclusion we evaluate the market reforms 'against' both definitions. At this stage, we want to clarify what is meant by 'desert-based' and 'needs-based' equity.

Desert-based conceptions of equity are founded on the contention that goods should be distributed according to merit or desert. This principle is seen to be vital to the healthy and proper functioning of a market economy because it is believed to provide an incentive for individuals to behave in productive ways. Merit has traditionally been defined by proponents of educational stratification in terms of intellectual ability. This is the conception of desert implicit in Kenneth Clarke's (1991: 2–3) critique of the British comprehensive system in which children were allocated to schools on the basis of residence:

> 'The way in which Labour made our schools comprehensive from the 1960s onwards damaged opportunities very seriously for children from poor families in deprived parts of our cities. Selection by

mortgage replaced selection by examination and the eleven plus route was closed for many bright working-class boys and girls.

However, in Conservative discourse and policy during the Thatcher/ Major era, the association of desert with motivation has been more prominent. Within the motivation-oriented discourse, the working class is effectively divided into two groups, corresponding to Victorian notions of the 'deserving' and 'undeserving' poor. The 'deserving' poor are characterized as respectable, aspiring, thrifty and industrious; if they are unemployed it is because they are the unlucky casualties of the recession; they desire to own their own homes; they care about their children's progress at school; and most importantly they are potential Conservative voters. The 'undeserving', on the other hand, are un-employed because they are lazy; they are happy to 'sponge off' the welfare state; they are the single parents who get pregnant in order to jump the housing queue; they do not care about education; they allow their children to truant and to become habitual young offenders; and they are unlikely ever to vote Conservative. They are a demonized and mytholo-gized group which, we suggest, exist more in the imaginations and rhetoric of right-wing philosophy than in reality; but they provide convenient scapegoats, allowing attention to be diverted from the Government's economic policies. Their 'undeservingness' may also be useful in helping to justify the redistribution of scarce public resources away from the most disadvantaged in society.

Conservative welfare policies since 1979 appear to have been designed to reward the 'deserving' and penalize the 'undeserving', that is to reverse what the Thatcher/Major claim was the organizing principle of the pre-1979 welfare state. In housing, the 'right to buy' policy and more recent attempts to change the rules of council-home allocation so that single parents are no longer prioritized, are aimed at benefiting those sectors of the population deemed more 'respectable' and hence 'deserv-ing'. Giving single parents preferential welfare treatment is believed to encourage what is presented as the objectionable practice of single parenthood. In health care, funds for preventative medicine have been channelled into health-promotion clinics to which individuals are ex-pected to refer themselves rather than into programmes likely to reach those with greatest need – a system of health income allocation designed to reward those who help themselves. The self-help message is also starkly represented in the redesignation of Unemployment Benefit as the Job Seekers Allowance and in schemes for the unemployed like Job Clubs and Restart.

From the perspective of adherents of the deserving/undeserving distinction, choice in education is viewed as another mechanism which will more effectively distribute social income according to motivation. One of the messages embedded in the English education market is that parents who make 'good' and 'responsible' choices are likely to be rewarded with a 'better' education for their children than those who choose 'badly' or 'irresponsibly'. Neo-liberal advocates of the market do argue that all students will benefit from the improvement in standards which greater diversity and competition can produce and that is an important argument. Nevertheless, it is assumed that families will be differentially positioned in the market and that this should be related to effort and 'good' parenting rather than any conception of need.

As will have been evident from the way we have represented the distinction between the so-called 'deserving' and 'undeserving' poor, we reject these categories. First, they offer a caricatured version of working-class families, and second, we object to the values which inhere in the distinction between 'deserving' and 'undeserving' groups in society. Nevertheless, in assessing the outcomes of recent education policy in England in Chapter 7, we will apply the conception of equity encapsulated in this distinction, that is, the distribution of resources according to desert. For the purposes of this activity, we define the 'deserving' as those families – in particular, low-income ones – desiring to take advantage of the new 'opportunities' offered to them by the extension of choice in education through the policy of open enrolment. In short, we are concerned to explore how successful the English education market is in terms of achieving one of the key aims its architects have constructed for it. However, we are not going to look for a perfect distribution of education income according to desert, bearing in mind Gray's (1993: 91) observation (following Hayek) that 'accepting market institutions involves accepting an unpredictable dispersion of rewards that is only partly connected with anyone's merits and deserts'. Our test will be whether the new education market is *improving* the chances of access to a better quality education for those deemed 'deserving' in Conservative discourse.

A *needs-based definition*, the second conception of equity we wish to consider is that which is embedded in left-wing arguments for choice. This is represented by the maxim, 'From each according to her capacity, to each according to her need'. A needs-based conception of equity is implicit in Crump's (1994) defence of markets in education. Programmes of choice which 'build on genuine democratic community interests' (1994: 2), he argues, have the potential to be more equitable than bureaucratically managed systems because they are more likely to make state schools responsive to the 'different needs and interests [of] low-income, minority, single-parent and other excluded groups'. For Crump, a major component of need is access to a curriculum which does not impose an alien culture but which recognizes and values the culture of children's families and their particular ways of seeing the world. Crump does not argue that choice is a perfect system of educational income distribution, but that it is the 'best lousy theory' (1994: 9) with the potential to 'improve existing conditions', and he takes critics of choice to task for their 'unrealistic expectations and measure' that choice should be in the interests of everyone (1994: 4).

While a desert-based notion of equity underpins the design and legitimatory discourse of the English market, needs-based conceptions appear to be alien to this discourse and are not incorporated in the design of the new system of provision, as we shall see. The English market differs in this respect from some of the experiments with choice and competition in the USA (see Domanico, 1989; Fliegel, 1990; Glenn, 1990). Many U.S. choice programmes have been designed for the express purpose of meeting the educational needs of those members of society deemed to be academically 'at risk' in zoned systems of provision, that is, economically disadvantaged and ethnic and language minority group students in inner-urban areas. Levin (1990: 268) defines a needs-based system of education income distribution as one in which 'persons from different social groups should have equal access to the types of resources that they need to succeed educationally'. If this principle is going to be translated into practice, Levin suggests (1990: 268), at least two requirements must be set:

> First, educational resources available for each student should favour those with greater educational need . . . and those with fewer private resources in the home and community to be able to meet educational needs – for example, low income and single parent families. Second, families from different social origins ought to have at least equal ability to exercise choices among all of the available alternatives. This requires equal access to information about alternatives as well as equal ability to exercise choice.

For the purposes of evaluating the needs-based equity implications of the English market we will use Levin's conception, as summarized above. But, as with the desert-based conception of equity, we want to apply the needs-based definition realistically, that is, bearing in mind Crump's assertion that we should not expect a perfect system of distribution according to need. Our test will be whether the English education market is resulting in a more equitable distribution of educational resources according to need than existed previously. While the architects of the English market might not recognize this as a relevant test, we do not wish to be confined in our analysis solely by what policymakers deem to be appropriate criteria of evaluation. We believe that there may be lessons to be learned from the English market experience, irrespective of the intentions of its architects, which might inform the construction of education programmes which *are* designed to engender a needs-based distribution of educational resources.

Research settings, samples and analysis

The particular settings and samples upon which the research reported here is based were selected initially to provide a context in which choice and competition were likely to be significant factors in the local politics of education and a concern impinging upon schools and upon parents choosing a secondary school for their child. The research was conducted over a three-year period from 1991 to 1994. Data collection was focused on three competitive 'clusters' of schools in three geographically contiguous LEAs in London: Northwark, Westway and Riverway. (All names used in the text are pseudonyms.) The LEAs were chosen to be very different in terms of social class and ethnic mix. Each has a different party in control of the local council and a different orientation to, and engagement with, the education market. (See Chapter 3 for more details.) The data collected at LEA level included:

- meetings and interviews with various officers and officials (eight in all);
- where available, material on parental choices and school enrolments;
- reports and performance indicators related to local schools; and
- minutes, plans and documents related to school choice and LEA spending and planning.

Across the three cluster areas, 137 interviews with parents were conducted in three tranches, one in each year of the study. The parents were approached through a sample of primary schools which 'feed' the 'clusters'. Respondents were elicited in a number of ways: by letters sent to Year 6 class groups; by headteachers at transfer interviews (when parents come to discuss their choice of secondary school); and by direct approach at primary school or public meetings on transfer. The sample was constructed inductively to match as far as possible the socio-economic and ethnic composition of the three cluster areas, that is, in the third round of interviewing we attempted to target groups which were not well represented in the opportunistic samples gathered in the first two rounds. A summary of characteristics of the sample is presented in Tables 1.2 to 1.7. We timed the interviews to take place while parents were choosing and before offers were announced to avoid the post-factum recollections or rationalizations of choice-making elicited in some previous research on parental choice. The interviews lasted from

Table 1.2 Classification of parental occupations by LEA and gender

Class*	Northwark		Riverway		Westway		Streetley		Totals			
	m	f	m	f	m	f	m	f	Total m	Total f	Total	Total (%)
1	2	7	1	1	2	6	1	0	6	14	20	8
2	13	12	3	5	18	17	1	1	35	35	70	27
3N	15	8	12	6	11	4	1	2	39	20	59	23
3M	2	11	2	12	0	3	1	2	5	28	33	13
4	6	4	6	1	1	1	0	0	13	6	19	7
5	1	0	0	1	1	0	0	0	2	1	3	1
Unemployed	1	3	1	6	0	3	0	1	2	13	15	6
House worker	4	0	5	0	4	0	2	0	15	0	15	6
Unclassified	6	4	6	3	4	3	0	0	16	10	26	10
Total**	50	49	36	35	41	37	6	6	133	127	260	100
Lone parents	3	2	3	2	4	0	0	0	10	4	14	5

m = mother
f = father

* Using Registrar General's Classification where 1 represents professional occupations, 2 intermediate occupations, 3N non-manual skilled, 3M manual skilled, 4 partly skilled and 5 unskilled occupations.

** These totals exclude 'missing' partners from one-parent families.

Table 1.3 Ethnicity of families interviewed by LEA

Ethnicity	Northwark	Riverway	Westway	Streetley	Total
White	39	41	28	4	112
Black	5	0	0	1	6
S. Asian	6	0	10	1	17
Others	2	0	0	0	2
Total	52	41	38	6	137

Table 1.4 Gender of children transferring to secondary school

Gender	n
Girls	60
Boys	77

Table 1.5 Gender of parents interviewed

Mothers only	82
Fathers only	20
Both parents	34
Other relatives	1

Table 1.6 Parents interviewed by LEA of child's primary school

Northwark	52
Westway	38
Riverway	41
Streetley	6

Table 1.7 Parents interviewed by year of research

Year	Interviews (n)
1991–2	70
1992–3	40
1993–4	27

thirty minutes to two hours and covered a range of issues related to choice including:

- perceptions of schools;
- information used;
- influences and criteria employed;
- decision-making in the family;
- constraints and problems; and
- visits to schools.

We also interviewed 18 headteachers in selected 'feeder' primary schools about their perceptions of the secondary school market and about parents' concerns on transfer and choice. In addition, we observed a number of transfer interviews conducted by these heads with Year 6 parents.

   Our 14 secondary schools, set in the three local competitive clusters, were selected on the basis of various criteria but particularly school type and market position. The sample included both LEA and GM schools, co-educational and single sex, a church school and a CTC (see Table 1.8). Among these were over- and under-subscribed schools. Only one school

Table 1.8   Schools participating in the study

Cluster	Description★
Northwark cluster	
CTC	City Technology College sponsored by multinational services firm
Martineau	Girls' comprehensive, obtained GM status during project
Milton	Mixed comprehensive, obtained GM status during project
Northwark Park	Mixed comprehensive
St Ignatious	Catholic comprehensive, obtained GM status during project
Trumpton	Mixed comprehensive, obtained GM status during project
Riverway cluster	
Fletcher	Mixed, 11–16 comprehensive
Goddard	Mixed, 11–16 comprehensive
Overbury	Mixed, 11–16 comprehensive
Pankhurst	Girls, 11–16 comprehensive
Parsons	Mixed, 11–16 comprehensive
Westway cluster	
Flightpath	Mixed community comprehensive
Lymethorpe	Mixed community comprehensive
Parkside	Mixed community comprehensive

★ GM = Grant-maintained.

Table 1.9   Cross-sectional interviews in schools★

Category of staff/governor	Interviews (n)
Headteachers	22
Deputy heads	25
Administrative staff	6
Heads of sixth form	5
Special Educational Needs staff	7
Primary liaison teachers	8
Union representatives	8
Newly qualified teachers	5
Teacher governors	10
Other staff	4
Chairs of governors	5
Parent governors	12
Business governors	2
Total	119

★ In a few cases, one person interviewed accounted for more than one role but these are not double-counted.

we contacted refused to participate and four of the schools had participated in a previous research project (Bowe *et al.*, 1992). The three clusters consist of schools which are in some kind of competitive relationship with one another, although competition also exists, in some cases, between the clusters, across LEA boundaries. Data collected in the schools related to their market behaviour and the impact of market forces on the values, stances, policies and planning of the school staffs and governors. In each school, with variations as appropriate, a set of cross-sectional interviews were conducted (see Tables 1.9 and 1.10). In some cases there were repeat interviews with key respondents. Altogether 119 school-based interviews were carried out. Open evenings were attended in all of the schools in each of the three years of the project. The school brochures and prospectuses were collected. In some schools we also attended governors' meetings and collected planning and report documents. As data analysis progressed alongside data collection, 'analytical' decisions were taken which led to a greater concentration upon some more 'theoretically interesting' schools and less attention being given to others.

The analysis of our qualitative data rests upon the techniques of coding and constant comparison developed by Strauss (1987). All the interviews were professionally transcribed and carefully coded in order to identify core categories and integrating concepts. Coding as an analytical process

Table 1.10   Secondary school interviews by LEA

LEA	Interviews (n)
Northwark	60
Riverway	33
Westway	26
Total	119

is a method for breaking down the 'natural' structure of data and reconstituting them in new ways. 'By breaking down and conceptualizing we mean taking apart an observation, a sentence, a paragraph, and giving each discrete incident, idea, or event, a name, something that stands for or represents a phenomenon' (Strauss and Corbin, 1990: 63). Coding produces conceptual development and theory building, but it also contributes to the making of research decisions via theoretical sampling, that is, insights from analysis are ploughed back into, and used to, organize further data collection. Our comparative work required the systematic examination of analytic categories (such as 'skilled/privileged' or 'reluctant implication') and the search for similarities and differences among the properties of the components of our structural 'sample', that is, among the schools, the actors in the schools, the three LEAs and the parents. Those differences and properties provide the basis for most of what is presented and discussed here. We want to underline the point that the procedures of coding are not simply mechanical or algorithmic: insightful interpretation, creativity and theoretical sensitivity are all involved in the process.

Our research strategy is eclectic but systematic. It is also reactive, that is, we have attempted to employ methods and approaches which escape from some of the problems and limitations which we see embedded in existing research. Nonetheless, a great deal of further work needs to be done: other settings need to be studied; more data on the second-order effects of choice and selection are needed; and changes over time as education markets begin to stabilize must be monitored. It is also important that some attempt is made to examine the overlaps and interplay between different sorts of planned or quasi markets in the public sector and the ways in which these multiple public-sector markets impact upon lives and effect the opportunities of particular populations.

Our emphasis here is upon critique. We are not unaware of some benefits and positive outcomes from the insertion of the market form into education, and some of these are noted in the text, but in evaluating the 'creative destruction' of market forces in education, our evidence leads us to give main emphasis to the destructive and divisive effects. The creative aspects seem minor and marginal in comparison.

Notes

1 In an effort to be precise and acknowledge local and legislative variations in the structure and operation of education markets in England, Wales, Scotland and Northern Ireland, we refer here specifically to England.
2 The Education Reform Act 1988 introduced the local management of schools, parental choice, open enrolment, formula funding and the national curriculum.

2

CHOICE AND CLASS: PARENTS IN THE MARKETPLACE

Introduction

At the level of political rhetoric, parental choice of school is presented as a mechanism which will extend personal freedom whilst making schools more responsive to their 'consumers'. Embedded within this rhetoric are caricatured versions both of how parents choose and of the effects of those choices. In this chapter we aim to separate out the simplicities and misrepresentations of 'choosing' embedded in political debates and some of the research on parental choice from the complexity of the choice-making process in real social contexts. As we argued in Chapter 1, most parental-choice research and commentary may be divided into two types. The first type treats choice as a decontextualized, undifferentiated and neutral mechanism. This research is itself caught up within the discourse of market theory; the meanings and processes of choice and the constraints upon it for different families are glossed over. The only interest in difference appears to be that of difference in the criteria used or in the 'availability' of choice. The second body of research and writing on parental choice takes matters of difference more seriously, indicating that choice systems discriminate against working-class families. In this chapter we want to build upon and extend that second body of research. We begin, though, by briefly describing how the concept of 'choice' is being constructed in the public arena both by its advocates and by a growing body of popular texts aimed at helping parents choose schools.

Conservative advocates typically set parental choice within the wider ideology of the market and wider discourses of choice. They present it as fairer than planned provision, because it is 'classless': everyone has the opportunity to choose and to decide upon the 'best' providers of goods and services to meet their needs (but planned interventions continue nonetheless). Greater choice is in itself 'a good thing' because it extends individual freedom. However such freedom requires individual endeavour, it has to be 'earned' and central to market choice is the assumption that responsible parents will invest a great deal of energy in ensuring that they have made the right choice. Opportunity and responsibility are the keywords here. In *The Parent's Charter* (DES, 1991; DFE 1994) choice is powerfully promoted as a personal matter, a question of individual parents taking responsibility for their children's educational future: 'You have a duty to ensure that your child gets an education – and you can choose the school that you would like your child to go to[1]. Your choice is wider as a result of recent changes' (1991: 8). These new rights, duties and responsibilities are all welded together into a 'language of choice' which has a very overt political role. Parents, or at least a significant number of parents, will need to exercise their individual choices. They will need to actively choose a school rather than allow 'allocation by default'. This appeal to parents to 'consume' education idealizes 'responsible consumerism', both typified and encouraged by the steady growth in consumer magazines and consumer programmes on TV and on the radio, all promoting the merits of being a responsible, rational consumer. In this respect *The Parent's Charter* is both *of* and *in* the social and political context, it emerges from and feeds the ideology of the market and discourses of choice, as well as actively encouraging choice as a right and seeking to construct an image of the responsible parent as one who will display the characteristics of the ideal consumer. This promotion of educational consumerism has spawned the publication of the *Good State Schools Guide* (Clarke and Round, 1991), the schooling-as-product equivalent of the 'consumer's bible', *Which?* Serialized in *The Observer* colour supplement and widely reported in the press, the book aims to identify 300 schools 'which are testimony to the *best* in state education' (emphasis in the original). It includes a seven-page guide, 'What parents need to know', which details parental rights (to choice), types of school, getting local information from the LEA and the school (prospectuses, exam results, visits – what to ask and what to look at), all intended to 'assist you in mounting the ladders and avoiding the snakes' (Clark and Round, 1991: 13). This call to consumerism is equally evident in the publicity accorded to 'league tables' and the appearance, in 1992, of other newspaper 'guides' to schools (*The Sunday Times* magazine; *The Independent*; *The Evening Standard* magazine) – now annual publications.

Opponents of educational markets have pointed out that the rhetoric of Conservative advocates of the market obscures the way in which choice systems privilege certain sorts of families and disadvantage others. A wealth of critical commentary accompanied the Education Act 1988, predicting the emergence of a tiered education system, in which working-class children in the cities would get the worst deal (e.g. Bash and Coulby, 1989; Flude and Hammer, 1990). Furthermore, there has been a growing body of research on parental choice both in the UK and the USA which supports the contention that educational markets are class-biased. First, the evidence suggests that where oversubscribed schools are allowed to select pupils, modes of selection tend to favour children from middle-class backgrounds (Moore and Davenport, 1990). Second, where choice systems operate, research shows that middle-class parents do more choosing than working-class ones. Edwards *et al.* (1989: 172) found in their study of the Assisted Places Scheme that whilst 'the scheme has certainly benefited large numbers of low income families', children of professional and middle-class parents were pre-dominant amongst place holders. More than half of their sample of 90 parents of assisted place pupils had themselves attended selective or independent secondary schools (1989:171). They conclude that 'class-related social, educational and cultural factors . . . not only inform 'choice' but, more importantly, they enable some groups to recognize its possibilities and execute it more advantageously than others' (1989: 215). The large-scale study of Echols *et al.* (1990) on the impact of open enrolment in Scotland supports that conclusion. They found that 'in the first year of the policy, parental choice was inequitable, in that take-up was more common among better educated parents and those of higher social class' (1990: 213) (for similar findings see also Stillman and Maychell, 1986; Moore and Davenport, 1990; Blank, 1990). Studies in the USA have indicated that the greater take-up of choice by middle-class parents can be explained at least in part by the complexity of the choice process which tends to discriminate against low-income and less educated families (Moore and Davenport, 1990).

What the existing research on choice points to is the importance of cultural resources, particularly what Edwards *et al.* refer to as 'educational inheritance' in determining access to choice. Thus although material resources might not always be necessary for the exercise of choice in a market system, cultural resources remain as, if not more, important than they have ever been. In this chapter we want to take these arguments further by considering precisely how cultural resources are used in the processes of school choice, in particular social contexts and what their effects are. There are two substantive points of focus, although these are strongly interrelated. The first is on the processes of, and constraints upon, choice-making. The second is on the role of choice in the maintenance of social class-related distinctions and educational differentiations.

Both aspects of the analysis draw upon Bourdieu's (1986) work on social judgement and taste in which he examines the specific logic that informs the 'economy of cultural goods'. In Bourdieu's terms, the choice of, and competition for, access to schools can be analysed as a 'social field'. The idea of a 'field' allows us to think relationally about human actions (choice is normally conceptualized individually by both politicians and researchers) which simultaneously take on multiple and complex meanings (choice means different things to different people in different settings). A field implies both common ground and a composite of apparently contradictory environments:

> I define a field as a network, or configuration, of objective relations between positions objectively defined, in their existence and in the determinations they impose upon occupants, agents or institutions, by their present and potential situations (situs) in the structure of the distribution of species of power (or capital) where possession commands access to the specific profits that are at stake in the field, as well as by their objective relations to other positions (domination, subordination, homology, etc.). Each field presupposes, and generates by its very functioning, the belief in the stakes it offers.
>
> (Bourdieu quoted in Wacquant, 1989: 29)

Our contextual analysis of choice and class goes to the heart of the ideology of the market and the claims of classlessness and neutrality. Choice emerges as a major new factor in maintaining and indeed reinforcing social-class divisions and inequalities. The point is not that choice and the market have moved us away from what was a smoothly functioning egalitarian system of schooling to one that is unfair. That is crude and unrealistic. There were significant processes of differentiation and choice prior to 1988 (within and between schools). Some skilful and resourceful parents were always able to 'work the system' or buy a private education or gain other forms of advantage for their children. But post-1988, the stratagems of competitive advantage are now ideologically endorsed and practically facilitated by open enrolment, the deregulation of recruitment and parental choice. Well-resourced choosers now have free rein to guarantee and reproduce, as best they can, their existing cultural, social and economic advantages in the new complex and blurred hierarchy of schools. Class selection is revalorized by the market.

The substance of this chapter draws heavily upon our interviews with parents of Year 6 children (10–11 years) who were in the process of 'choosing' a secondary school for their child. As detailed in Chapter 1, three sets of interviews were conducted, in the years 1991–2, 1992–3 and 1993–4. The interviews were spread across three 'clusters' of 'competing' secondary schools. However, the extracts from interviews quoted below are more than usually inadequate in what they can convey; they are very much ripped out of context and lose impact and effect as a result. Choice-making is typically accounted for by parents in terms of long narratives or a complex social calculus of contradictions, compromises and constraints. The quotations are representative examples only – to provide a sense of things (see Gewirtz et al., 1993a). Both presences and absences in the data are important to our argument, what is said and what is not said by families in different class groups.

Class choosing

Our analysis is structured by the presentation of three types of chooser identified within the data set: the *privileged/skilled chooser*, the *semi-skilled chooser* and the *disconnected chooser*. The typology is strongly class-related: the disconnected choosers are overwhelming working class; the privileged/skilled choosers are overwhelmingly middle class; and the semi-skilled are a mixed-class group. Perhaps in Bourdieu's terms, the privileged may be seen as 'inheritors' and the semi-skilled as 'newcomers'. But there are exceptions to the general pattern: as we know, class is an indicator rather than a determinant of family traits. Further, significant social and economic changes over the past twenty years mean that social-class categorizations are increasingly slippery and difficult to apply. While the class references here, and the relationships between class and choice, are presented fairly simply and straightforwardly, as Bourdieu suggests they rest upon 'a network of secondary characteristics' like age, gender and race. However, our central point throughout is that choice is thoroughly social, it is a process powerfully informed by the lives people lead and their biographies – in short, their position within a social network. Differences in choice-making are not a matter of relative deficiencies or of social pathology in which certain parents are less responsible, or efficient or effective choosers. Our use of the term 'skill' is intended to denote particular cultural capacities which are unevenly distributed across the population but which are valorized by the operation of the education market. In Bourdieu's terms, the market constitutes a particular cultural arbitrary which presupposes 'possession of the cultural code required for the decoding of the objects displayed' (Bourdieu and Passeron, 1990: 51–2).

We want to underline the point that the categories generated by our analysis are ideal types rather than naturalistic categories. Nonetheless, they represent certain very clear trends, relationships and patterns in the data. Thus, the majority of families interviewed fit well within the ideal types, although a few families display contradictory or mixed qualities or dimensions in their choice-making. We nevertheless wish to argue that the types illustrate or allude to a 'singular configuration' of explanatory factors related to school choice. These are constructed 'in order to account for a state of the distribution of a particular class of goods or practices, i.e. a balance sheet drawn up at a particular moment of the class struggle over that particular class of goods or practices' (Bourdieu, 1986: 113). (In this case the particular 'class of goods' refers to secondary schools.) The groupings identified below are thus 'the form taken, in that field, by the objectified and internalized capital (properties and habitus) which defines social class and constitutes the principle of the production of classified and classifying practices' (Bourdieu, 1986: 113–14).

Privileged/skilled choosers

There are four key qualities to this type of chooser. First, there is a strong inclination to choice; that is, the idea and worth of having a choice between schools is valued. Thus for many privileged/skilled families, choice of school becomes a major concern over an extended period of time. However, a number of families inclined to choice also noted some disadvantages or problems associated with the policy of choice.

Second, there is a strong capacity to engage with and utilize the possibilities of choice. Economic, social and cultural capital are all important here. These choosers were able to 'decode' school systems and organization, to discriminate between schools in terms of policies and practices, to engage with and question (and challenge if necessary) teachers and school managers, to critically evaluate teachers' responses and to collect, scan and interpret various sources of information. In respect to all of this, they also maintain a degree of 'healthy' scepticism about the meaning and value of impressions and information. Many of those families who fall within this ideal type had some kind of 'inside' knowledge of education systems and the way they work. But not all 'insiders' displayed these understandings. These parents tend to be oriented to high-status, élite 'cosmopolitan' schools (see below), some of which have difficult or obscure systems of entry, which are 'known' to the privileged/skilled parents. Such parents are often able to employ forms of direct contact and negotiation which can be vital in accessing these schools. *This is where social and cultural capital plays a crucial role, knowing how to approach, present, mount a case, maintain pressure, make an impact and be remembered.*

'She wasn't offered a place at Princess Elizabeth school, on the sort of first round, but as I understand [it] a lot of girls that are offered places there have also applied to private schools and get a place at private schools and so they drop out, and there was a meeting there with the headmistress for all the families who thought they were going to appeal for a place, and we went along to that, and we then had a chat with the headmistress afterwards about our particular case and what we felt were our reasons for wanting Nicki to have a place there and about a week and a half later we had a phone call one evening from the headmistress saying that she had a place for Nicki, so that's where she's going.'

(Mrs Knighton, 17 September 1991)

'I know someone who is an educational consultant and if you pay . . . if you go to see her, basically she gives you advice on what your child would need tutoring on . . . what schools would be suitable, she's independent . . . and so rather than sort of paying out for tutors for across the board education, go and have a look to see what Lisa would actually need if she went for a scholarship.'

(Mrs Giggs, 24 October 1991)

There is also an established pattern of transfer from certain primaries to particular secondaries. Thus, for privileged/skilled parents, the choice of primary school is often the first of several strategic decisions involved in the careful construction of their children's school career. Furthermore, the primary headteachers often play a key role in influencing or deflecting parental choices and in providing crucial 'access' and application information. For example, knowing which schools only consider 'first choices' is extremely important.

'I'd like to talk to him . . . [Lisa's primary headteacher]. I'd just like to say to him, Princess Elizabeth [school] want two referees. One is fine from the headteacher, but they want another one. All her extracurricular activities are associated with the school, so we can't actually give another one. I'd just like to ring him up and say look, is this a problem with Princess Elizabeth because he obviously knows the headteacher there pretty well.'

(Mr Giggs, 24 October 1991)

These families also possess the financial resources to be able to move their children around the school system in a variety of senses.

Third, from the interplay of unclear or contradictory social principles, of diverse aspirations, desires and concerns related to their children and their children's futures, and of multiple sources of impression and perception, choosing a school often emerges as a confusing and complex process. In some ways, the more skilled you are, the more difficult it is. The more you know about schools, the more apparent it is that no one school is perfect and that all schools have various strengths and weaknesses.

> 'I found that the more choice we had, the more we went round in circles.'
>
> (Mrs Morden, 31 December 1991).

The more possibilities, the more potential for confusion. The other two main ideal types do not display the same degree of complexity and paradoxically their relative lack of information often results in a more clear-cut and definitive outcome to their decision-making. The privileged/skilled choosers frequently end up with a compromise decision or are left with a degree of equivocation or ambivalence about their choice. Alternatively, they will use seemingly arbitrary factors to reduce the pool of schools from which the final choice is made. That is, they will deliberately not consider all the schools they could. Questions of distance, travel and safety are all important here, as they are for parents in the other choice types. Some privileged/skilled parents went to considerable lengths to make distance possible and safe for their children. However, travel and distance emerge as contingent factors, not priority or determinate ones.

> 'It is something to consider. It turned out for our son that there was a feasible British Rail route. At one point I was resigned to chauffeur him for years, not being very happy with it and for our daughter, although it's not as far in miles, there is no public transport . . . so I'm not quite happy with that, and as it turns out she will have company, but I will work something out but she could walk sometimes with friends . . . and I will ferry sometimes.'
>
> (Mrs Ferguson, 14 October 1993)

> 'I couldn't put a figure on my radius because it was fairly flexible, because it wasn't just a circle . . . we also took into account the ease of transport . . . so perhaps . . . a school over in Westing wouldn't be possible because the transport . . . would be difficult . . . but Fletcher [school] wouldn't be too bad because it's one bus. It's a long walk but then it's one bus ride to Fletcher . . . so the radius changed depending on the transport arrangements.
>
> (Mrs Dearing, 23 June 1991)

> 'When Robert came home from Fletcher school on the first day, what I did was . . . I didn't actually stand at the bus stop with him, because he would have felt a bit silly, but I followed the bus on my bicycle behind and checked everything was okay, and watched him get off

the bus, and met him at home. So summing up, it's not a major
consideration but obviously you have to take it into account.'

(Mr Giggs, 24 October 1991)

Finally, in common with many other choosers across all of the ideal
types, they identified their impressionistic, affective, personal responses
to schools, derived from visits or open evenings, as often providing the
clinching factor in arriving at a final choice or eliminating a final
alternative. *The role of the affective, of ethos, atmosphere, 'feel', impression,
sense, climate is absolutely fundamental to choice.* (The significance of these
factors and this aspect of choice have been systematically neglected in
much of the previous parental-choice research.)

One of the key factors which underlies the inclination to choice and
which generates complexity is that the privileged/skilled choosers are
engaged in a process of *child-matching.* That is, they are looking to find a
school which will suit the particular proclivities, interests, aspirations
and/or personality of their child. For some, this is often the *only* primary
concern and is driven by very precise academic concerns and aspirations
related to their child. In these cases the matching is based on a future/goal
orientation in which choice of secondary school is regarded as a major
life-course decision for their child with decisive implications for the
child's whole future. The child is often complexly constructed in terms of
traits, needs and talents. This in itself complicates choice, especially when
combined with 'insider' knowledge of the school system. For some
parents, the identification of the 'best' school is made more difficult
because the cross-matching between child and school becomes increasingly precise. For others, the matching is more generalized or is related to
more immediate concerns about their child's happiness or ability to cope
or flourish at school (Coldron and Boulton, 1991). One parent was
concerned with precision.

'I think it's very difficult to choose a school for a kid when you don't
know what . . . their strengths are particularly going to be, and also
. . . the school's strengths could change – I mean it's five or six years
before GCSE. So all I know is at the moment he is very keen on
maths, so I wanted a school that was strong on maths.'

(Ms Bond, 30 December 1991)

The following extract illustrates more general concerns about matching
child to school.

'He's different from his brother, so what I'll be looking for for him
might be very different . . . You've got to choose something that
you feel your child will actually adjust to and be happy with. My son
[Christopher] is quite introverted, very shy, a lot of his friends are

hopefully going on, if they get in as well, to Lockmere [school]. This was quite an important transition for me, because of my child's personality. I mean I know they do adjust and they are adaptable, children . . . but Christopher is particularly quiet. So it was quite important to me to choose what we felt happy about and he felt happy about.'

(Mrs Roding, 12 December 1991)

As Mrs Roding indicates, the matching process often results in different choices for different children in the same family. Various aspects of a school – size, ethos, academic orientation, social mix, etc. – and the child, come into play in the matching. Rather than employing clearly prioritized criteria, these parents are looking for a composite, a balance and blend of factors specific to the needs of their child. Here we begin to see a 'decoding' process at work. In order to achieve a 'good' match, the parents make use of their grasp of how schools work and what makes them different from one another. We return to this below.

In all this, examination results can play a part in 'sizing-up' schools but is one indicator among others and is rarely of overriding importance. Echols and Willms (1993: 22) note a similar finding among Scottish parents.

We thought issues of academic quality would dominate reasons for rejecting and choosing a school. This was generally not the case . . . social/reputational reasons and disciplinary climate were the dominant themes for both the reasons for rejection (push) and reasons for selection (pull).

These parents are making a choice for the whole package, they do not want an examination factory. They are concerned much more with what Bernstein (1975) calls the expressive order of the school, that is the complex of behaviour and activities in the school which are to do with conduct, character and manner.

We have a school very near here called Trumpton, and the acid test that I use, and it's probably not a very good one, other than their academic records, is to stand outside the school and have a look at the kids coming out and see how they behave and how they dress and that . . . and I did that at a number of schools in the borough and none of them were suitable. It's a sad fact that Fletcher [school], being in a predominantly middle-class area, does tend to have a more supportive PTA, the kids are better encouraged at home, it's generally a better school academically than what was on offer round here, but more importantly, there was a big emphasis in Fletcher on pastoral care . . . How can I put it? There is a liberal attitude that prevails at that school but it is one that doesn't result in anarchy, there's a fine balance there that they seem to have achieved . . . and for our son those particular attributes of the school are very important rather than purely the emphasis on academic achievements or [the] academic record of the school.'

(Mr Giggs, 24 October 1991)

This expressive order is the medium for the recontexualization of the student's out-of-school life and is often 'a formalisation, crystallisation, even idealisation, of an image of conduct, character and manner reflected by some, but not all, groups in the wider society' (Bernstein, 1975: 30, 38, 49). This is part of what Slaughter and Schnieder (1986) call 'holistic' choosing.

Nonetheless, while they are still often significantly influenced by atmosphere, impression and 'feel', the more 'goal-oriented' parents do take examination results seriously and work through them comparing school performances in particular subjects. They also attend to the strengths and weaknesses of schools in particular subject areas. Other parents are not unconcerned with examination results but they also raise questions about the adequacy and appropriateness of these as a fair measure of the quality of a school. A significant number of parents offered versions of the 'value-added' argument as a source of scepticism about results.

'Yes, we did. Yes we did long and hard with Joe, more so with Helena, although we did again look through the figures again. You read what you will at the end of the day. I remember we sat with friends the first time, analysing and reanalysing the percentage of this, percentage of that and this, that and whatever . . . and at the end of the day you can play the exam results game however you want to play. I think the one head that made the most sensible comment, I felt, was the headmaster at Goddard [school] who basically said, you have to assess the children that you've got coming in and then assess them as they're going out and then you have a true picture of what a school can do.'

(Mrs Morden, 31 December 1991)

'I don't think that you can choose a school on the basis of those results. You know that children from advantaged backgrounds are statistically likely to come out in the top third and so obviously if the local school had had maybe only 14 per cent of children getting five or more grades A to C, or whatever, the thing is, you would have questioned that, but given that they're all in the range of around sort of 30, 35 per cent, it isn't a very useful criteria [sic] to use'.

(Mrs Parker, 7 November 1992)

Some of the skilled/privileged choosers, those committed to particular educational outcomes and futures for their child, conveyed a particular sense of urgency about the school-choice decision. Sometimes this produced a sense of frustration when no school is quite perfect and compromises have to be made. Other parents, looking for a more general, all-round education, are by no means unconcerned. They are committed to making the right decision, but typically arrive at a situation where more than one school is acceptable.

> For many parents, the task is not to sort out the complexities of sundry educational alternatives and make the right choice. Rather, their task is to find the nearest available 'suitable' school.
>
> (Echols and Willms, 1993: 23)

At this stage, for the latter, once unsuitable schools have been eliminated, the child's role is important and the final decision can be left to them and concerns like where the child's friends are going can come into play.

Leaving aside these subtle differences, it is important to underline and illustrate the role played for the privileged/skilled (and other) parents by affective responses in the choice-making process, as signalled earlier. The 'feel' of a school, its ethos and atmosphere, as conveyed by teachers' and students' attitudes and behaviours, the state and nature of the buildings, the location, the headteacher's speech, etc. play a major role in the final decision about which school to choose. Schools are selected and eliminated by this means. Many parents are clear that this is a factor of major importance in their choice-making. Their ability to convey or explain their responses and to pin-point the sources of them vary but they are usually able to identify some factors which contribute to this. One very important thing to note is that different parents will react to the same schools in these respects in very different ways – partly because the very aspects which repel some attract others and partly because the interpretations of atmosphere differ in themselves. Schools in this sense are polysemic. But these interpretations are not random, they are patterned.

> 'I liked it very much. Instinctively I just felt that this was the place where Sarah [daughter] would do really well. It's ever so difficult to explain but for Alexander [son] I just knew instinctively that the

CTC was the only school that he would do well at, it had everything that he wanted to do and liked . . . I had the same feeling about Martineau [school].'

(Mrs Dempsey, 11 January 1993)

'The facilities . . . the feeling, it seemed a happy school as I went around. I felt comfortable in it, as I was walking around. This is the funny thing, it's quite interesting how people perceive things differently because . . . when I talked to some of them, no way would they consider Parsons [school]. You know what I mean, it's just how you interpret the feeling of the school, and I got slightly stressed about this because I thought, well I certainly didn't like Overbury [school] at all, and that's the one everyone seems to choose as their second one'.

(Mrs Roding, 12 December 1991)

'I feel Lockmere [school] is very cramped . . . they've obviously had to take in more to make up the numbers . . . We liked Lockmere first of all, we chose it for Joe two years ago, and we tried to influence him for Lockmere, but he really didn't like it because he felt overwhelmed by it, he felt the buildings were coming in on you and he felt there wasn't space, and going round the second time I feel that . . . this time. There's a lot of Portakabins and the Astroturf – although they're allowed on the Astroturf, it's an area that you have to have trainers on before you can go . . . but I mean the children that we know that go there are perfectly happy'.

(Mrs Morden, 31 December 1991)

Of course, this begins to raise interesting issues about the extent to which such impressions are based on the effects of deliberate planning by schools and the extent to which the elements of a school 'ethos' can be changed or fostered or manipulated. But the skilled/privileged parents certainly display a marked scepticism about the attempts at impression management involved in the production of school prospectuses and in the organization and choreographing of open evenings and school tours. As Bourdieu (1986: 466) suggests, these affective responses are acquired dispositions to differentiate, and 'function below the level of consciousness and language'. But these responses do not have to be regarded as simply personal or mysterious. They cannot be completely explained or rationalized but there is certainly *an element* of class discrimination in the perception of, and response, to schools. There are class-related messages/signs to be read off from the school setting, the demeanour of the students and the attitude of staff. We can relate these processes of response and choice to Bourdieu's discussion of taste.

Taste is the practical operator of the transmutation of things into distinct and distinctive signs, of continuous distributions into discontinuous oppositions: it raises the differences inscribed in the physical order of bodies to the symbolic order of significant distinctions. It transforms objectively classified practices, in which a class condition signifies itself (through taste), into classifying practices, that is, into a symbolic expression of class position, by perceiving them in their mutual relations and in terms of social classificatory schemes.

(Bourdieu, 1986: 175)

Thus, responses, as socially differentiated dispositions, are modes of distinction and classification and via their operation serve to reproduce oppositions and associations between classes and schools. They function 'as a sort of social orientation, a "sense of one's place", guiding the occupants of a given place in social space towards the social positions adjusted to their properties, and towards the practices or goods which befit the occupants of that position' (Bourdieu, 1986: 466). Thus, choice is oriented to, and informed by, class thinking.

How can we identify or discern these class-related classifications at work in the way that parents talk about choice? Some indications of this were offered earlier and there are certainly other indications and traces of such class-significant distinctions and classifying practices in our interview data.

'I thought they were absolutely awful. Every class we went into in Overbury [school] somebody was being told off – mainly it was boys, but not only boys. The behaviour was very much . . . oh *Grange Hill* [fictional school on TV], it seemed almost like to me, and I felt Lockmere [school] was very much a boys' school, a boys' dominated school, very large, the playground was very small, everything was up on stilts . . . very crowded and we were there at playtime as well and they all come rushing out and pushing past you and . . . no holding any doors open for you, this sort of thing.'

(Mrs Snaresbrook, 16 December 1991)

These comments point up the importance of gender as well as class in the habitus of these schools. And the use of '*Grange Hill*', a television version of the 'underside' of school life, as a model of bad taste, is interesting.

'Yes, he's very keen to go to Lockmere [school], but again it's the flavour of the month again, since the head's changed . . . It seems to be a very good school. When our eldest son [Chris] had to go there, it was a horrific school, I mean they had knife fights and it was a different place altogether, wasn't it Chris? I mean, he was terrified to go there. It's a very different place since they've let the girls in and the head's changed.'

(Mrs Collier, 30 January 1991)

Clearly, class-orientation, symbolized through behaviour, dramatically represented here in the 'knife fights' is transmitted and circulated in the currency of reputation. Again, male violence is employed as a significant marker and is seen as a key constituent of the school's culture.

'I think it's got what my husband and I would term as a slight yob element. I think there are an element of children who could cause trouble, which we didn't notice so much at the other schools . . . we looked at, maybe because they're girls' schools.'

(Mrs Mills, 12 February 1993)

'He'll go to Suchard [school], and if things prove very difficult we'll move him. The main reason we want Max [son] to go to Suchard is because he tends to gravitate towards the rougher children in the school and they're nice enough kids but they're not very motivated, they're not very bright, and he tends to work at the level of the children he's working with'.

(Mrs Brent, 19 December 1991)

Here class is closer to the surface: the euphemisms are 'yob element' and 'rougher' and this latter is associated with 'not very bright'. The Brent's preference here is for a selective grammar school in an adjacent LEA. This also points up the key role in these aspects of choice of social mix and social mixing. What is important is with whom your child goes to school. We are not arguing that this is the only factor in choice, but that it is a decisive constituent of choice-making. For some parents it is of crucial importance; it is less so for others, but it is rarely unimportant. The Colliers chose to try for a private sector school for their son and their reasoning is similar to the Brents.

'I think in the end that was why we decided – well partly, because William's [son] head suggested that we should put him in for the exam . . . not because he's brilliant or anything, but because of the . . . behavioural difficulties, that he might possibly get in with the wrong groups.'

(Mrs Collier, 19 December 1991)

Again, all of this is tied up with discipline, social order, orderliness and security, the dangers of the 'wrong groups'; there are undertones of tainting effects, of impurity. The concomitant of all this is separation and differentiation. Thus, Bourdieu (1986: 31) makes the point that

[It] should not be thought that the relationship of distinction (which may or may not imply the conscious intention of distinguishing itself from the common people) is only an incidental component in the aesthetic disposition. The pure gaze implies a break with the ordinary attitude towards the world which, as such, is a social break.

Safety, security and orderliness are seen partly as a product of social composition and partly as a product of school policies and practices.

'One of the problems of Overbury [school] . . . is that they have a very large intake from the Bridge estate which is just up the road from them in Westway [LEA] where there's an enormous number of problems. So problem kids are going to Overbury, particularly as Overbury has a reputation for being a caring school. Because it's caring, people with kids with problems send their kids there and I'm a parent with kids with problems, but I don't want my problem kids to get into a school with all the other problem kids, because the attention will be shared out more thinly. That's a fact of life, you want the best for your kids.'

(Mrs Osterley, 13 December 1991)

Here we have a lexicon of 'wrong types', of 'kids with problems' and indications of the competition and struggle for scarce resources in schools, like special needs support. The dual aspects of class choosing are evident. One aspect is concerned with subjective meaning – the signs and expressive features of schools, and their affinity with or antipathy to the habitus of the family. The other is concerned with the structure of objective relations and class antagonisms within the social field of schooling. Here social positions within the field, the 'limits between groups . . . are also strategic emplacements, fortresses to be defended and captured in a field of struggles' (Bourdieu, 1986: 244). These aspects are part of class struggles over the appropriation of cultural goods – struggles conducted with great subtlety and with little visible or palpable conflict.

The symbolic struggles between the classes have no chance of being seen and organised as such, and are bound to take the form of competitive struggles helping to reproduce gaps which are the essence of the race.

(Bourdieu, 1986: 251)

Significantly, for one parent the issue of school habitus was addressed the other way round – the problem is the children who do *not* go to the Riverway comprehensives.

'If comprehensive education was really what it's supposed to be, if all the children went, then that would be okay, but the cream is all going somewhere else. And so therefore when they go, they haven't got the competition, they haven't got the children at the top that they should have, it isn't comprehensive education . . . Everybody who can afford to, sends their children to independent schools, especially in this particular part of the LEA. So therefore he's just not going to have the competition that he should have, in the groups that he has.'

(Mrs Charing, 19 December 1991)

Another parent highlighted the relationship between social space, social identity and class, and again the affective antipathies of habitus clash.

'Goddard [school] we felt was probably too . . . it was across the dual carriageway, so it either meant going over the road or under the underpass . . . and we wouldn't have been happy about that, and I don't think she would have been and it just feels geographically different. It doesn't feel part of this community, it feels part of the Goddard community. There's that slight distance with the road. The road really carves up between Tidewash and Goddard . . . although they had a new head there . . . it had a poor reputation in the past.'

(Mrs Latimer, 12 December 1991)

Here again, geography, distance and social setting are all important. Goddard is essentially a working–class school in a working-class setting. For Mrs Latimer, it is marked by its otherness, it 'feels' alien, unfamiliar. This is also related again to a poor reputation.

Even when it is in no way inspired by the conscious concern to stand aloof from working class laxity, every petit bourgeois profession of vigour, every eulogy of the clean, sober and neat, contains a tacit reference to uncleanliness, in words or things, to intemperance or imprudence.

(Bourdieu, 1986: 246–7)

Considerable interpretative work is involved in decoding the school and its locality. One parent adds a further twist to this: she is attracted to Goddard by the good work done by a new headteacher (which Mrs Latimer also mentioned) but again Goddard is a different place, 'cut off from civilization'.

'I think he's doing very good work there. And he does have a way to go, as he says – he's got the dual carriageway cutting him off from

civilization, because there's the main dual carriageway just at the side
of the school between it and the rest of Riverway.'

(Mrs Osterley, 13 December 1991)

For some parents, such class-related rejection of certain schools was
more generalized and they made deliberate choices *out of* their local
comprehensive system. This was particularly evident in Northwark
LEA. This is partly based on an historic antipathy to Northwark
(ex-ILEA) schools – an interesting class-related perception that the ILEA
was engaged in social engineering not in the interests of aspiring
middle-class parents.

'We only went to Fletcher [school] for Robert . . . yes, that was the
only one we went to for Robert. I just refused point blank to consider
the schools in Northwark . . . It was very soon after the change as
well . . . and I thought they wouldn't have had time to settle down
anyway.'

(Mrs Giggs, 24 October 1991)

'Oh yes, my neighbour across the road has three daughters who've
done very well, they're taking A levels at Trumpton school . . . so
yes, I mean we did speak to other people locally . . . I was just going
to say that a lot of people, particularly . . . very locally here, tended
to send their children out of LEA anyway, unless they were very very
worried about their travelling at eleven'.

(Mrs Bruce, 4 September 1992)

As indicated already, a crucial part of the construction of class-related
choice is shared perception and understanding.

The agents only have to follow the leanings of their habitus in order
to take over, unwittingly, the intention immanent in the corresponding practices, to find an activity which is entirely 'them' and with it,
kindred spirits.

(Bourdieu, 1986: 223)

An identification with the institution and its 'clients' is an important
component of choice. Social networks transmit actual and symbolic
forms of information. 'Taste is what brings together things and people
that go together' (Bourdieu, 1986: 241).

'Oh very crucial, I think the headmaster is actually the one that
makes the school . . . but because I have a few friends whose kids

have gone there before . . . I think that all the children seemed very happy, and that was a very important thing for me.'

(Mrs Roding, 12 December 1991)

'We tried to find as many people as possible who had children at the various schools, yes, we did discuss it with friends and neighbours.'

(Mrs Brent, 19 December 1991)

Again, this approach is remarkably subtle; it certainly side-steps what Bourdieu (1986) calls the 'brutality of discriminatory measures' and instead displays 'the charms of the apparent absence of criteria' (1986: 162). This suggests a complex sense-making process, a cultural competence to 'read' schools in particular ways and to move within the 'stratum of secondary meanings, i.e., the level of the meaning of what is signified' (Bourdieu, 1986: 2). If we can stretch the parallels with Bourdieu's analysis of taste a little further, then we can begin to see the work of decoding that is done here.

Consumption is, in this case, a stage in a process of communication, that is, an act of deciphering, decoding, which presupposes practical or explicit mastery of a cipher or code. In a sense, one can say that the capacity to see (*voir*) is a function of the knowledge (*savoir*), or concepts, that is the words that are available to name visible things, and which are, as it were, programmes for perception . . . A beholder who lacks the specific code feels lost in a chaos of sounds and rhythms, colours and lines, without rhyme or reason.

(Bourdieu, 1986: 2)

The point is that social class groups engage with and decipher schools in different ways. What they 'see' and 'know' of school is different and is related to different systems of values and relevances. But their degree of confidence, their ability to use the language of schooling and their depth of perception are also different. The role of decoding is, we suggest, fundamental to the relationship between class and choice that is evident in our study and others (see Willms and Echols, 1992).

Let us stretch the point and take this argument one stage further. A general review of the views and concerns of the privileged chooser would suggest that their sympathies are certainly liberal, if not progressive. That is to say, apart from a preference for school uniform, there is little evidence of the rampant traditionalism that Conservative commentators perceive among parents nor any marked hostility to comprehensive education. Thus, not untypically, Mrs Latimer rejected one school for her daughter because she thought it 'too grammar schoolish'. However, one issue of 'progressive/comprehensive' practice was regarded with *concern* (we use this moderate term deliberately), that is, mixed ability grouping.

Among those mentioning the issue, there was a preference expressed by a majority for setting[2]. This was used as one criterion for distinguishing between schools. The point we wish to make is that the distinctions and 'dividing practices' which are used to distinguish between schools, extend to internal differentiation. For some parents there is an educational and reproductive calculus involved here related to maximizing their child's objective chances of obtaining valued certificates. But this is set, in Bourdieu's terms, in 'the new system with its fuzzy classifications and blurred edges' (Bourdieu, 1986: 154). (In some ways, the market contributes to this blurring as new types of schools are invented and the ideology of choice is extended.) But as Bourdieu (1986: 155) goes on to say,

> . . . the blurring of hierarchies and boundaries between the elected and the rejected, between true and false qualifications, plays a part in 'cooling out' and in calm acquiescence at being cooled out.

It is worth recalling that the impetus to mixed-ability grouping was launched from a rejection of the 'cooling out' effects of streaming (Ball, 1981).

> 'And another thing I was pleased to learn about was that there is still an element of streaming in the school. They don't have mixed ability classes for the main subjects, for the core curriculum.'
>
> (Mr Giggs, 24 October 1991)

> 'They don't set for the first two years and then they set most subjects, I think they're set into three bands, for different subjects, so that if a child is bright at maths they'll go into the top set . . . if they're not so bright at English, they'll go into the second set for English. I think it's very flexible which I think is important . . . that they don't sort of stream just sort of across the board.'
>
> (Ms Bond, 30 December 1991)

> 'Several of my friends' children who are now at independent schools have chosen it because in the GCSE classes they weren't streaming them. I mean there was non-streaming. I mean you cannot teach non-stream GCSE, it's just not possible. And at several of the schools, and Lockmere [school] was one of them, there were non-streamed GCSE classes.'
>
> (Mrs Collier, 30 December 1991)

> 'I think the other major factor for us was the fact that they do set them at Arthur Lucas [school], as they do at Coombe [school], and we

haven't found this to be the case with any other school. And they are set within the first two weeks of starting the school.'

(Mrs Bruce, 4 September 1992)

In part, these comments represent a simple self-interest, the objective choices of reproduction. The parents quoted feel it possible that their child would be disadvantaged by mixed-ability grouping and advantaged by setting: attention, particular sorts of teaching, pace, etc. are scarce resources. But this is not naive, backwoods condemnation. There is an understanding of pros and cons and of variations in policy. Again, a sophisticated decoding of policies and practices is in evidence. These preferences rest upon establishing and maintaining identities, key distinctions and categorizations, by means of arbitrary exclusions and selections.

Semi-skilled choosers

The families represented by this type of chooser have strong inclination but limited capacity to engage 'effectively' with the market: their cultural capital is in the wrong currency and they are less able to accumulate the right sort. Although many of the semi-skilled are oriented to the same 'cosmopolitan' schools as the privileged/skilled, the biographies and family histories of these families have not provided them with the experiences or inside knowledge of the school system and the social contacts and cultural skills to pursue their inclination to choice 'effectively'. They are less 'at ease' in the medium of school choice than the privilege/skilled choosers. For example, unlike the 'skilled' choosers these parents do not see themselves resorting to appeals procedures if frustrated in their initial choice. This type is defined as much by its difference from the other two as by its own intrinsic qualities. In Bourdieu's terms, all types are defined relationally.

In the intermediate position are the practices which are perceived as pretentious, because of the manifest discrepancy between ambition and possibilities.

(Bourdieu, 1986: 176)

Significantly, the accounts generated by those families who fit the profile of the semi-skilled are simpler and starker than the privileged. In the most obvious sense, they are shorter and less detailed. Complexity is often reduced and schools are portrayed in terms of general qualities – positive and negative. There is an appearance of confidence in the judgements being made but at the same time there is also a degree of confusion and uncertainty surrounding the parents' perceptions of schools:

'With David [son], being the first one, if you like, we thought well we better do it fairly thoroughly, so we got all the local schools . . . we got all the prospectuses from the local schools and we actually visited, I don't know, how many schools did we visit Prue [wife]? It must have been what, eleven or twelve? We went right out to Sunfold and . . . and I think at the end of that we were totally confused because obviously . . . some schools are good at some things and not at others and in the end we thought, well what do we do? Finally we decided to go for – all due respect to . . . I hope this doesn't get back to Westway LEA council, we are not a lover of Westway Council's education . . . for various reasons – and we actually decided on . . . Overbury in Riverway, because we thought, okay its very easy for him to get to.'

(Mr West, 14 January 1992)

These families talk about potential school choices as outsiders, often relying, at least in part, on the comments or perceptions of others. For the Wappings, who did not attend open evenings, and the Pritchards, newspaper reports assumed considerable significance.

'Yes, that was strongly influenced by things I'd read in the newspaper about it, one thing was that it had been chosen by London Weekend Television for a survey on comprehensive education in the country and, having visited there and started filming, they discounted it because they said it wasn't representative, that they thought it was too good to be considered representative of comprehensive education . . . so I thought then that said an awful lot.'

(Mrs Wapping, 19 December 1991)

'(a) It's received very good press, (b) in the papers it always has good academic results, and I talked to several people who have children, because I'm sort of a fairly old mother, my children are young for my age . . . so the people I know have older children, have already gone to senior schools, and I've heard very very good reports on it.'

(Mrs Pritchard, 13 October 1993)

The Colindales were unable to attend open evenings and also relied heavily on second-hand sources of information and impression.

'Basically we didn't actually get to go to Trumpton [school], because we were in America on holiday at the time so my brother went to the open evening there for us . . . and he was quite impressed with it, he thought it was one of the better ones. We missed quite a few of the

schools actually, because we were away and it was at that time . . .
when they were actually doing the open evenings and that, so we
made our choice basically on hearsay from others and what was
actually in the booklet that was supplied to us.'

(Mrs Colindale, 10 January 1992)

The Leytons only attended one open evening and relied primarily on
schools prospectuses and brochures and the advice of friends. Second-
hand accounts were also important in discounting certain schools.

'Parsons [school] came out, I'm going back to when I was at school in
Bridges, Parsons in those days was always seen as quite a good school
but from what we've heard lately I think they've got a lot of
problems. I hear they've got a very large drugs problem at Parsons
school, we was told by somebody.'

(Mr Leyton, 21 February 1992)

'I don't like the school, I knew somebody who was a teacher there
who has now left and they didn't like teaching there. Now somebody
else who I knew, who was doing a project there, probably much the
same as you're doing; she was involved in looking at several schools
right across London and she said she'd never actually been in a school
that had an attitude like Parsons [school] and she said she found it
very disturbing, and that, well, coming from a professional, that put
me off completely.'

(Mrs Wapping, 19 December 1991)

In a way, the semi-skilled find themselves unable to distinguish between
schools, unable to decode the polysemic messages with which they are
confronted:

'When you actually go and look round the schools, to be quite honest
you can't really find anything wrong with any of them . . . So you
learn very little by going round really.'

(Mr Plaistow, 14 January 1993)

The boundaries and classifications which are so significant to the 'skilled'
choosers become slippery and ill-defined.

Researcher: Right, and what kind of impression did you gain from
looking at the brochures?
Mr Leyton: Well they were all much, they all gave the impression
that they were all much the same, their sort of high standards.
Mrs Leyton: Yes, a lot of the brochures seemed to be, well, these are
our exam results and it just listed the children's achievements and
. . . with the Pankhurst [school] one . . . it did give you the exam
results but it . . . there came across a more caring attitude to all the

children and how they . . . help them to achieve to the best of their ability. They didn't seem to be overimpressed with exam results. They wanted to tell you how they could bring the best out of the children, which I think is nice.

(Interview, 21 January 1992)

In a sense these parents know what they are supposed to do as 'responsible' parents but find it difficult to act independently. There is less reliance on 'feel' and 'affective' response. The semi-skilled seek reassurance from those they see to be 'informed' or more 'authoritative' in such matters. They appear to want to render choice into a more certain and objective process but seem not to do this on the basis of their own judgements. In the absence of reassurance from others, the parents generally find themselves in difficulty when it comes to evaluating schools. Semi-skilled choosers appear to feel themselves to be on the outside looking in on an education system radically different from their own school experiences.

'We sit there as parents and we don't know. I think unless you're actually in the education system, employed by it, you don't really know what's going on in the system and how it's really run, you only really get told what they want you to know.'

(Mr Plaistow, 14 January 1993)

'Obviously with my parents, they didn't have a choice for me, you either went to the secondary modern school or you went to the grammar school, it was one or the other, and that was the only choice in the LEA. There was either the girls' grammar, the boys' grammar or you went to the secondary school which was mixed . . . so in fact, in a way, I feel we've got too much choice, there's too many schools to pick from. In a way I'd rather not have to have the choice.'

(Mrs Dankworth, 29 September 1993)

Perhaps as a result, rumour and reputation are much more likely to be taken at face value. Overall, the views and accounts of schools produced by these parents are considerably less well grounded in the contemporary discourses of education than those of the skilled/privileged. There is little evidence of personal interpretive work in the decoding of school practices. These families are 'outsiders' to education and are 'uncertain of their classifications' (Bourdieu, 1986: 326). However, like the skilled/ privileged, differentiations based on social mix play a part in their evaluation of schools. For example, some of these parents appeared concerned about the proportion of ethnic minority students in the local schools. The skilled/privileged parents did not refer to social mix in these terms. This may be because the skilled choosers are more reticent about their racism and more skilled in disguising it.

Paradoxically perhaps, for the semi-skilled parents, the publication of examination results is not necessarily a help, rather, in some cases, a source of further uncertainty. The difficulties they experience in making sense of the figures and in relating the figures to the concrete qualities of schools actually produces a further barrier to their appreciation of schooling and the possibilities of discrimination. There were also doubts about the veracity of the published figures. In a sense, the more varieties of information there are, the less clear are differences between schools.

> 'Well I did look at them but they all seemed to be between 48 and 50 per cent and I think they've got ludicrous now and I can't actually . . . looking at them at all, because they all average round about that, and I think this desperate thing to get it up a few per cent is now getting very irritating, because they're all the same. And I don't think these figures mean anything to anyone really, they're so compli-cated.'
>
> (Mrs Buckhurst, 16 December 1991)

One parent, commented (before the publication of 'league tables'):

> 'Yes, I think they tend to tell you how many of them actually got grade A, or if they didn't necessarily get very good marks, they give you a percentage of what the overall pass was, where it would be better if they just had one general, right, so many passed, but so many were above whatever grade, because that's all changed since we were at school as well, because there's all different exams now.'
>
> (Mrs Colindale, 10 January 1991)

Overall, for the semi-skilled the process of school choice is abstract, more a matter of finding the 'good' school, rather than the 'right' one. This is a 'pure but empty goodwill which for lack of the guidelines and principles needed to apply it, does not know which way to turn' (Bourdieu, 1986: 323). The qualities of the children are very rarely a criterion for choice. The careful child-matching of the privileged choosers is absent. In contrast to the privileged choosers, there is a kind of 'wait-and-see' fatalism about the outcomes of education and their children's future. In this respect, they have more in common with the disconnected choosers (see below).

Mr West: Victoria [daughter] is not going to set the world alight. She's going to be middle of the road most probably all the way

through. She's not going to be bottom of the class, she's not going
to be top.

Mrs West: As long as she's happy going to school.

(Interview, 14 January 1992)

'You can't force a child to do well academically. If it's there you can
encourage it – well we feel that you can encourage it – but if they
switch off, or it just doesn't happen, nothing on earth will make it
happen.'

(Mrs Plaistow, 14 January 1993)

The disconnected – 'choice as necessity'

This type of chooser approximates to those parents Vincent (1993)
describes as 'detached'. They are disconnected from the market in the
sense that they are not inclined to engage with it. It is not that these
parents have no views about education, or no concerns about schools and
their children's experiences and achievement. They do, but they do not
see their children's enjoyment of school or their educational success as
being facilitated in any way by a consumerist approach to school choice.
For these parents, the idea of examining a wide range of schools is not
something which enters their frame of thinking. Whereas skilled/
privileged parents sometimes find the many differences between schools
somewhat baffling, the disconnected parents typically see schools as
much the same.

'I think they are much of a muchness really. Perhaps one may have a
better library, another one may have better sports facilities, but
we've decided we're going to look at the two schools, and as long as
there's nothing academically vastly different or better with one
school then David [son] can make the final choice. We feel he's got to
be happy.'

(Mrs Sutcliffe, 28 September 1993)

While the skilled/privileged choosers often ended with two possible
schools from their process of elimination and comparison, the disconnected almost always began with, and limited themselves to, two. These
would be schools in close physical proximity and part of their social
community. There is little or no attempt to collect information about
other schools and little awareness of other schools apart from those
within the locality. Choice here means something different from the
process gone through by the privileged or the semi-skilled. Choice for
these parents typically seems more or less predetermined, often a process
of confirmation rather than comparison. The reasons articulated in
interviews are normally the reasons for the choice that is made rather than

an account of a process of choosing. Visits to schools were often for the purpose of seeing the school already selected – 'a look around' – rather than part of a choice-making process. There is even sometimes a degree of haphazardness or chance to 'the choice':

> 'We didn't know the area and we'd heard . . . all things . . . You hear some people say, "This school is good, no that school's good". So in the end we thought we'd wait and see what came and, as it was, the very first thing that happened was that Tania's [daughter] school organized a visit to the local school down here, Lymethorpe, and the whole class went off for the morning . . . She came back saying she . . . had a very good time.'
>
> (Mr Tufnell, 30 January 1992)

That was how Tania came to choose Lymethorpe. There is a reactive response to events here rather than the proactive or demanding engagement typical of the skilled/privileged. In a few cases choice is abdicated altogether to the child. The Fairlops were a case in point:

> 'We didn't think it was worth going too far . . . so it was really, for closeness I suppose, it was a choice of two schools, Parsons and Flightpath. And most of her friends were going to Parsons, which surprised me why she chose Flightpath, but she chose Flightpath and that was it. I mean, we didn't go to look at any of them . . . We wasn't really that bothered as I say . . . because to me, all schools are the same. I mean I'd have liked her to have gone to the same school I went to, because I liked it there, but it's a bit further still than Flightpath school, so she'd have had to have caught a bus or something, every morning, messing about like that. As I say, we left it to her and she chose Flightpath, so we were quite happy with it.'
>
> (Mr Fairlop, 16 December 1992)

The happiness of the child is of great importance to this type of chooser, but happiness is generally a matter of social adjustment, friendship and engagement with 'the local', rather than the achievement of long-term goals or the realization of specific talents,

> 'I think he's always just thought, well I'll go to Lymethorpe.'
>
> (Mrs Dublin, 28 September 1993).

Again, as with the semi-skilled, this is sometimes related to a fatalism about schools and about achievement, the idea that achievement is about doing your best and waiting to see what will happen. This is also rooted in the idea that schools are all basically the same and is all part of what Bourdieu (1986: 380–1) describes as resignation, realism and closure:

> 'The second one is doing better than the eldest one, she's quite bright, the second one, but it's not the school.'
>
> (Mrs Stockwell, 22 November 1992).

This kind of perspective may be grounded in a belief that the child's willingness or ability to learn is fixed and innate, regardless of the learning environment (Carspecken, 1990; Vincent, pers. comm.).

Disconnected parents want a 'good' education for their children in their local school and do not see the need (nor do they necessarily have the resources) to 'seek out' a 'good' education elsewhere. A 'good' education is not measured by the examination performances of schools: examination results were not used to discriminate between schools nor did an awareness of poor results lead to rejection. Indeed, examinations were rarely mentioned without prompting.

> *Researcher*: Did you look at things like exam results?
>
> *Mr Tufnell*: Not particularly, because they really didn't mean anything to me, because he goes to school, he does his best, if he doesn't pass then it won't be for the want of trying . . . so he can only do his best and it really doesn't matter to me, how many – like Flightpath [school], even if it had a very poor record I would still send him there, because they've got the stuff there to do the job, and if the teachers are training the kids, you can't blame the teachers if the kids can't learn, do you see what I mean?
>
> (Interview, 30 November 1992)

Factors such as facilities, distance, safety, convenience and locality are of prime concern to the disconnected chooser. In contrast to the issues of child personality, grouping, school policy and teaching methods talked about by the skilled/privileged, this is a realm of material matters. This then is class-choosing of a different kind.

These parents might be described as working on the surface structure of choice, because their programmes of perception rest on a basic unfamiliarity with particular aspects of schools and schooling. Usually this type of chooser left school early themselves and has little confidence in their ability to understand or interpret the language of teachers. They are more confident with the material realities of plant and facilities. Thus, Mrs Debden clearly knew something about her local school and was impressed with the building and equipment but nevertheless felt herself 'bamboozled' by 'what they were saying to us'. As Mrs Perivale put it, 'what do I look for?'

'They had a lot more to offer, Flightpath [school], but when we went round there on the open evening, I thought . . . what have I got to sort of look for, and we had no idea . . . They were good, they showed us round all the labs, well everything they showed us round, what the children were doing, they had children there, doing things so we could see what they were doing, and what Billy [son] would be doing. But I'm walking round thinking, "What do I look for, a good teacher?" and think, "well are you a good teacher or not? . . ." I didn't know, I really didn't know.'

(Mrs Perivale, 24 November 1992)

Disconnected parents do not speak the language of secondary educational meanings. Authoritative accounts are sought from within local social networks or from direct experience – rather than from sources of 'public' information. Mr Perivale attended a local school himself and has other local knowledge to draw upon. These things are important as positive bases for choosing, but so too are the 'impressive facilities':

'The choice is really practically between the two schools, Lymethorpe and Flightpath, and because of my miserable time at Flightpath . . . although it is a vastly different school, I still feel it's too big and our neighbours' eldest daughter goes to Lymethorpe and she's done very well . . . I think they've got eight science labs, something like that, computers, everything. He loves drawing, they've got . . . art workshops . . . the facilities are tremendous.'

(Mr Perivale, 14 November 1992)

The information networks of disconnected choosers are limited in scope but nonetheless rich and useful. These networks themselves are indicative of the relationship between local schools, families and community.

'Well, Parsons [school] . . ., my sister-in-law's children go to Flightpath [school] and each one has done very very well. I've known children to go to Parsons and they haven't done well . . . As I say, I've got two nephews and one niece at [Flightpath] . . . and they were always talking about the diaries and I just asked what it was for.'

(Mrs Harper, 7 November 1991)

There is a collectivity to choosing, in contrast to the individuality of the child-matching strategies of the privileged. Thus, there is frequent mention of friends, neighbours and relatives in framing choice. Furthermore, the choices of disconnected choosers are much more likely to be located within the specifics of other decisions and preferences within the same family:

'No, we was quite happy when we took the eldest one down the first time, she's in the third year now, we was quite happy with the school, and we're quite happy with her work over the past two years, three years, whatever . . . so I can't see the point in going to other schools when I'm satisfied with one school.'

(Mrs Wooley, 18 October 1993)

In south Westway, other notions of community and familiarity underlay the rejection of some schools by some families. For many white, working-class parents, the racial composition of Gorse school excluded it from consideration and elicited a range of racist comments.

'Because it's all nig nogs, isn't it? It's all Asians and it is a known fact that they hold ours back. And the last I heard actually, some of the kids, they were complaining as well, you see, because some of them, while they're at home they talk English, some if they want to go to school they're alright, but you get the others . . . the kiddies while they're at home speak in Punjabi or whatever it is, so that when they come to school they can't understand a bloody word, you see? And this is what's happening down there, and there's no way that he's going there. I mean I know somebody that goes there, and in her class there's about 35 I think, five are white, the rest are . . ., so he's not going down there. He's definitely not going there.'

(Mr Tufnell, 30 November 1992)

Mrs Perivale: It was a good school on the whole, the actual education was good, wasn't it? But I think in the back of your mind, I don't think you would have sent Ben [son] there, would you? Because of the race . . .?

Mr Perivale: No, it's 90, no, probably 80 per cent Asian pupils there and it's geared that way, or it seemed to be, it probably isn't, but it seemed to be geared that way, as well, the main intake is going to be from Westway [LEA].

(Interview, 24 November 1992)

'No, there's too many Indians there.'

(Mrs Stockwell, 22 November 1992)

This 'racially-informed' choosing works in reverse for some South Asian parents. For them, Gorse school is attractive because it is regarded as safe, and it has a strong and very overt emphasis on educational traditionalism and academic achievement.

'Yes, I did see the exam results and my [niece and nephew] have been in that school . . . and secondly . . . the education of that school and the principal – it's very strict, you know, like the kids, if they're not in uniform or they haven't done their homework, things like that, if they muck about, they'll be told off and at the end of the day they're not so – you know all the time misbehaving in the school, things like that.'

(Mr Kahn, 17 January 1992)

In contrast, the predominantly white Flightpath school is regarded with some suspicion as, or as having been, 'a bit rough' – which is probably a euphemism here.

> 'Yes, I did think a lot about this other school . . . Flightpath, but I've never seen . . . Flightpath school . . . I haven't been in there, but I've seen the kids, they go from building to building over the flyover up there . . . and in fact some time ago we did read in our local paper what sort of school it was . . . the kids were a bit rough up there sometimes, things like that . . . I think some action has been taken by the education department . . . But it had a really bad name.'

(Mr Kahn, 17 January 1992)

And for a few white parents the presence of South Asian children at Gorse school is seen as a positive attractor in their choice of school.

> 'Gorse has a very high Asian count of children and it seemed that the Asian children, they are very much on education and discipline, and I think that rubs off on everybody else.'

(Mrs Cole, 13 October 1993)

These racialized choices are related to communal interests and are based around social and family networks and informal sources of information, even if negatively and antagonistically constructed.

Choice of school, despite the way it is written about by many researchers and commentators, cannot be made separate from the interpersonal relationships, patterns of parenting and material environments which constitute and constrain the lives and opportunities of families. For the disconnected and some semi-skilled choosers, choice of school enters into a complex terrain of other concerns and necessities. School has to be 'fitted' into a set of constraints and expectations related to work roles, family roles, the sexual division of labour and the demands of household organization. The material and cultural aspects of this are difficult to separate. For the privileged/skilled and some of the semi-skilled, it was much more common to find family roles and household organization being accommodated to school. For the disconnected choosers, social reproduction is, as we have seen, more closely tied to a sense of locale and community, of which the family is a co–extensive part. The local school is in Cremin's (1979) terms part of a 'functional community' and is chosen positively for this reason. That is, reproduction is defined and constrained and achieved within a spatial framework. Family life, and things such as school choice, are played out within, and over and against, a space and time budget. For the disconnected choosers, space and family organization were very often the key elements in choice-making.

'Too far . . . I mean, supposing something was to happen, God forbid, that means I would have to go miles to get her . . . or get any of the children. I'd rather have a quick way of getting there.'

(Mrs Harper, 7 November 1991)

'Really only because her brother goes there and its local as well, because she'll have to pick up her sister as well, so she's got to have something local . . . Because my husband really wanted him to go to Crawford Park [school], because he'd come from there, but we thought it was too far for him to go . . . that we wanted something really local and by having Trumpton [school], like my husband said, they can all go there, because it's a mixed school, which is good.'

(Mrs Nevin, 18 July 1991)

In transport studies, activity analysis 'examines inter-dependencies within the household in respect of the scheduling and time – space constraints placed upon individual household members' (Grieco *et al.*, 1991: 1) and suggests that 'household organisation lies at the heart of the understanding of travel behaviour' (1991: 4). Among low-income households on time-constrained budgets, the limitations of private and public transport play a key role in a whole range of decision-making. These constraints and the forms of household organization which develop as a result are particularly associated 'with the gender roles of women' (Grieco, 1991: 4).

Women in many such households are able to meet their daily domestic responsibilities and to respond to crises only by 'borrowing' time and other resources from other houses (principally kin) in their social network.

(Grieco and Pearson, 1991: 4)

Access to a car, the pattern of bus, tube and train routes, the local transport timetables, the pattern of busy roads and open spaces and the physical location of schools all affect the possibility and the perception of choice. 'Spatial and temporal practices, in any society, abound in subtleties and complexities' (Harvey, 1989: 218). In part, these horizons (and the complex relationship of space to distance) relate what Harvey calls the 'representations of space' to 'spaces of representation' or imagination; particularly in the latter, 'unfamiliarity' and 'spaces of fear' are important.

Mrs Harper: She'd go across the crossing.
Researcher: Through the park?
Mrs Harper: Oh no, she won't go through the park, definitely not! There's a pathway, it goes all the way round, past the library and then under that footway bridge and then round the corner. She's been taught she don't go in parks, no way!

(Interview, 7 November 1991)

Where transport deprivation leads to the social isolation and segregation of particular social groups in particular localities, *social enclaves* are created. The existence of such enclaves reinforces the importance of *the local* and the need for complex intra- and interhousehold dependencies. The existence of enclaves can also be related to informational dynamics and local information structures (Weimann, 1982). These patterns and processes of time and space management and the existence of social enclaves and social networks are of prime importance in understanding school choice-making for certain class groups. Such an analysis begins to highlight the important interrelationships between market schooling and the other deregulation policies of the current Government, such as transport, housing, health, social welfare and employment training (see Carlen *et al.*, 1992). Differences in the perception of time and space are related to differences in 'finite time resources and the "friction of distance" (measured in time or cost taken to overcome it) [which] constrain daily movement' (Harvey, 1989: 211). The distribution of 'time – space biographies' is class-related – and in this way 'the organisation of space can indeed define relationships between people, activities, things, and concepts' (Harvey, 1989: 216).

The complexities of choice for the disconnected parents reported here are created by the intersection of the values and constraints of locality. There are vestiges apparent here of the 'localism' which Clarke (1979: 240) refers to as 'a pervasive mode of working class culture'. But there are also a set of frictions and limitations and fears and concerns which tie disconnected choosers to their local schools. The sense of locality in disconnected choice and the more cosmopolitan activities of the privileged/skilled parents suggest that parents are orientated to different circuits of schooling and we turn to an analysis of these in the next section.

Circuits of schooling

It is possible to take the analysis of the relationship between social class and choice of school one stage further through an overview of the local markets with which we are concerned. Our data point to the interplay between social class, cultural capital and choice within differentiated *circuits of schooling* in this market system. Across the three LEAs and adjacent areas in which this research is situated there are three clear circuits of schooling which relate differently to *choice*, *class* and *space*.

1 First, there is a circuit of *local, community, comprehensive schools* (A) which recruit the majority of their students from their immediate locality, have highly localized reputations and which have policies and structures which relate to a comprehensive school identity. They are oriented to fairly definite locales, which is in Giddens' terms a 'physical region involved as the setting of interaction, having definite boundaries which help to concentrate interaction in one way or another' (Giddens, 1984: 375)

2 Second, there are *cosmopolitan, high-profile, élite, maintained schools* (B) which recruit some, or often many, of their students from outside of their immediate locale, which have reputations which extend well beyond their home LEAs, some of which are (overtly) selective, i.e. grammar schools, others of which have 'pseudo-selective' or limited catchment criteria. These schools are usually oversubscribed.

3 Third, there is the *'local' system of day, independent schools* (C). These are schools which, in effect, compete with the maintained sector and which provide alternatives or possibilities for parents who also make a choice to maintained schools, although of course they also attract parents who are interested exclusively in the private sector.

4 There is also a fourth parallel but separate circuit of *Catholic schools* (D), which has its own hierarchy, pattern of competition and spatial structure (see Chapter 3).

The schools in each of these categories which fall into the remit of our study and which are regularly mentioned by parents in interview, are listed below. Most of these schools were referred to in the extracts from data quoted earlier.

A Trumpton, Milton, St Ignatious (also D), Northwark Park, Martineau, Ramsay Macdonald, Corpus Christi, Parsons, Overbury, Flightpath, Parkside, Gorse, Blenheim, Lockmere, Lymethorpe and Goddard.

B Suchard Grammar, Princess Elizabeth, Arthur Lucas, Fletcher, Hutton, Pankhurst, The CTC, Nancy Astor Girls, Florence Nightingale, Cardinal Heenan (also D).

C Trinity, Camberwick High, Madeley High, Harrod.

Some parents are clearly oriented to only one of these circuits and are unlikely or unwilling to consider other schools. Working-class, disconnected choosers are most likely to associate themselves with the A circuit (except of course when a B school is their local school). Middle-class, skilled/privileged choosers are more likely to associate themselves with the B and C circuits.

'We went to Martineau [single sex girls], Fletcher, Camberwick High and Madeley High and Princess Elizabeth. We went to the CTC, but it wasn't quite . . . it's actually having an open day next week. Trumpton I didn't go to though. I had been going to because I felt I ought to, being as it was on the doorstep . . . I wasn't really interested and at the same time felt I ought to go, but it didn't work out.'

(Mrs Knighton, 17 September 1991)

'Lockmere school, well that's the one we've put at the top of the list and I assume that she'll get a place there because we're linked to that and Suchard for girls, yes, but they have to take an exam. She's taken the exam but I don't think she'll get in, but the other school we considered is Pankhurst school for girls.'

(Mrs Mills, 12 February 1993)

'We applied to two independents, Camberwick High and Madeley High, and to the CTC college and to Princess Elizabeth's. I really wanted her to go to one of the independents, you know, the results were that much better . . . and then Princess Elizabeth . . . she didn't get in there . . . and then the CTC, and Northwark schools were bottom of the list.'

(Mrs Dearing, 23 January 1991)

However, the boundary between A and B is not absolute and fixed and there are borderline (or reputationally mobile) schools – Fletcher and Martineau are examples. And the arrival of the CTC has 'disturbed' the local system – as it is intended to do. Similarly, some families in a sense also hover on the borderline or move between circuits, particularly between B and C, the cosmopolitan state and private schools, and consequently express a whole range of uncertainties and ambivalences.

'When it turned out that the only schools Nicki [daughter] had places offered, was Martineau [school] and the CTC, I was very unsure about the CTC . . . one week I felt that it was going to be a marvellous place, then the next week I'd be thinking, be trying to talk to people about what they thought about it, and whether it would really suit me, because the terms are longer, and being a working mother and . . .'

(Mrs Knighton, 17 September 1991)

Nicki finally went to Princess Elizabeth.

'We put Martineau [school], and we did that because . . . we thought it was 99 per cent certain she was going to go in the private sector, and that if she did end up in the state sector, the amount of time she'd save on travelling and the amount of time she'd have to do other things, would be made up for by being local, and there being quite, probably quite a reasonable group of people going to Martineau, compared with the group who were likely to be going to Milton.'

(Mrs Tulley, 19 January 1993)

'We had a look at Milton [school] and thought that was probably the best of – I mean I didn't go to Trumpton school, but I've been past there at lunchtime and I didn't like what I saw, so decided that that definitely wasn't to be looked at. If he had not been successful in choosing the CTC, then we were going to pay for him, because we didn't consider anything else.'

(Mrs Moran, 27 November 1991)

'We've come from a family where the tradition has been for the boys to go to the local grammar school, which is now an independent school. So brothers, uncles, cousins are all there and have been there. So there was a very strong inclination for the first son to go to the independent school, Harrod . . . and if he failed that, my only other, or our only other consideration was a local church school . . . out of LEA, because I wouldn't consider Parsons [school]. It had a very bad reputation and had had for many years and it would not have been my choice.'

(Mrs Richards, 16 July 1991)

Conclusion

We began this chapter by indicating the complexity of parental choice of school but we can end it by pointing to at least two very simple and straightforward conclusions. First, choice is very directly and powerfully related to social-class differences. Second, choice emerges as a major new factor in maintaining and indeed reinforcing social-class divisions and inequalities. Again, in stating that, we do not seek to celebrate or romanticize the *past* here. There is a degree of significant continuity in the crucial role played by social class in educational opportunity. The point is that one set of class-related processes is replaced by another set. The 'balance sheet of the class struggle' over educational goods is changed. Choosing is a multifaceted process and there are clear indications here of class, 'race' and gender dimensions to choice. That is, despite some commonalities, the meanings (and implications) of choice vary distinctively between classes: 'different classes have different ways of life and views of the nature of social relationships which form a matrix within which consumption takes place' (Featherstone, 1992: 86). Where most recent analyses of class differentiation in education have stressed the work of selection and allocation done by schools and teachers, here selection and differentiation is produced by the actions of families. (Not that selection of the first sort has disappeared from the system, as we shall see in Chapter 6.) The onus is now more on the 'classified and classifying practices' of the proactive consumer. Education is subtly repositioned as a private good. The previous interrupters of class schooling (ineffective as they often were), like comprehensives with balanced intakes and mixed-ability grouping, are now being displaced. The ground rules of the class struggle over educational opportunity have been significantly changed.

The use of cultural capital in the decoding of schools and interpretation of information and in the 'matching' of child to school is a crucial component of choosing and then getting a school place, although economic capital is also important, most obviously in relation to the independent sector. Here we can see the actual realization of social advantage through effective activation of cultural resources (Lareau, 1989: 178). By linking biography to social structure, the analysis of school choice in relation to class and capital also illuminates the reproduction of class position and class divisions and points up the changing form and processes of class struggle in and over the social field of school choice.

Notes

1 Significantly, this phrase was changed in the 1994 *Updated Parents' Charter* to, 'You can say which school you would prefer your child to go to' (DFE 1994: 9).
2 Setting is the practice of grouping students for lessons according to ability.

3

AN ANALYSIS OF LOCAL MARKET RELATIONS

Introduction

The market in school-level education is, arguably, the most highly developed and ideologically charged of any of the new public-sector markets in England and Wales. That is, it comes closest to the ideal-type 'real' market, at least in so far as consumer choice acts directly upon producers and in many locations stimulates competition. However, the overall operational framework of the school market (open enrolment, per capita funding, devolved budgets, etc.) offers only a very crude sense of the workings and effects of specific local education markets. The diversity of local settings and the particularity of their politics, social geographies and histories make it difficult to generalize about market forces in education. Any meaningful conceptualization of the market in schooling must incorporate aspects of these local factors. This chapter offers some modest starting points towards such a conceptualization.

In highlighting the importance of 'the local' we also intend to indicate the continuing significance of the role of LEAs in the constitution and dynamics of local education markets. We suggest that it is a mistake to simply 'write-off' LEAs as a significant factor in the 'planning' of local systems of education, despite the inroads into their powers made by the Education Acts of 1988 and 1993 and the concomitant autonomy given to schools. The material presented here also serves to underline our point that the English education market is very much, in Hayek's (1980) terms, a form of 'ordered competition' which is organized 'so as to achieve *particular* social and economic goals'.

We proceed by presenting an overview of the recent history, patterns and dynamics of the local markets in our three case-study LEAs. In each case we will also illustrate the market 'position' of particular schools within each LEA. The point of these presentations is not simply to highlight the specifics of the 'cases'. We are aiming to isolate those major local factors which will shape and 'distort' the realization of the national-policy framework within 'lived' markets. The market in education is not simply a product of the Education Reform Act 1988 or of LEA decision-making; markets in particular settings have long and complex histories. Those histories are part of the local folk knowledge that parents draw upon when choosing schools. Those histories construct and confer reputations upon schools (although, as we will discuss in Chapter 5, schools are increasingly aware of, and increasingly sophisticated in, the management of impressions and reputation building). Education markets are also informed and constrained by the social meaning of locality and community. Some schools have strong locational identities. In particular, as we saw in Chapter 2, the attraction of the local school remains strong for many working-class parents and is a major criterion in their choice of school. For others, however, particularly many middle-class parents, this is of limited importance and they are willing and able to move their children around the system to get the particular schooling they want (see Chapter 2). In more general terms, changing social demography and the stability, or otherwise, of the local population will also have effects upon patterns of recruitment to schools. The spatial location of schools is itself important in relation to enrolment. This is the one thing that schools have little or no control over: patterns of public transport provision, natural barriers, traffic flows and local housing policies all impose limitations upon the possibilities of recruitment and hit certain schools hard and benefit others – irrespective of their 'quality'. Some schools find themselves isolated or disadvantaged by arbitrary factors related to their location while others are protected by the existence of 'natural' catchment areas. The outcomes of previous governmental and LEA decisions, which were driven by very different economic and political priorities from those now in play, such as the history of school building, of school closures and amalgamations also have a continuing impact in relation to the dynamics of local competition between schools.

Social class, in some cases ethnicity, and social geography are also key factors in the dynamics of the market in other ways. There is evidence of relationships between certain class factions and preference for certain styles and ethos of schooling. The class and ethnic composition of schools

Table 3.1 Characteristics of case-study LEAs

Characteristic	Northwark	Riverway	Westway
Socio-economic	Mixed class	Predominantly middle/upper middle class	Predominantly working class
Ethnic mix	Mixed ethnically	Mainly white	Mixed ethnically
Demographic fluidity/stability	Fluid local population, gentrification and so changing population of schools	Mainly stable local population but affected by fluidity in Northwark	Stable population – parents and grandparents attended same schools
Local systemic histories	History of comprehensive schools but strong tradition of status hierarchies	History of comprehensive schools, mutable status hierarchies, strong independent sector	Tradition of community schools
Parental inclination to 'choice'	Many parents willing for children to travel some distance to out-borough schools	Many parents willing for children to travel some distance to school in the borough (and to out-borough Roman Catholic and Church of England schools)	Strong localism and disinclination to travel
Transport	Good transport links	Good transport links	Poorer transport links
Existence of 'natural' catchments	Declining-disrupted 'natural' catchments	Increasingly unstable 'natural' catchments	Stable 'natural' catchments
LEA policy	LEA encourages competition and diversity	LEA encourages corporatism	LEA takes hands-off approach
Extent of competition	Strongly competitive	Muted competition within borough, strong competition with private and out-borough schools	Muted competition with borough, stronger competition with out-borough schools
Extent of hierarchy	Decomprehensivization, intensification of hierarchy, social segregation	Fragile stability, status hierarchy still mutable but greater awareness of hierarchy	Community comprehensive ethos retained and enhanced

Table 3.2   Profile statistics of case–study LEAs (1993–4)

Statistic	Northwark	Riverway	Westway
Midyear population (1993)	258 300	160 500	206 500
Standard Spending Assessment total education	£88 261 476	£36 952 966	£81 775 216
Total net expenditure on education	£96 411 000	£40 934 000	£84 674 757
Net expenditure on education per head of population	£373	£255	£410
Total general schools' budget	£60 013 000	£41 837 000	£79 879 000
Students per qualified teacher (secondary)	15.7	16.5	16.1
GM school students	7020	No GM schools	2123
Students on free school meals (%)			
Primary	30	13	28.8
Secondary	10	10	21.6

The figures represented in this table are collected from the following sources: CIPFA (1993)
Education Statistics 1993–4 Estimates; Society of County Treasurers (1993) Standard Spending
Indicators 1993–4; and Northwark, Riverway and Westway LEAs.

is also, for some parents, a criterion in their selection of schools (as we saw
in Chapter 2). Social class is yet another key factor, we suggest, in
understanding the movement of students between LEAs and the
recruitment strategies of particular schools. As we shall see, the policies of
Riverway and Northwark LEAs are certainly indirectly related to
retaining or changing the social-class and ethnic profiles of their schools.

Table 3.1 summarizes the key points of difference between the
case-study LEAs, as factors in the conceptualization of local markets. In
Tables 3.2 and 3.3 some profile statistics on the three LEAs are given.

Northwark LEA

Northwark is a socially and ethnically mixed area with a significant
degree of population change in recent years. In particular, in certain areas
of the authority, a marked process of gentrification has taken place, and
the authority has sold off a significant proportion of its council housing.
At the last Census, 20.2 per cent of the local population were from ethnic

Table 3.3 Funding per pupil components of aggregated schools budget formula for LEAs 1993–4 according to age

LEA	11	12	13	14	15	16	17	18
Northwark	£1594	£1594	£1594	£2591	£2591	£2989	£2989	£2989
Riverway	£1472	£1472	£1472	£1866	£2004	–	–	–
Westway	£1351	£1351	£1351	£1970	£1970	£2228	£2228	£2245

Source: CIPFA (1993) *Education Statistics 1993–4 Estimates*.

minorities, the largest single group being Black-Caribbean which formed 6.1 per cent of the total population. Tube and bus routes in the LEA are fairly comprehensive although some areas are less well served. There is a clear history of status differentiation among the state secondary schools, of which there are nine. There is also a large and expanding independent sector.

The Conservative-controlled LEA of Northwark is committed to competition, choice and diversity of provision and has actively pursued a policy of developing a market in schooling. The LEA was previously part of the Inner London Education Authority (ILEA) and the majority party on the council makes no secret of its antipathy to ILEA policies. In a local magazine article (October 1992), the leader of the council wrote:

> Until April 1990, education in Northwark meant ILEA: a uniform diet of all-purpose comprehensives. Every one the same and some of the worst examination results in the country. They even blew the whistle on competitive sport. And don't take my word for it. While the pupils were rattling around in half empty classrooms, their pals from across the street were voting with their feet. 4500 local secondary school places were going begging while four out of ten youngsters went to school outside the LEA or in the independent sector.

Lying behind the concern about surplus places there is also the issue of recoupment. The LEA must pay the per capita costs of students educated in schools in other LEAs. In effect they pay twice – once for the surplus place and once the recoupment.

The development of a market is being pursued in a number of ways. The LEA is attempting to make the secondary schools into 'magnet' schools with specific curriculum specialisms and selection by aptitude and ability. The chief education officer (CEO) of Northwark, Mr Quick, explained the LEA's policy in the following way:

'You can't have parental choice without greater diversity, you cannot have diversity without greater specialization, you cannot have specialization without selection.'

(BBC radio interview, November 1992)

Hence the LEA encouraged the setting up of a new City Technology College (CTC) in Northwark, as well as converting an existing poorly-subscribed school, Carbridge, into a local authority-run Technology College. Mr Quick explained, in interview, the thinking behind the move to establish the Carbridge Technology College:

'There was no way in which the present majority party could be persuaded to go along with the formula of the neighbourhood comprehensive school which has so patently failed. A few years ago there were four schools in Carbridge – many of them flourishing. Within a relatively short period of time there was next to none. So there would be no question of the council going along with – "well we're just going to turn the school round by giving ourselves more of the same medicine".'

(CEO, 25 July 1991)

These initiatives have resulted in five LEA schools using 'opting out' as a way of escaping from the LEA's policies. These schools were unanimous in seeing grant-maintained (GM) status as a way of maintaining their comprehensive identity and avoiding the specialization and selection policies being pursued by Northwark. However, the practical and ideological commitment to comprehensive education did – and does – vary from school to school. The paradox here is that, in 'driving out' some schools which want to protect their 'comprehensive identity', the LEA is hampered in its attempts to pursue its objective of creating a 'diversified' school market. Despite the history of surplus places in the authority, the LEA also encouraged the relocation of a Church of England secondary school from a neighbouring authority. The plan was meant to increase diversity of choice for parents within the LEA, but was also part of the LEA's corporate competition with its neighbours and its efforts to reduce its recoupment costs.

'A thousand Northwark children go out of the LEA for their education, for a Church of England secondary education . . . The argument is, if we had a Church of England school in Northwark, it would represent no threat to the remaining schools because it would be dealing with a constituency which is already finding its education elsewhere for which the LEA has to pay a heavy recoupment. So it must be costing £2–3 million a year because we haven't got a Church of England school in Northwark.'

(CEO, 25 July 1991)

As it turned out, a poor Ofsted inspection report in 1994 led the LEA to abandon its plan. In 1991, the LEA began to publish surveys of attendance, examination and test performance for primary and secondary schools. New tests have been introduced into primary schools as part of this process of comparison and accountability. From 1992, figures on school exclusions and ethnic minority student performance have been published. These are intended to provide effectiveness indicators and general information for parents who are choosing schools. The LEA also established a 'Choice Shop' – a shop-front information centre to help parents in their choice of school.

Overall, the Northwark CEO is committed to a model of educational provision which purports to give maximum independence to schools and a minimal role to the LEA and which involves competition between schools and school providers. This position, intriguingly, led Mr Quick to vociferously oppose those aspects of the 1992 education White Paper *Diversity and Choice* which emphasized the need, based on cost, to remove surplus places. Mr Quick, like many others, recognizes that the removal of surplus places would curb the market and possibilities of parental choice and shift market power back to the producers but he also sees it as likely to stultify innovation and limit diversity. Nonetheless, in 1990 the LEA announced the closure of two secondaries, one boys' school and one girls' school. The girls' school attempted to obtain GM status and were strongly supported by parents but were turned down by the Secretary of State on a technicality – that notice of closure had been announced before the moves to GM status were formally initiated.

The relationship between the LEA and its schools is at best tense and typically antagonistic and combatitive. However, despite the decision of five of the LEA's eight secondary schools to opt for GM status, the interventionary market policy of the LEA continues to have a dramatic impact on the form of the local system of secondary education. In particular, the determined pursuit of specialization and selection has made an impact. The sequence of events here is worth recording in some detail.

During 1991, various attempts were made by the CEO and chair of the education committee to 'interest' the secondary schools in some form of magnet system of specialization. As noted already, over a short period of time this pressure for change resulted in four of the LEA-maintained schools as well as the Catholic secondary opting out of Northwark control. The three remaining schools, all undersubscribed and seeing little to be gained from opting out as far as recruitment is concerned, were offered various sums for rebuilding and redevelopment work in exchange for an acceptance of specialization linked to a system of selection by aptitude. Northwark Park, an undersubscribed school, was offered £3 million.

> 'We were called up . . . to talk about specialization . . . And we said, "Well look, if there's more money, we're bound to look at it." I mean that's really the bottom line at the moment, if there are resources that can be got, we will do it. But we said we didn't want to be located in what is seen as a non-academic area of the curriculum exclusively [Art]. So we said, "How about a second area?" . . . So within a week there was a committee paper saying that we were to specialize in Modern Languages. The head was given a day and a half to produce a plan . . .
> (Chair of governors, Northwark Park School, 9 November 1992)

It was eventually agreed with the LEA that Northwark Park would reduce its standard number and allocate half of the Year 7 intake numbers to places based on aptitude tests for Languages and Art. Meanwhile, a high-profile innovative headteacher was appointed to the newly desig-nated Carbridge Technology College (September 1992). Ramsay Mac-donald school agreed a package with the authority for a system whereby half the school's intake would be based upon 'selection by reference to general ability' (Northwark LEA Consultative Document, October 1993) in exchange for a £4.5 million building programme. However, the LEA now faced a problem: in offering a selective education to boys they were in danger of transgressing equal opportunities legislation, that is, that the same opportunities should be made available to boys and girls. Northwark's consultative document offered two possible solutions: either that the LEA establish a new 540-place girls' grammar school 'admitting girls on the same basis as applying to Ramsay Macdonald [school]', or that Martineau girls' school (now GM) change is own admissions criteria to match those of Ramsay Macdonald. In effect, Martineau found themselves out-manoeuvred by the LEA. In autumn 1993, Hutton school (also GM) unilaterally announced plans to introduce a system of 50 per cent entry by selection. The headteacher of Martineau explained the course of thinking in her school:

> 'Northwark [LEA] has this consultation document out on Ramsay Macdonald school, the boys' school up the road, and that is going to be 50 per cent selective on general ability. It was made quite clear to us that if we didn't look at our admissions procedures, another school would be invited into the old Elizabeth Anderson girls' site . . . and that it would be a three form entry grammar school. I thought about this a lot, and obviously with certain governors and others in the

school, I felt that Martineau [school] going partially selective would
be better than having a grammar school up the road. We would seek
to go selective by ability for 90 pupils, which is 30 per cent of our
intake. We're getting those anyway, so it's about protecting what
we've got . . . Unlike Hutton [school], we're not seeking for more,
we're seeking to protect what we've got. It's the only pragmatic way
I can see at the moment of safeguarding the school. I appreciate that
others who believe in pure comprehensive systems wouldn't see it
like that, but the governing body have and it's now gone to
consultation.'

(Headteacher, Martineau school, 24 November 1993)

In November 1994, the Secretary of State turned down Ramsay
Macdonald school's application to partially select its intake. This decision
meant that the threat to Martineau of the LEA establishing a girls'
grammar on the old Elizabeth Anderson site in order to comply with
equal opportunities legislation had now disappeared. Nevertheless,
Martineau decided to go ahead with its own plans for introducing
selection, on the grounds that other schools in Northwark were already
selecting or were in the process of becoming selective. It was felt by the
headteacher and a majority on the governing body that selection was now
essential at Martineau if the school's 'balanced' intake was to be
preserved.

Trumpton school (another of the GM schools) also took quick action in
response to the specialization and selection developments in the authority
and the planned import by the LEA of the Church of England school. The
latter, it was indicated, would specialize in Music, and be moved to an
empty site less than a mile from Trumpton. Speedy decision-making by
the senior staff and governors produced an application to the Department
for Education (DFE) for Technology College status for September 1994.
This received enthusiastic support from the Northwark council leader. In
interview, the headteacher explained that she saw this as the only strategy
open to the school in the face of increasingly direct and cut-throat
competition for students in Northwark. At both Martineau and Trumpton, a number of staff expressed strong opposition to the responses made
by the senior managers and governors. The senior managers found
themselves caught between their principles and the defence of their
institutions in a 'cut-throat' market environment (see Chapter 4).

The policies of Northwark LEA contain a number of contradictions
around the issue of *planning* versus *choice*. As noted above, in 1990 the
LEA made the decision to close Elizabeth Anderson girls' school despite
the school's application and parents' support for GM status. The CEO
has described himself in public as 'agnostic' on opting out and told parents

at a public meeting on opting out in another school that they should not believe that 'opting out will allow you to escape from Government policies; it won't'. One of the effects of the LEA restructuring of its secondary schools is intended to be the destruction of the neighbourhood comprehensive principle. If this is achieved, parents who support the neighbourhood comprehensive principle will find this choice unavailable to them. Where in the past LEAs have been seen to be imposing uniformity upon schools, Northwark is determined to impose diversity and selection. The Consultative Document (October 1993) states that:

> Selective education occupies a powerful place in the English educational tradition. It is not an option available to Northwark residents unless they are prepared to pay. If non-fee-paying selective education can be provided economically, and if it meets proven demand, there is every reason why it should resume its place in the local education system in Northwark.

Northwark LEA has supported and advanced 'choice' and competition, paradoxically by adopting a highly interventionist strategy. The independence of schools, which the CEO advocates, rests on terms set by the LEA. Here we see the LEA continuing to be a major player in defining the shape and character of the local education system. And the much lauded autonomy of GM schools takes on a very different complexion: as the headteacher of Martineau [school] commented (24 November 1993), 'in some respects GM status has turned out not to be the liberator one thought'.

Milton school provides a somewhat cruel example of the interventionist, political nature of the market created out of the Education Reform Act 1988 and reinforced by Northwark's policies. It is a school with an unsavoury past and it has been steadily recovering its position and reputation over a number of years. It is a school which has an unusual, socially mixed recruitment and a difficult geographical position. In 1991, Milton opted out of Northwark LEA, in an attempt to escape the selective/specialist policies being pursued by the authority. It then billed itself, interestingly, as a GM comprehensive school. However, also in 1991, within ten minutes' walking distance of the school, the CTC was opened.

We discussed the impact of the CTC on Milton recruitment with the primary liaison teacher by looking at the changing recruitment from local feeder primary schools.

> *Researcher*: . . . Another one is Angrave [school]. That's gone from 20 in 1990 to four in 1991.
> *Primary Liaison Teacher*: A lot of their children got into the CTC. They were very much a targetted school. The CTC had them in

before it opened in the holidays for a week, half term, all kinds of things that we couldn't do. We don't have these resources. We weren't even aware of them until after the event . . . I suppose it's the aspiring working classes, I think, who make their judgements about education, about uniform. They think . . . the long hours and all of the other things that are sold to them . . . are actually the most important things about a school.

(Interview, June 1992)

The impact of the arrival of the CTC (together with other factors) is evident in the overall pattern of Year 7 recruitment between 1989 and 1992, as shown in Table 3.4.

Table 3.4   Milton school: Year 7 entry

1989	1990	1991	1992
199 (210)	245 (262)	218 (262)	190 (245)

Standard numbers are in parentheses.

Contrary to popular opinion, GM status is not a recipe for market success or even a guarantee of stability in the market (Power *et al.*, 1994). As well as the arrival of the CTC, Milton school must still struggle with its historical reputation which is well entrenched in parental folk knowledge of the Northwark area. The idea that Milton is a school with a bad reputation cropped up several times in our interview data, for example:

Researcher: Why are you so set against Trumpton and Milton?
Mrs Ablett: God . . . terrible schools . . . I know a lot of parents whose kids go there . . . and . . . I don't really want her having O levels in how to sniff glue and roll joints and God knows what . . . they're wild, just wild . . . In my day, Milton was a really rough school . . . and although they say now the rate of education is higher in the schools, the discipline's still really naff, and I think that at that age she is going to need discipline, because it is very easy to go off the rails, and those two schools just haven't got it, so I don't want her there.

(Interview, 24 October 1991)

Milton is a non-uniform school, one of very few in the Northwark area; it is a school that represents comprehensivism with some pride, although this may be weakening (see Chapter 5); it is a school with high levels of achievement in Music and Drama. These factors are staunchly defended by staff and have served to attract a small but significant number of 'liberal' middle-class students from a wide area. In a sense, perversely, Milton has a niche in the market: it is a specialist school, it is chosen by many parents for its unique qualities and it contributes to the diversity of schooling in Northwark but in a way that is not recognized as valid by the LEA. The pressure is now on Milton to conform, to standardize itself, to minimize its differences from other schools. The paradox here is that one of the effects of the political market in Northwark (and elsewhere) is to reduce diversity and stultify risk and experiment. Milton's paradigmatic comprehensivism is anathema to the majority party on Northwark council. Milton must face up to the possibility of a future where it competes with other schools in Northwark and Riverway on their terms, not on its own. Here the market effect is not a release of energy and inventiveness, it is a regime of anxiety and fear.

The pressures on Milton are not helped by its odd location. It sits in the centre of a council estate of low-rise flats. To the south behind the flats is a large wooded common which is a transport barrier and a disincentive to some parents worried about their children's safety to and from school. The estate itself was opened in the 1960s with a population of young married couples, many of whom naturally sent their offspring to Milton. The stability of the estate population has meant few new young marrieds have moved in so that the most immediate source of recruitment is drying up. To the north of Milton and the estate is an area of noticeable affluence, large detached houses with off-street parking. According to Milton staff, many of these families choose the independent sector for their children. Altogether, the school is increasingly aware of its competitive environment.

'The CTC is one [competitor] and Fletcher [school in Riverway] is another. I mean, I should think we lose more able pupils to Fletcher because there's always been a westward drift anyway. The numbers we lost to Fletcher [school] we might have gained from Carbridge [school on the north east side of the LEA]. So there's this movement out, but now we've got the CTC there as well. And one of our big problems is the recruitment of girls. Although we don't see Martineau [school] as a particular rival because it's a girls' school, it causes us problems because it takes girls away from here. So yes, we do look upon other schools as rival establishments.'
(Parent governor, Milton school, 21 October 1992)

It is important to note in market terms that the CTC, Milton's most direct competitor, has an overall effect on the Northwark schools by taking a disproportionate number of children with a higher measured ability. The Northwark intake analysis document (October 1992) noted that in 1991

> . . . The college selected a high proportion of more able readers (37.0%) [the same as Milton] and a low proportion of less able readers (13.0%). The mean London Reading Test score for the intake was 104.2, the highest for any secondary school in the LEA. Expectations for pupil achievement in the coming years at the CTC should be correspondingly high.

Contrary to the claims of the CTC movement's supporters and as anticipated by its critics, the CTC at least is selecting in terms of ability even if ability is not one of the stated criteria for selection.

The overall social impact of Northwark's policies on choice and recruitment is difficult to gauge in the short term and the competitive position of Northwark as an LEA is becoming increasing difficult to monitor as more and more of its schools opt out. Nevertheless, data produced by Northwark LEA using reading test scores suggest that generally some 'high-ability' students are being lost (mainly to Riverway and to 'élite' cosmopolitan schools; see Chapter 5) and 'low-ability' students are being attracted into Northwark, mainly from the adjacent Streetley LEA. Knowing what we do about the relationships between performance on such tests and social-class background, these findings suggest that such movement of children is part of a westward drift of middle-class students, both Black and White, from inner-city to sub-urban schools. Push and pull factors play a part. Streetley LEA is poorly perceived by many middle-class parents and Northwark looks good by comparison. As far as outflow is concerned, Northwark's history as an ILEA division also looms large. As indicated in Chapter 2, a number of the middle-class parents we interviewed in our research clearly regarded ILEA education policies as operating against the relative advantage of their children and continue to regard the Northwark schools with suspicion. Furthermore, according to DFE (1993) figures, Streetley LEA is the largest net loser of students in England, showing as at January 1992 a net loss of 5764. The same report shows Northwark with a net loss of 48.

Northwark is hardly a typical LEA. Its interventionist, pro-market policies have very few counterparts. But it demonstrates the continuing possibilities for LEA 'steering' of their local markets. These policies also underline some of the continuing contradictions embedded in the politics of the education market. The Northwark schools are subject to the dual pressures of ideological policy intervention and market forces. The competition in Northwark was already keen and may now well be described as cut-throat. The surplus places in the LEA and the setting up of the CTC have forced the pace of promotional and substantive change in the schools. Schools like Trumpton and Northwark Park (see Gewirtz *et al.*, 1993b) have responded to the changing competitive context by moving away dramatically from their previous comprehensive identities; Hutton has acted to reinforce its historic status advantages; Martineau has exploited to the full its position as the only girls' school; and Milton has reluctantly begun to rework its image in response to its competitors. (See Chapter 5 for a detailed discussion of some of these developments.)

Riverway LEA

Riverway is a predominantly White, affluent, middle-class area: just 5.5 per cent of the local population are from ethnic minority groups, the largest of which is Irish (2.9 per cent of the total population). There are good road, rail, bus and tube links in and across the authority. The LEA, which is controlled by a Social Democrat council, contrasts dramatically with Northwark. It is supportive of comprehensive education, acts to maintain a high level of corporate identity among its eight secondary schools and, as far as it can, tries to dampen competitive behaviour. There is a well-established but perhaps fragile consensus among the secondary schools that unconstrained competition would be damaging. Thus, the LEA produces schools' prospectuses in a common, low-key format (although the schools are now producing glossy supplements). It also manages the admissions to schools centrally (except for Corpus Christi) and has an officer responsible for marketing and statistics. A system of 'linked' primary schools operates (which we will describe below), together with a mutually agreed 'no poaching' agreement. An annual 'event' organized by Riverway CASE (Campaign for the Advancement of State Education) is held for parents whose children are about to transfer to secondary school to which all secondary heads in the authority generally attend. The LEA is generous as regards capital spending of schools:

> 'We're quite keen that none of us should opt out, because we actually operate quite well within the LEA. There's evidence that our capital programmes are bigger than they would be if we opted out, the revenue budget is actually quite buoyant at the moment, and in my capacity as chair of governors, we tell the LEA that they need to keep funding us if they want to keep us there.'
>
> (Chair of governors, Fletcher school, 3 May 1993)

Thus, within the constraints of the Government-established education market, the LEA works hard to ameliorate what are seen as its negative effects. However, the CEO of Riverway does not view his LEA as having a history of strong central direction.

'The authority is quite *laissez-faire* and [gives] considerable auton-omy and freedom to schools . . . If you talk to the head of Parsons [school], who came from the ILEA, she would say that this is an authority with one policy – that we don't have any policies.'

(CEO, 4 September 1990)

Paradoxically, the CEO sees the Education Reform Act 1988 as leading to an increase in LEA initiatives: 'if anything we are more proactive than less'.

Riverway currently recruits just under 40 per cent of its secondary intake from primary schools outside of the LEA. Indeed the out-of-LEA intake increased by 13 per cent between 1985 and 1992, although the trend has reversed slightly since the 1988 peak of 39.6 per cent. This overall in-crease in inflow is in part accounted for by the growth in secondary places in Riverway but is also a mark of the relative 'attractiveness' of Riverway schools compared with its adjacent LEAs. In some neighbouring authori-ties during the same period surplus places have increased and schools have been amalgamated and closed. The location of most of the Riverway schools close to the LEA borders also encourages choices from 'outside' based on simple propinquity. But both the stability and the 'middle-classness' of the Riverway schools make them attractive to out-of-LEA parents. The idea of 'The Riverway Schools' as an entity was often re-ferred to by parents in our interviews. In effect, Riverway is a market player in education and it competes corporately to attract students in from other LEAs and this inflow success is 'built into' Riverway policies on the management of school places and capital expenditures. In terms of the dy-namics of the internal market and relations between schools, the possi-bility of 'filling up' with students from out-of-LEA serves to further moderate competition between the Riverway schools. However, despite the corporatism, the schools are keenly aware of changing patterns of re-cruitment and feel that they have to be image and publicity conscious to continue to attract their in and out-of-LEA choices.

'To some extent Riverway schools have always had to be fairly com-petitive, because in secondary schools, when you had falling rolls about ten years ago, there wasn't a decision to rationalize, and we've maintained our number of schools by importing from neighbouring LEAs.'

(CEO, Riverway, 4 September 1990)

The schools themselves appear to recognize that the very positive percep-tion of Riverway LEA and schools in their local area is a benefit to them all. They also fear that the development of intensified competition as a result of one or more schools opting out would damage that positive perception. The gains and losses of opting out remain unclear and some of the Riverway headteachers who might be attracted to opting out on financial or recruitment grounds are ideological opposed to the idea. But it is doubt which seems to be the key factor in maintaining the status quo.

However, the apparently *muted* competition between the schools in Riverway to an extent obscures a second level of tension and struggle which is related to the issue of the type rather than number of students recruited. Parsons school is a case in point and the recent history of recruitment to the school points up both the complexity of local market dynamics and highlights in particular the powerful social class subtext which informs and inflects patterns of choice (Bowe *et al.*, 1995).

> 'I am conscious that a number of parents who don't choose us, don't choose Parsons school for social reasons. We are more of a working-class comprehensive school, with a bigger working-class proportion of children than say Blenheim school or Overbury school or Pankhurst. And that is just a statement of fact. We're actually on the LEA boundary and we recruit one third of our intake from Westway [LEA]. Two of our closest feeder primary schools are in Westway, and it's not the middle-class end of Westway at that.'
>
> (Headteacher, Parsons school, 21 May 1992)

Parsons loses potential recruits from its immediate locality to other schools in more middle-class areas of the LEA. It loses middle-class boys and girls to adjacent independent schools and nearby Riverway comprehensives. Patterns of class choosing disrupt any possibility of a natural catchment area for Parsons. As the headteacher indicates, the school is therefore heavily dependent on cross-border recruitment from working-class areas of Westway. Parsons is currently undersubscribed.

> 'I think of Lockmere [school] as a competitor for pupils who should naturally come to us. I see Pankhurst as a competitor for able girls, because it's the middle-class able girls who tend to drift off towards Pankhurst, not only, but that tends to be the case . . . I think we tend to attract more people from Westway [LEA]. Dare I say it, they perhaps see the school as a step up, whereas there are people in this locale that might regard it as a step down.'
>
> (Headteacher, Parsons school, 21 May 1992)

What the headteacher is indicating here is a class-related status hierarchy among schools (see Chapter 2). This hierarchy and the competitive dynamic which it animates includes both the LEA schools and a number of local independent schools. Overall, approximately 50 per cent of

Riverway's secondary age children are educated in the independent sector. For some of the Riverway secondaries, competition with the independent sector is at least as important as their rivalry with other state schools.

> 'In terms of competition our competitors are not the other Riverway mixed schools, so much as Suchard girls [school] which is a grammar school . . . and the independent sector . . . The independent sector seems to me at the moment to be at the vagaries of the economy, and that's a very unstable feature for us, because parents might decide that their businesses are at risk and they'll send their daughters to us this year and then it'll pick up and we lose them next year, and that's very difficult, because if the roll fluctuates then because of LMS [local management of schools] it does make budgeting very difficult.'
>
> (Headteacher, Pankhurst school, 17 June 1993)

The independent sector also has a significant impact on Fletcher. The gentrification of the school's immediate environs in the early 1980s means that many local children now attend independent schools. Thus Fletcher has to market itself further afield and now relies on a spatially scattered intake.

> 'It never used to be that. It used to be very local. Parents used to know the school very well, they used to support it very well. Now there's been a drift and one of the things that's caused that drift . . . is house prices around the school. When they rose, they rose significantly . . . Those children who came from this area [in the past] had quite liberal minded parents [who] would actually send their children here and they didn't mind the comprehensive nature. There is a perception that children from those particularly expensive houses . . . [now] tend to go to private schools, they go to a [state] junior school and then off to a private school, and therefore we don't have what we call the payroll mafia.'
>
> (Teacher governor, Fletcher school, 17 November 1992)

These developments have affected the social-class profile of the student body. Fletcher also feels keenly the presence of Pankhurst, the girls' school in Riverway, which affects both the gender and ability balances of the school. The social class and gender make-up of the intake are matters of concern to the senior management team (SMT) and the governors. In addition, the disparate nature of Fletcher's intake makes 'marketing' to and liaison with its (approximately 50) primary schools difficult to manage.

Because of its location near the border with Northwark, Fletcher recruits the majority of its students from that authority (75 per cent of the

Year 7 intake in 1993–4 were from Northwark). This is part of the westward drift noted above. In the past, the school has benefited from the antipathy of some Northwark parents to the ILEA but recent policies of Northwark LEA, particularly its attempts to retain more of its students and the opening of the CTC, are perceived as a real threat to the continued high level of recruitment of out-of-LEA students:

> 'When I started, Northwark [LEA] was part of ILEA and they had a clear commitment to . . . all through comprehensive systems and you were competing with those, in effect. Well that has changed, and is changing now . . . to the extent that we have a sort of a variety of provision . . . with which we are competing, ranging from city technology colleges, to the opted-out comprehensive schools to schools . . . possibly magnet schools.. that are remaining within Northwark. So there is a whole . . . variety of provision . . . and we have to make sure that what we are offering is what the parents actually want, so that they will continue to send their children here.'
>
> (Headteacher, Fletcher school, 6 July 1992)

Fletcher's intake poses problems for the school in terms of its relative performance in the local league tables. With its large Northwark intake, the school sees itself as being compared unfairly with other Riverway schools when performances are evaluated. The chair of governors expressed the view that the uninformed observer, relying on raw scores alone, might not appreciate the good work done by the school.

Fletcher is a good illustration of the idiosyncrasies of local markets, of the impact of class, gender, social geography and location on the market position of individual schools and on competition between schools. In a sense, both administratively and contextually, the school is out of place and there are mismatches between its actual intake and immediate competitive environment. As a result, the governors and SMT display a particular sensitivity to marketing issues while attempting to retain some of the markers and much of the ethos of comprehensivism (see Chapter 5).

While most of the LEA schools continue to recruit healthily, the status quo in Riverway is likely to remain intact. But the LEA is attempting to retain a strange and difficult balance: it needs healthy recruitment of out-of-LEA students in order to sustain its schools, but on the other hand wants to ensure against its schools being flooded from outside to the detriment of local council-tax payers. In this regard, the Greenwich judgement in the High Court creates particular problems in Riverway. In the past, pre-Greenwich, the LEA was able to defend its schools from out-of-LEA choices without much difficulty, by using residence as a criterion for priority. In effect, the market position of the LEA meant that the schools could be filled up from inflow choices (with the possibility of subtle forms of selection) while ensuring that all Riverway parents who wanted one got a place for their child in a Riverway LEA school. Greenwich changed all that, as LEA of residence can no longer be used as an entry restriction. The Riverway solution is a scheme of 'linked' primary schools with priority at secondary transfer being given to 'link'-school students. Some out-of-LEA primaries are designated as 'linked' schools.

There are two major problems with the scheme. First, the geography and designation of the secondary schools (there is one ecumenical school and one girls' school) makes the 'linked' scheme difficult to design, and some schools have lobbied hard with the LEA when they have felt discriminated against. Second, some parents feel themselves denied choice by the workings of the scheme. If they exercise choice by nominating other than their 'link' school for their child they may risk not getting their first choice – because first priority is given to 'linked' students, followed by siblings and distance. If their 'link' school is their second choice they may not get a place if the school fills up on first choices.

The problem for the LEA, in selling its scheme to 'consumerist' parents, is that the effects of the use of other criteria for entry (like distance) are unclear to individual consumers. Allocations based simply on propinquity and sibling attendance would increase the proportion of non-Riverway students in Riverway schools. The likelihood is that many fewer Riverway parents would get their first-choice school than do so now. The difficulty for the LEA, in part at least, is that they are pursuing a policy based on the collective best interests of their council-tax payers when the prevailing climate is one where individual parents are encouraged to exercise choice in terms of familial self-interest.

There is a further dimension to this problem. The attraction of the Riverway schools for many (especially middle-class) parents is their socio-economic constitution. Open entry would be likely to change the social class make-up of the schools, particularly in the north and east of the LEA. Again though, individually self-interested parents are unlikely to be aware of this aspect of collective interest. Alternatively, the use of a 'closed-shop' strategy by Riverway denies free choice of school to parents outside of Riverway, even though in many cases a Riverway school would be geographically their nearest school. In negative terms, the protection of the local system through the 'linked' school arrangement protects the class privileges of Riverway parents while ensuring that the schools remain full. It has the additional effect of reviving and reinforcing social-class divisions within the LEA. The scheme is also subject to local micropolitical and party political pressures.

'The vice chairman of governors at Blenheim is hugely influential on the education committee, and wishes to retain the children coming from the middle-class Chinon school in Pendry [north Riverway] . . . and yet geographically it's crackers. Their nearest school is Fletcher. But Fletcher is largely a working-class Northwark [LEA] school, with a heavy contingent of the more Arts-involved professionals in the west Northwark area, so there's that bit of the equation. Like many things in Riverway [LEA], policies are scarce, and when they are made they're based on pressure group politics and not on principles . . . and we've been quite rude to councillors [saying] you are there as an LEA to even-out differences . . . to ensure people have their entitlement, and to make sure that there is equality of provision throughout the LEA . . . but you would have to make yourself unpopular to defend equality of opportunity within the LEA, and they can't make themselves unpopular, because they would lose the ward in Pendry, and the balance between Liberal Democrat and Conservative in the LEA is a very fine one.'

(Headteacher, Parsons school, 12 November 1993)

A Riverway LEA admissions officer commented that if the 'link' scheme were to fail or schools to opt out, then

'the situation is now so volatile that it is impossible for anyone to predict what would happen. The situation is such that it is increasingly difficult to manage the system in the best interests of students or schools.'

(Admissions officer, 20 January 1993)

The 'linked' school system offers most of the secondary schools a degree of predictability and security in the marketplace but this should not be overestimated. Schools still find it very difficult to match offers against admissions year on year, as many parents now make multiple-place applications, and they are constantly surprised by changes in patterns of recruitment. In the case of Goddard, Blenheim and Parsons schools, the variations in the year-on-year change in admission numbers is close to or greater than one class size.

The relationships of minimal trust between the schools are maintained via a regular meeting of headteachers at which a code of conduct for promotional activity has been hammered out; for example, an agreed date for the publication of examination results. Again though, these agreements are sometimes strained by competitive pressures. Bartlett (1992: 23) notes a similar situation in Avon LEA.

'I was angry with Parsons [school] last year because we felt that we had a heads' agreement, made in the tired state that one gets to at the end of term . . . And I reckoned that we ought to be more worried than anybody, and yet we didn't break the agreement, and then I did see other schools as doing that.'
(Headteacher, Overbury school, 1 August 1992)

'My job is to keep the school full, even if it flies in the face of what other colleagues want from me. So I am much less likely to adhere to a corporate decision of the heads now and much more likely to serve this school's interests. And if these interest fly in the face of what has been corporately judged to be the best thing then I shall pursue what's best for Parsons, and I'm sure the heads of the other schools would do exactly the same.'
(Headteacher, Parsons school, 17 July 1992)

Competitive awareness and the year-on-year anxieties about recruitment patterns in Riverway LEA thus still produce a climate of inchoate suspicion, of 'looking over one's shoulder', of the need to search for a competitive edge. One school in particular is viewed as 'straining' the agreement or 'breaking ranks'.

'[Lockmere school is] more aggressive, and it is felt that there is more of a sell rather than a reflection of the truth'.
(Headteacher, Overbury school, 1 August 1992).

Overall, in Riverway, the demand for places is buoyant and the pressure on accommodation has led to investment in a school-building programme. But despite the corporatist policies of Riverway LEA and the buoyancy of secondary-school recruitment, the market dynamics of competition and choice are still complex and difficult to predict, and the insidious effects of the education market are still in evidence. The local-market dynamics in Riverway have a set of particular characteristics which complicate, ameliorate, deflect and nuance the realization of the national policy framework. The existence of a church school and a girls' school (Pankhurst) in the LEA, with their recruitment cutting across the other schools, is one complication; the social geography of the LEA and the spatial distribution of the schools is another (most situated towards the boundaries of the authority); competition with the private sector and the internal patterns of social-class recruitment is another; and the attempts made by rival LEAs to retain their students is yet another. The Riverway example also points to ways in which market forces both threaten and reinforce class divisions and class advantages.

Westway LEA

Westway is a Labour-controlled authority. It has a mixed population but
in the south of the authority, the area with which we are primarily
concerned, the population is predominantly working class and markedly
stable: 24.3 per cent of the population belong to ethnic minorities and the
largest single ethnic-minority group is Indian – 14.3 per cent of the total
population.

Westway appears to represent a 'third way' as regards market
dynamics. It has 14 comprehensive schools spread over a wide area. Two
of these, Graham Greene and Hulme House, both Catholic and both of
which take large numbers of out-of-LEA students, are now GM. Voting
at the one LEA comprehensive to move for GM status resulted in a heavy
(84 per cent) 'no' vote. The council is opposed to opting out on principle,
but compared with Northwark and Riverway, the LEA is radically
non-interventionary. Its major policy thrust during the 1970s and early
1980s was the creation of community schools with integrated adult
education and sports facilities. The LEA has several distinctive local-
education markets and some very localized and distinctive social communities or urban 'villages', as one deputy headteacher describes them.
Compared with Northwark and Riverway, public transport is somewhat
less well integrated and the LEA is crossed east – west by several major
roads which create natural barriers around the 'villages'. Despite a
considerable surplus of places in the past, the LEA has not moved
decisively to close schools and recently the changing demography of the
area (the school-age population was higher in 1994 than it was in 1971)
and inflow from adjacent LEAs has turned this into a physical capacity
deficit in secondary schools:

> 'three years ago, in secondaries we had about 19 per cent surplus
> places and I think we were down to 5 per cent and we are heading for
> a crisis in secondary school accommodation.'
> (Admissions officer, Westway LEA, 9 February 1994)

In the south of the authority there is a history of small-scale outflow to
Riverway schools, particularly to Parsons, Pankhurst and Overbury.
Some primary schools in south Westway are Riverway 'linked' schools
(see above). In 1994, 84 per cent of applicants obtained a place in their first
preference secondary school compared with 98 per cent in 1990. In
1992–3, the LEA had a net inflow of students into its schools of 1144. But
however, even when there was the potential for 'cut-throat' relations
between schools, this does not appear to have led to the sort of
antagonisms or suspicions evident in Northwark. This is despite the fact

that two of our three case-study schools, Flightpath and Lymethorpe, are undersubscribed. It was commented that:

'I've a feeling things are loosening up somewhat, but I think schools still feel a little bit guilty about competing against each other.'
(LEA admissions officer, 9 February 1994)

Westway LEA is *laissez-faire* in its market orientation compared with Riverway's corporate stance and Northwark's ordered competition. Apart from the geographical factors noted above, two other factors seem to account for the lack of a cut-throat approach, at least as regards our case-study schools. First, all three are community schools and community-oriented. They are striving to retain students from their community rather than 'poach' from elsewhere. Second, Parkside and Lymethorpe (and it would seem other schools in the LEA) are more aggressive in their attempt to attract out-of-LEA students: Parkside from Eldridge and Fromley LEAs and Lymethorpe from Brokerage LEA. Flightpath also has a major competitive relationship with two out-of-LEA schools, that is Parsons and Goddard, in Riverway.

The situation of Lymethorpe illustrates the system of 'natural' catchments and highly localized markets in Westway. The headteacher sees his task as maximizing the 'local' community choice for the school rather than attempting to attract 'outsiders' in. He sees the local community as fairly distinct socially and geographically. There is a history of local families attending the school – children, parents and grandparents. And the school is a fully functioning community school, which helps to develop the local identity of, and identification with, the school. Part of the 'whole-school' marketing strategy is based upon getting adults into the school in the day and evenings. The headteacher also encourages an emphasis on the curricular 'strengths' of the school (as reflected by its intake) – such as Drama and a 'brilliant football team . . . I don't pretend that this is the most academic school in Westway because it isn't'. The headteacher talks about getting the school accepted on the basis of his agenda

'rather than the agenda that might be imposed from the outside . . . rightly or wrongly, I don't see the potential of the school to expand very much outside its natural community boundaries.'
(Headteacher, Lymethorpe school, 5 June 1992)

Riverway is too far away for competition but the school loses students to, and attracts some from, Brokerage County Authority.

We're not in competition [with Riverway LEA], it's too far away. Flightpath [school] are . . . but we're not and Gorse [school] are very much so, but we're not. Brokerage [LEA] is our competition. This is a very strange confined area. Lymethorpe is a village in many respects, it has a lot of extended families in it, quite a significant number of our parents have attended the school themselves and grandparents who still live here. There are often three generations of families in this area. Now that's quite unusual.'

(Headteacher, Lymethorpe school, 5 June 1992)

Here geography and community enable the headteacher to distance himself somewhat from hard-nosed competition.

'I don't criticize other schools, but they are both good schools. Obviously I'm interested in recruitment, but it's based on what we do, not what other people do, so whether that's market forces or not, I don't know. I think it's completely unprofessional to knock other schools and I won't do it. There's a bigger thing out there that we all need to be worried about.'

(Headteacher, Lymethorpe school, 5 June 1992)

It may be coyness or naivety but the Westway interviews seem to carry a different 'structure of feeling'. There is plenty of talk about marketing but an across-the-board emphasis on positive and cooperative relationships with neighbouring schools. *This is a low-key market.*

The primary strategy at Lymethorpe is to prevent 'leakage' from the school's 'natural' constituency by, first, working on the public perception and presentation of self of the school and, second, firming up the intakes from local feeder primaries, particularly its three 'partner' primaries. However, the headteacher does see the broadening of horizons over time, that is doing more to attract parents from 'border' primaries who are otherwise travelling 'away' from Lymethorpe. Lymethorpe is now, although technically undersubscribed, on a small scale, an 'attractor' rather than a 'loser' school.

'A very small percentage, but nonetheless an increasing percentage of students are . . . coming on a bus and stuff like that which would never have happened. Once upon a time you'd literally get them from round the corner and nowhere else.'

(Senior teacher, Lymethorpe school, 17 February 1994)

Another aspect of recruitment at Lymethorpe and Flightpath, which illustrates an aspect of the general market dynamics in Westway, is ethnicity. Lymethorpe and Flightpath and their communities are mainly White and as a result few South Asian parents are attracted to the schools. Equally, few White parents are attracted away from the area to Gorse which has a majority of South Asian students.

'Gorse [school] I don't see as particularly in competition with us. There is an ethnic element in this actually because Gorse attracts a large number of Asian students, which we don't. I would like to see more Asian students recruited here, but it is a predominantly White area, as I'm sure you observed, and there is therefore a barrier. I don't wish to dress this up . . . and suggest it's more than it is . . . but there is actually a barrier, I think, to movement in that direction, towards Gorse school, from the White population here.'

(Headteacher, Lymethorpe school, 5 June 1992)

Significantly in all this, the LEA seems to be marginal. There would seem to be no obvious attempt to forge a 'corporate' LEA identity for marketing purposes, or any form of intervention into the 'natural' processes of competition between schools. But equally there is no evidence of hostility between the LEA and its schools that exists in Northwark. The headteacher at Lymethorpe commented:

'Not wishing to be unkind, but if the LEA disappeared tomorrow the school would still run . . . In the last year there has been less work with the LEA than there has been before. I have found that they're interestingly more remote from the school and my own relationship with my governors and my staff being more significant.'

(Headteacher, Lymethorpe school, 5 June 1992)

However, he later said,

'We still have good relationships with the LEA, so I'm not in any way suggesting that we've chosen that path . . . We're not unhappy with our relationship with our LEA. I think that there are many inefficiencies in the LEA and I'd like to see far more money delegated to schools, and if that's done by the LEA then I can see little advantage in opting out, financially . . . If I can get a capital grant of £300 000 for opting out, in a year's time, then I'd be interested, but I very much doubt that that'll be there.'

(Headteacher, Lymethorpe school, 17 February 1994)

We can see the arbitrariness of the market here. Lymethorpe appears to have a 'natural' community which is large enough to sustain the school without enormous efforts to recruit from elsewhere. The school has to work hard to ensure it keeps its community happy and cannot be complacent, and the class/cultural orientation of the intake will not 'look good' in the league tables but the pattern of housing, transport services, geography and the location of other schools creates a 'defensible' and identifiable enclave of recruitment.

Flightpath is a similar school to Lymethorpe in many respects. Its community is essentially White and working-class. It is a fully functioning community school. But it has a more 'exposed' and competitive market situation than Lymethorpe. In contrast to Lymethorpe,

Flightpath's headteacher thinks the school may be losing more able children in the new marketplace and in recent years the intake has been dropping, from 270 (1991) to 251 (1992) to 245 (1993).

> 'We're becoming more aware of our public image in the broader sense of the word. We are aware of some bright children being removed from the school because they don't feel they're getting adequate tuition so that we're having to look to our laurels a bit more.'
>
> (Headteacher, Flightpath school, 11 June 1992)

Both Lymethorpe and Flightpath see themselves as interacting on the whole with a fairly educationally unsophisticated clientele. They believe that they need to be more active and inventive when it comes to the 'motivated' parents of 'more able children' (who are viewed as particularly valuable 'commodities' in the marketplace – see Chapter 5). However, Flightpath also has a fairly well defined and demarcated catchment area. Like Lymethorpe, Flightpath sees its primary concern as defence

> 'Probably 90 per cent of our children come from six schools . . . They are a natural part of our catchment area . . . [We are] defending our . . . market share rather than aggressively trying to expand our catchment area.'
>
> (Headteacher, Flightpath school, 11 June 1992)

It may well be that Lymethorpe's expanding horizons have had an impact on Flightpath. The headteacher comments that:

> 'The numbers in primary schools have increased and whilst we have held ourselves very steady there, we have noticed that our near neighbour, who didn't enjoy such a good reputation through the late 1980s, has actually grown considerably – that's Lymethorpe . . . I think we just have to watch that our near neighbours aren't competing so strongly that they take away what is the natural thing for children to do, to come to their nearest secondary school.'
>
> (Headteacher, Flightpath school, 11 June 1992)

This is an indication of the stark contrast with Northwark where such a 'natural' market has been systematically destroyed by the LEA, and is in any case less well respected by middle-class parents.

Like Lymethorpe, Flightpath is aware that it has a built-in advantage of good facilities and recent buildings of high standard, but is also aware that this, in itself, is not enough to sustain numbers. Crucially, Flightpath has a more direct competitive relationship with out-of-LEA schools – in particular Parsons and Goddard in Riverway. The Flightpath – Goddard pairing is frequently mentioned by parents in local primaries as the either or of their choice-making. Two primaries, Smith Street and Ladybird Junior, are particularly disputed territory. Gorse is a different sort of competitor. As indicated already, its major attraction is to South Asian parents, many of whom are equally discouraged from choosing Flightpath because of a reputation of 'White racism'. We have reported in Chapter 2 on the views of some White parents about Gorse, although the headteacher at Grasshopper primary mentioned a few White parents being attracted to the school by its reputation for discipline and an academic orientation.

> 'I had one [parent] in today talking to me about this . . . Gorse [school] has got a lot of Asian pupils, and they see it as a very well-disciplined school, and also . . . she was saying . . . Asian parents have high expectations and she wanted her child to go there because of this, so that was interesting.'
>
> (Headteacher, Grasshopper school, 13 June 1991)

Also, according to the headteacher at Ladybird, Goddard is attractive as an alternative to Flightpath in the view of more middle-class parents. There is also confirmation here of the way in which Flightpath is currently losing numbers to other schools.

> 'In theory, the children would go predominantly to Flightpath [school], and that is what has been widely accepted as the norm. But I think lately there is more of a seepage to other schools, particularly Goddard [school]. There is also the racial balance of the different schools, where Flightpath is predominantly a White [pupil] school . . . Flightpath is . . . being crude, a White racist area. Gorse [school] therefore is very much, and I don't know the percentage, but very much a school for children from different cultural backgrounds, particularly Asian families . . . and they have at least one or perhaps two . . . Asian or Black deputy heads, I know, which will affect the appearance of the school. And it tends to be, I think again . . . parents who are perhaps . . . and I don't use the word class . . . but perhaps more thinking who will decide that they want Goddard for their children, rather than one of the other schools.'
>
> (Headteacher, Ladybird school, 20 June 1991)

But choice is still set within a restricted social geography and the primary headteacher does not see Parsons as a natural part of the local social geography.

> 'I don't know. Parsons [school] do try hard on the marketing of the school, from their point of view. I wonder whether it's less accessible. It's also possibly that they know less where it is. Goddard

school has a site where everybody knows where it is, it's the school that you pass on the main Chaplin Road. They all know where Flightpath school is, less so Gorse [school].

(Headteacher, Ladybird school, 20 June 1991)

Despite leakage, most Ladybird students, 60 per cent, still go on to Flightpath; 30 per cent go to Goddard.

Parkside, our third case-study school in Westway LEA, serves a different area of Westway and is not in direct competition with either Lymethorpe or Flightpath school. Again, we refer to it briefly here as part of our attempt to portray and analyse the ethos and dynamics of the Westway marketplace. Parkside is an ethnically and class-mixed school which serves what the deputy headteacher describes as 'a sort of upper working-class neighbourhood basically'. The school is oversubscribed and has parents going to appeal.

'[Parental choice is] done centrally, but we have this figure of 155 for the year group, but then we go to appeals, so we do increase that number, usually to around 165. Our present Year 9 I think is around 180 or something, but that was based on appeals above our standard number. I mean we're constantly getting little notes from the LEA . . . saying delete one, add one, and then when you do your sums you find you're still bobbing around the 155 mark.'

(Primary liaison, Parkside school, 16 May 1991)

The school recruits a high proportion of its intake from five key primary schools (one of which shares the Parkside site) but being close to Eldridge LEA, and because of changes to the education system there and the age of secondary transfer, students are being attracted across the LEA border.

'We have five main feeder schools, but we've got, for instance this year we've got 19 children coming from Eldridge [LEA] into the school. I find this year we've got enough coming to warrant a visit to the two Eldridge schools, whereas when it's only one you feel you can't spend an hour going out to meet one child.'

(Primary liaison, Parkside school, 16 May 1991)

Being oversubscribed, the school is mainly working to 'maintain our market share' rather than make up for undersubscription, as at Lymethorpe and Flightpath. As with those schools, the deputy head-teacher played down the role of competition. Indeed

'Five years ago or so . . . it was getting out of hand . . . The secondary heads spoke about it and had some sort of agreement . . . Running down the other schools, if you do that, I think it's a very dangerous thing to do, because parents will think of that as unprofessional.'

So although a sixth-form consortium with two other schools in the authority 'has died', there is

> 'a healthy respect for what each of the schools does and we don't see ourselves as competing against them . . . We're trying to recruit into this area of Westway from outside the authority, and we're all succeeding in doing it.'
> (Deputy headteacher, Parkside school, 16 May 1991)

As in Riverway, the history and sense of community and locality, however tenuous, that attaches to LEA boundaries, creates a structure of identity and locality which discourages intra-LEA competition but makes out-of-LEA schools (in Eldridge and Fromley) fair game.

Catholic schools

In the discussion thus far we have had little to say about the Catholic schools in our local markets. It would seem to be the case that Catholic schools operate in a separate market from other secondary schools. St Ignatious, in Northwark, the one case-study Catholic school in our three clusters, like many other Catholic schools in the area, is now able to fill its places entirely with Catholic parents. There are strong and enduring links between the school and local Catholic primary schools. But St Ignatious parents are drawn from a wide catchment. In effect, the school competes with other Catholic schools rather than neighbouring LEA or other GM schools. In particular, St Ignatious loses local, 'academically able' boys to a high profile opted-out boys' Catholic school some distance away. Given a fairly poor past reputation, the headteacher of St Ignatious knows he must work hard to increase retention from his target Catholic primaries.

> 'I mean it sounds rosy but we have to work at it, we get about half of theirs. You see there are places like Cardinal Heenan [school] which is just across the river, which is a grant-maintained school, has sort of a reputation of sixth form, a whole lot of things . . . so we have to work hard to, well, I say work hard, we sort of keep in touch to get the children from the Catholic primaries, and that's the aim, isn't it, to have every child from [our Catholic feeders] coming here? This year I've gone across the river to Fanshaw to a couple of primaries over there, because we're an easy journey for some of them. I've invited all of the primary heads in Northwark [LEA] for lunch here,

during the course of the year, and . . . there's three that I want to
invite from across the river . . . just to have a link really, so that you
know who you're speaking to . . . and so that they see the place and
they can actually, if a parent says, "What do you know of?" . . . they
can say, "Yes, I was up there and this is my impression of it" . . . so
. . . it's just making them aware that we're here really.'
(Headteacher, St. Ignatious school, 7 May 1992)

Two things are worth noting here. First, the Catholic system across our
case-study areas has its own pattern of internal market relations and
dynamics and a system of clear competition and choice that pre-dates the
Education Reform Act 1988. Second, the social geography of the system
means that many more parents require their children to 'travel' than is the
case in the LEA-maintained system. But there are other factors working
to support St Ignatious' recruitment.

'Well, we've actually got a new parish priest. Now the old parish
priest retired last July, and he used to get very, very cross indeed with
his parishioners, if they decided to send the children into fee-paying
schools, particularly non-Catholic schools, and he wanted everybody in this school to transfer *en masse* to St Ignatious. He felt they
should support their local Catholic secondary school.'
(Headteacher, St Bernadette Primary school, 27 June 1991)

Conclusion

It would be difficult to characterize these school markets as free markets.
In general terms, through its attempts to control the information system
of the education market (via national testing, local league tables of results
and other published performance indicators) the Government is asserting
a planning function while pursuing the rhetoric of autonomy and choice.

The school market is subject to manipulation and intervention in a
variety of other ways. Riverway and Northwark LEAs both constrain
and plan their local markets, although in different ways and with different
effects. The former is seeking to maintain comprehensive education and
the class advantage of local residents. The latter is seeking to deconstruct
comprehensive education and create a new diversity among schools
related to selection. In neither case could we see the outcome as some kind
of 'spontaneous order', an aggregate of individual actions. The implan-
tation of the CTC in Northwark is also a planned distortion of choice, an
intervention which increases surplus places while other 'popular' schools
are being closed. The analysis of Northwark, Westway and Riverway
LEAs, as market players, also raises more general questions about the role

of LEAs. As competitive units, attempting to maximize the use of their school-place provision and minimize recoupment costs, they act as corporations rather than small businesses (e.g. closing down unprofitable subsidiaries, investing in new developments and maximizing market share). However, their geographical boundaries are ultimately arbitrary in market terms. They cut across 'natural areas', catchments, or spatial localities. Nationally, in 1992, a total of 186 000 students crossed LEA borders to attend school (DFE, 1993). Riverway's policy of importation has avoided the necessity of school closures and, indeed, has led to an expansion of accommodation and facilities for students attending Riverway schools. In effect, these developments have been funded by other LEAs. Northwark is committed to reduce its loss of students and its recoupment costs by radical innovation and the expansion of the LEA's school portfolio. In their different ways, both authorities exercise some 'interpretive potential' (Duncan and Goodwin, 1988) in and around the provisions of the Education Reform Act 1988. Westway is clearly more *laissez-faire* and its non-intervention has proved, in the long run, to be a sensible policy choice, given the changing demography of the area.

We are suggesting here that in order to begin to conceptualize the operation and effects of the policy of using market forces as an organizing principle for school provision in England, and in order to understand the 'situation' and 'response' of individual schools in the education market-place, a multi level analysis is needed. That is, we need to see schools as situated and contexted in a variety of ways (see Figure 3.1). Clearly, the framework of national policy is crucial and this impacts on all schools to some degree. There is no escape from the effects of the market system. However, at a second level, schools are affected by the policies and roles, past and present of their LEA. The effects of the legislative framework can be mediated and refracted here. Local policies may support and exacerbate the effects or interrupt and modify them. Further, schools are situated within a local market with its own particular characteristics which we have identified and discussed above, drawing on our case-study data. An important part of any local market is the socio-economic and ethnic constitution of the 'consumers' – the parents. Choice and choosing differs between social class and ethnic groups, and different choice orientations and patterns of choice will animate local markets differently. Finally, markets are also driven in part by the 'behaviour' of 'producers': school engagements and responses are constructed by the initiatives and accommodations of the staff, in particular the senior management of individual schools. In Chapters 4 and 5 we will address in some detail this latter level of context – parental choice and school engagements and responses. What this kind of analysis begins to display is a complex interplay of *planned, political, historical, spatial, producer and consumer factors*

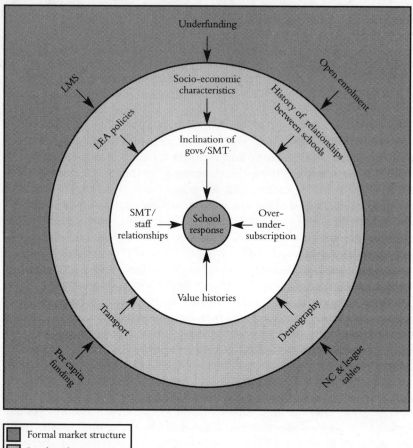

Figure 3.1 Factors influencing school responses to the market. LMS = local management of schools; NC = national curriculum; SMT = senior management team.

that constitute the education market. In all this, the LEA continues to have a role of some significance. None of the currently employed concepts – such as planned or regulated markets, consumer sovereignty, freedom of choice – do justice to this complexity or begin to describe or anticipate its effects either in terms of quality and efficiency or social justice and patterns of educational opportunity.

4

MANAGERS AND MARKETS: SCHOOL ORGANIZATION IN TRANSITION

In Chapter 3 we identified some of the factors, within local education markets, which produce contextual differences for schools, affecting their operating environments. We attempted to give substance to the simple but important point that the forces and disciplines of the market do not impinge upon and affect all schools in precisely the same ways. We shall now explore differences between schools further. Here we want to sketch in some of the institutional factors which affect and inflect the ways in which individual schools construct their responses to their local markets. This involves attending to the stances, perspectives and styles of the senior managers of schools (particularly the headteachers) and to the micropolitics of the schools (Ball, 1987) as responses are struggled over between different interests and value positions in the schools. However, we need to reiterate the basic point that the possibilities of resistance to, or deflection of, the pressures of the market are related to the market conditions within which the school operates. We do not want to convey the impression here that the market behaviour of schools is simply a matter of different value positions that people take up and that is all that counts. That is clearly not the case. The disciplines of the market are very real, the pressures on headteachers to ensure the survival of their schools are very real and the dilemmas they face are very real. But neither do we accept the view that responsiveness to patterns of choice in the education market is the working through of an inevitable and neutral mechanism or the playing out of simple coercive pressures.

In this chapter we will focus particularly on the headteacher who plays a key role in setting the agenda for school participation in the market (although the attitudes and values of school governors are also important; see Gewirtz *et al.*, 1993b). We will argue that a set of transformations are occurring within school management, but that the processes of change are far from straightforward: new languages, and evolving management styles, strategies and values co-exist in a strained and complex relationship with existing languages, practices and values. We will consider, first, how devolved management and the market has redefined the role of school headship. We will then go on to consider some of the sometimes subtle *personal* differences in the ways that individual headteachers and senior managers experience and construct their responses to the tensions which their new role produces. Finally, we will discuss the micropolitical circumstances of 'new management' responses. We will draw on the perspectives of teachers, senior managers and governors in our case-study schools, and will try to make sense of these, making use of existing analyses of change in the public sector (Considine, 1988; Mclaughlin, 1991; Clarke and Newman, 1992).

Reconstructing headship

The policy of devolved management in combination with open enrolment and per capita funding was, in part, designed to unleash the creative potential of school managers whilst constraining and undermining the alleged stultifying bureaucracy of LEAs. The idea, which drew on new business management theories, was that by giving headteachers and governors control over their budgets and by making school income dependent on attracting custom, senior managers in schools would have both the tools and the incentive to behave in more cost-effective, flexible, competitive, consumer-satisfying and innovative ways. In other words, schools would behave more like 'commercial enterprises'. (However, the *kinds* of commercial enterprises schools are supposed to be emulating tend not to have been specified by the political architects of devolved management, and in the legitimating rhetoric the term 'business' has been effectively deployed as an undifferentiated category; see Keep, 1992; Bottery, 1994). Thus local management of schools, the grant-maintained schools policy and the education market generally combine to interpolate and articulate a new kind of headship and leadership in schools. Both in terms of focus and in terms of style, a new role has been constructed for the headteacher. That is not to say that headteachers have either accepted that role uncritically or are necessarily acting it out. We discuss, below, how the headteachers in our case-study schools are responding to the new environment in which they now have to operate. However first we will discuss the direction in which senior managers are being 'encouraged' to move by the disciplines of the market and devolved management.

Most fundamentally, as regards focus, headteachers (in conjunction with their governors) are now responsible for the survival of their institutions, and that concern for survival can be broken down into a number of key tasks. First headteachers need to ensure that their institutions are responsive to consumers, i.e. parents (or at least particular groups of parents, see Chapter 5). Second, headteachers are responsible for retaining or developing a 'competitive edge' over other local schools. Third, they are responsible for managing the budget efficiently and cost-effectively, which includes making decisions about the appointment, utilization and dismissal of staff as well as the purchase and use of physical resources. Finally, headteachers are faced with the task of having to manage any conflict that their new role confronts them with. The market sets up a potential divide between management and staff. Indeed our evidence indicates that as income maximization, the image and marketing of the school and good management of the budget become for headteachers the prime and most pressing aspect of their role, so there is a tendency for headteachers to become increasingly distanced from the work of teaching – and hence also from their staff (Bowe *et al.*, 1992). The 'gap' can lead to conflict and has to be 'managed' somehow. As a deputy in one of our case-study schools put it:

'We need to galvanize people . . . into realizing it's not just the school as some anonymous object which either survives or falls. It is they, as individual teachers, that also have a role to play in ensuring the survival or growth of the school . . . We're setting out on quite a long journey because you've got to win their minds.'
(Deputy headteacher, Parkside school, 16 May 1991)

Thus it would now appear to be part of the job of headteachers (and senior managers) to somehow 'encourage' staff to accept, to some extent, that, to survive, schools need to be consumer-responsive and cost-efficient and that, as we discuss below, management decisions may 'need' to be made more quickly and stridently than was previously the case. Staff may also need to be 'encouraged' to accept the possibility or reality of redundancies.

All of these tasks create a pressure for shifts in management styles and strategies as well as new values and subjectivities. To cite Coopers and Lybrand (1988: 50) in a report commissioned by the then DES 'to provide independent advice on the implementation of financial delegation':

What is required is a fundamental change in the philosophy of the organisation of education [at the school level]. Thus the changes required in the culture and in the management processes are much wider than purely financial.

(1988: 6,8)

The need to survive or to retain or assert a 'competitive edge' in the marketplace and to balance the books creates pressures which drive management decision-making within schools towards *commercial* and away from *educational* or *social* considerations, although these are not always mutually exclusive. As regards management *styles*, the first three of the tasks identified above, if they are to be acted out 'effectively', require speedy decision-making. This derives mainly from the sense of urgency and uncertainty fostered by unpredictable and changing budgets and results in a decisive assertion of 'the managerial prerogative'. The managerial prerogative requires a reduction of, and changes in, the nature of staff participation in decision making and also produces a marginalized role for trade unions. To cite Coopers and Lybrand (1988: 34) again: 'it will be important to ensure that any . . . consultation [with staff and pupils] does not unduly slow down decision-making, nor reduce management flexibility'.

It is therefore possible to argue that the market may be facilitating an assertion of '*technical rationality*' in school management over and against '*substantive rationality*' (Considine, 1988). The emphasis of technical rationality is upon the development of techniques, procedures and organizational practices which are intended to facilitate speed of decision-making, coordination, the setting and reviewing of objectives, good financial controls and information, cost improvement, responsiveness and consumer loyalty. The emphasis of substantive rationality is upon the intrinsic qualities of the 'product – process' – here education, teaching and learning.

Another useful way of conceptualizing the reconstruction of school management is provided by Clarke and Newman (1992) (drawing on the work of Mintzberg (1983) and Johnson (1972) amongst others). They suggest that the restructuring of the welfare state by the New Right represents an attack on an 'internal regime' of 'bureau-professionalism' and an attempt to replace it with a 'new managerial regime'. An internal regime is defined as 'the articulation of modes of power which connect the structures, cultures, relationships and processes of organisational forms in specific configurations'. Bureau-professionalism embodied 'the Fabian archetype of expertise coupled with the systemic organisation of services through the regulatory principles of administrative categories' (1992: 4–5). Amongst the things that were valued in this 'old' regime were 'collegiality, service, professionalism and fair dealing' (1992: 11).

By contrast with the professional, the manager is customer focused and is driven by the search for efficiency rather than abstract 'professional standards'. Compared to the bureaucrat, the manager is flexible and outward looking. Unlike the politician, the manager inhabits the 'real world' of 'good business practices' not the realms of doctrinaire ideology . . . The significance of management as a regime lies in the claim that managers 'do the right things'. It is this which underpins management as a mode of power and is associated with an insistent demand that managers must be given the 'freedom' or the 'right to manage'.

(Clarke and Newman, 1992: 6)

A further characteristic of new managerialism has been identified by Storey (1992: 14) as an

increased emphasis upon 'individual' as opposed to 'collective' relations with employees [as manifested in the utilization of more] direct forms of communication and involvement: team briefings by each line manager, the use of quality circles, problem-solving teams and the like. Commensurate with this are the developments in integrated reward systems and the linking, in one form or another of remuneration to performance rather than to 'rate for the job'.

Such shifts in management strategies are, of course, facilitated by mass unemployment and by legislation aimed at weakening trade unionism. It might be added that within a bureau-professional regime, managers tend to be socialized within the field and values of the particular public-sector area they are working in. Thus, in education, senior managers in schools or LEAs have traditionally emerged from the teaching profession. In a managerial regime, managers are more likely to be *generically* socialized, that is within the field and values of 'management'. The main character-istics of the two regimes are summarized in Table 4.1. which represents an *idealised* version of the two regimes. Both sets of characteristics rarely, if ever, existed or exist in an undiluted form and should be treated as extreme ends of a continuum of possibilities. We also want to emphasize here, as Clarke and Newman do, that *in practice* 'managerialization' has not involved the 'displacement' of one internal regime by another. In practice, we shall see that real managers inhabit the discourses of both regimes. Our argument in this chapter is that the restructuring of education provision has opened up a space for new management values and practices, but, as we go on to discuss, precisely how that space is filled depends on the degree of latitude allowed by local market conditions, as well as the stances of particular managers and the micropolitical contexts in which they are operating. Meanwhile, we want to complete our account of the reconstruction of the headteacher by considering the role of the new management literature in contributing to that project.

Table 4.1 Main characteristics of the bureau-professional and new managerial regimes

Bureau-professionalism	New managerialism
Public-service ethos	Customer-oriented ethos
Decisions given by commitment to 'professional standards' and values, e.g. equity, care, social justice	Decisions driven by efficiency, cost-effectiveness and search for competitive edge
Emphasis on collective relations with employees – through trade unions	Emphasis on individual relations, through marginalization of trade unions and new management techniques, e.g. Total Quality Management (TQM), Human Resource Management (HRM)
Consultative	Macho
Substantive rationality	Technical rationality
Cooperation	Competition
Managers socialized within field and values of specific welfare sector, e.g. education, health, social work	Managers generically socialized, i.e. within field and values of 'management'

The 'new managerialist' conception of school management implicit in the policies of the market appears in some senses to be supported and legitimated by the publication and circulation of a growing range of technical manuals on school management. Significantly, the Open University Press's 1993 'Top Twenty Books for Teachers' included the following titles: *Marketing Education* (Gray, 1991) *Total Quality Management and the School* (Murgatroyd and Morgan, 1993), *Human Resource Management in Education* (Riches and Morgan, 1989), *The Income Generation Handbook* (Warner, 1992) and *Managing Educational Property* (Warner and Kelly, 1993). In these texts, headteachers are being encouraged to develop business plans and promotion strategies (see also Kirby 1992a, b) and apply business consultancy approaches (Gray, 1991). They are being taught how to use management techniques borrowed from commerce, such as Human Resource Management (HRM) (Riches and Morgan, 1989) and Total Quality Management (TQM) (Murgatroyd and Morgan, 1993) in which 'performance is driven by customer perceptions of quality'. Headteachers are being advised to carry out SWOT analyses and produce corporate images (Pardey, 1991). Such publications support and inform the growth in management training programmes and courses offered to senior managers. More *generic* business management courses like MBAs are now being taken by teachers. For example, Keele

University's MBA (Education) course details suggest that a 'successful graduate will be equipped to manage successfully in Education as well as in other contexts . . . for example, . . . in the Health Service and other parts of the Public as well as the Private Sector' (Keele University Prospectus, 1993).

It would be inaccurate to suggest that the new breed of technical manuals which have been appearing in recent years are entirely affirming of the model of management implicit in the policies of the market which we described above. There is certainly the potential for school managers to use concepts such as 'quality' and 'excellence' which are central to these texts to carve out a space within the new managerial discourse 'to which "professional" values about good practice (and best practice) can be connected' (Clarke and Newman 1992: 18). There are, however, at least two important general senses in which the kinds of texts cited above uphold and legitimate the 'technical' conception of management implicit in the market. First, as Angus (1994: 81) has argued, they encourage 'school participants not to question the social and political conditions of their work but to get on and do the job by focussing on their own little domain of the school'. (See also Bottery, 1992; Ozga, 1992; Smyth, 1993.) This is important if the market is to work in the way that its architects intended, as Coopers and Lybrand (1988: 8) warned in their report to the DES:

> The success or failure of a financial delegation scheme will be crucially dependent on the attitudes of the schools and of their staff. If headteachers see the scheme as a means of giving them more administration plus the blame for education cuts, the concept is doomed to failure.

Angus was referring specifically to the best-selling publication, Caldwell and Spinks' (1988) *The Self-Managing School*. His analysis can be equally applied, however, to virtually all of the new practical guides to school management. Thus, for instance, Murgatroyd and Morgan (1993: 2) explain that their own book 'is not intended to discuss the ideology of schooling, but to sensitize and help those now leading primary and secondary schools understand and respond to new contexts that governments have legislated'.

The second way in which such texts affirm the policies of the market is by providing practical guidance for headteachers on how to 'manage' conflict within schools, the potential for which, as we noted above, is exacerbated in the new context. Such advice is modelled on a variety of new management theories in which collaboration is used for the instrumental purposes of manufacturing consent for a set of predetermined goals, and the work of Peters and Waterman (1982) is particularly influential. For example, in *The Self-Managing School*, 'collaborative' strategies are recommended within a 'loose – tight' framework (Caldwell and Spinks, 1988: 7):

> They [Peters and Waterman] found that excellent companies are both centralised and decentralised, pushing autonomy down to the shop floor or production team for some functions but being 'fanatical centralists about the core values they hold dear'. The parallel in education is the centralised determination of broad goals and purposes of education accompanied by decentralised decision-making about the means by which these goals and purposes will be achieved, with those people who are decentralised being accountable to those centralised for the achievement of outcomes.

One of the key means by which the leader's goals and purposes are achieved is through the 'communal institutionalising of a vision' (Caldwell and Spinks, 1988: 175):

- The leader implants the vision in the structures and processes of the organization, so that people experience the vision in the various patterned activities of the organization.
- The leader and colleagues make day-to-day decisions in light of that vision, so that the vision becomes the heart of the culture of the organization.
- All the members of the organization celebrate the vision in ritual, ceremonies and art forms.

'Bilingual' headship

We now want to turn from a consideration of the new version of headship implicit in the policies of the market and the recent school management literature to how real headteachers are confronting the new role expected of them. The new school-management manuals are being purchased by senior managers in schools. The question remains as to how far either the ideology inherent in, or the practices recommended by, these texts and 'encouraged' by the new structure of provision has actually permeated the thinking and culture of headship.

We certainly have evidence of a shift in the language of management within schools. Increasingly the headteachers and senior managers in our study refer to their 'unique selling propositions' (USPs), they talk of 'getting the product right' (deputy, Flightpath), analysing 'market trends' (headteacher, Fletcher) and developing 'corporate images' (headteachers of Milton, Martineau and Lymethorpe). Senior managers are beginning to refer to 'poaching', 'industrial espionage', 'knocking copy' and 'underhand moves' (always on the part of other schools, incidentally). They are establishing 'marketing groups' in their schools (Northwark Park, Trumpton, Pankhurst, Flightpath, Overbury and Fletcher) and new administrative positions have been created, in some cases replacing deputy headteachers. The holders of these posts are variously known as bursars (Martineau, Milton), financial directors (Martineau), senior finance and administrative officers (Trumpton), finance managers (Overbury, Fletcher), promotions managers (Flightpath), and press officers (Martineau). Caretakers in most schools have been redesignated 'premises managers'. The CTC has a Chief Executive and the headteacher is known as 'Managing Director (Academic Resources)'.

This new language of schooling is indicative of transformations which are occurring at a deeper level. We have evidence of a decisive shift in the values informing and reflected in management decision-making, as educational considerations are being increasingly accommodated to image and budget-driven ones. These aspects are discussed in Chapters 5 and 6, but what we term 'values drift' (see Chapter 5) involves a redistribution of resources and a shift in emphasis away from the most educationally vulnerable towards the most academically able. We are also seeing school management and organization increasingly geared towards realizing instrumental, narrowly-focused academic ends as schools respond to the national curriculum, OFSTED expectations and league tables (see Chapter 6). Some schools are also employing techniques like total quality management (TQM) and quality assurance (QA) to formalize, disseminate and inculcate the messages of performance evaluation, feedback, measurement and comparison. Within the existing policy complex the emphasis of such techniques is primarily upon indicators of academic progress and performance and in particular they are geared towards maximizing the examination achievements of those students who seem most likely to enhance overall school performance in key public indicators (like GCSE grades A–C). We have also observed a perception amongst staff in many of our case-study schools of a tendency towards speedier and non-consultative or pseudo-consultative decision-making by management. All of this is generating new (or exacerbating old) tensions between management and staff. These tendencies are exemplified by the case of Trumpton which we discuss below. Another perception of teachers we interviewed in a number of our case-study schools was of a marginalization of the role of unions within individual schools and across local school systems consequent upon the devolution of employment responsibilities to headteachers and governing bodies.

'I'm a member of the NUT and I was the NUT rep in school for quite a long time but . . . because of LMS [local management of schools] – the union used to have a fairly big role locally, and it was really hand in hand with the Director of Education and the Education Department, and that was always their way of working which meant it had quite a lot of influence with schools . . . and I think they have very little influence now. I mean . . . I think unions are very important, people are more isolated, and it works school by school rather than on a local authority-wide basis . . . now.'

(Head of Department, Pankhurst school, 18 March 1992)

At Martineau, a number of union issues have been redefined by the head as personnel issues.

'My time for being a union rep has been decreased this year on the basis that we've now got a deputy head who is in charge of personnel and other things as well and therefore lots of these issues ought to go to him rather than to me, which I think, is a complete misunderstanding of what a union rep is and what a senior management in a school is, but that was the sort of reason given to me.'

(NUT representative, Martineau school, 18 June 1993)

Despite these fundamental developments, our research suggests that it would be simplistic to suggest any *straightforward* shift from bureau-professional values and modes of operation to new managerialist ones. It is easy to caricature or over simplify headteachers' responses, but the roles and relationships and the people involved are complex and changing. Furthermore, the headteachers in our study take up a variety of value stances towards the education market – although the differences on the whole are subtle – and there are variations in the ways in which the new headteachership is acted out by its incumbents. All the management teams in our study take the market very seriously indeed, but the degree of proactive engagement with the market varies, as does the relationship between principles and shrewdness in the calculus of competition.

One way of understanding the headteachers we worked with and the data presented below is in terms of what Clarke and Newman (1992: 19–20) term 'becoming bilingual' or 'learning to talk management'. As they explain:

This metaphor expresses how profound the impact of managerialism on the culture of the public sector has been and how foreign it appears to many of those working within it. It also carries a recognition that old discourses and vocabularies are no longer enough or appropriate. Not to be able to speak management leaves one marginal, disenfranchised or rendered speechless – using words which are no longer recognised. The metaphor also sums up our own ambiguities about the process of managerialism and our role within it. It references the problems of how to translate between old and new languages; how to use the new effectively and how to 'manage' the tension between speaking a discourse and being spoken by it.

Headteachers and senior managers generally can be identified as placing themselves differently in the tensions and dilemmas exposed between the old and new vocabularies of schooling. There are headteachers who appear to have enthusiastically embraced the new language and culture of management. Trumpton's head has found that the market environment provides a powerful weapon with which to 'hammer' reluctant staff steeped in the 'complacency' and 'dependency culture' she believes was cultivated by ILEA. (We consider Trumpton's management approach in some depth in the next section of this chapter.) Martineau's headteacher, Mrs Carnegie, has also readily entered into a new managerialist discourse. She is looking for new markets in which to participate and is willing to spend money on active marketing.

> 'We'd also like to get the British Kitemark for management because, again, a lot of the things that that requires, we do. It's a case of going through the motions and getting those things here and then we'd be able to put them on our stationery . . . and a charter mark. And that's where we're going. It's difficult to know if the Government will push that one too hard . . . but I think we'd be ready to move in that direction.'
>
> (Senior teacher, Martineau school, 16 July 1992)

Mrs Carnegie has embraced TQM – both as a means of fostering a culture of performance monitoring and evaluation (see above) and as part of a broader strategy of unifying parents, students, staff and management around a specific central 'vision' or 'corporate identity'. Martineau is a school which, like many others, is moving towards the use of more setting and selection and towards a narrower focus on academic activities (see Chapter 6). These are strategies which many teachers, socialized within ILEA and within the values and practices of comprehensivism, object to on philosophical grounds. The policies of setting and selection therefore generate tensions between staff and management (see also Trumpton case study, below). TQM through the specific techniques of 'determining vision and strategy' (Murgatroyd and Morgan, 1993: 90) is a mechanism designed, in part, to iron out conflict and resolve tension: it is meant to make staff feel they can have an input into school decision-making (although in reality the parameters of debate are pre-set by senior management). One of the aims of TQM is to encourage 'individuals within an organization . . . to modify or transform their taken-for-granted assumptions about the organization and its processes so as to be in alignment with the vision' (Murgatroyd and Morgan, 1993: 90).

> 'A truly integrated and permeating vision energises people and can resurrect disgruntled, routinised, burned-out employees. It provides true challenge and purpose. It makes each person feel that he or she can make a difference to the world. It becomes a rallying cry for a just cause – their cause.'
>
> (Whiteley, 1991: 28)

Martineau's headteacher takes seriously the TQM-inspired task of 'institutionalizing' a vision through the production and utilization of symbols, what the TQM literature refers to as 'symbolic management':

> What is important is that those in leadership positions in the school seek to legitimate the vision and strategy by their choice of metaphors, words or models . . . Leaders can influence a great deal of thinking in a school through tuning and finessing symbolic meaning.
>
> (Murgatroyd and Morgan, 1993: 92)

At Martineau, feminist symbolism plays a prominent role as a focal point around which conflicting interests within the school can coalesce. It is too early to fully assess the effectiveness of new management techniques in achieving staff cohesiveness and loyalty in schools like Martineau, as these techniques have only fairly recently found a place within the repertoire of school management. However, at Martineau, teachers who are strongly opposed to particular developments which are seen as 'uncomprehensive' and who are critical of the management of the school, at the same time indicate a strong attachment and loyalty to the goal represented in the school motto – 'Educating the Women of the Future'.

Even in cases such as Martineau, however, where the new managerialism appears to have taken hold quite decisively, the old vocabularies and values have not gone away. Thus Mrs Carnegie, the headteacher of Martineau, defends her 'hawkishness' in the marketplace on the grounds that she is defending 'comprehensive education', and she is ambivalent about competition, finding it 'hard to come to terms with'. She says that 'at the end of the day I think one has to accept it's competitive, but I'm not so happy with that idea'. The CTC provides a poignant, if unusual, example of how headteachers can inhabit two apparently conflicting discourses. The new managerial imagery as reflected in job titles, the non-recognition of trade unions for negotiating purposes, the consumer orientation and internal language is striking; but the headteacher, or to use his official title, Managing Director (Academic Resources), articulates in one of his interviews with us a vision of progressive comprehensivism which given the emphasis on open learning, collaboration, 'real world' problems and an integrated curriculum, would not sound out of place at Stantonbury or Countesthorpe. (Although in another sense the vision reflects the practices of 'vocational progressivism' which have much in common with post-Fordist production strategies (Ball, 1990)).

Each CTC is actually unique. They have different emphases and different interests and for us in the college what we're focusing on is a holistic curriculum, where Science merges into Technology, into Physical Education, into Music and Drama. We've created a cross-curricular map, which allows us to make sense of the national curriculum and identify attainment targets, for Science perhaps within Technology or within Mathematics . . . But also we can coordinate the learning experience for children, so that throughout the school day there will be a variety of approaches to learning, some of it in front of VDUs, some of it traditional paper-and-pen work, experiential work, group work, discussion work, role play, a whole variety within one day, and breaking the day up in timetable terms to suit the curriculum need. Instead of having a timetable which says you will learn on a Monday morning for an hour French, then it'll be Geography, the timetable is there to be manipulated and moved around so there will be elements of a term when in fact half days will be devoted to a particular area, a project or we'll have a series of short sessions. It will move around to meet the needs of the teaching and learning imperatives.

(Managing Director, CTC, 26 July 1991)

There were other headteachers in our study, the majority in fact, who were far more grudgingly accepting of the market. These headteachers exhibited marked discomfort, resentment and cynicism, stemming from a belief that commercial practices and values are inappropriate in an educational context. They were not fully fluent in the new languages of marketing and management. Milton, Northwark Park and Overbury are typical of schools *reluctantly implicated* in the market. A strong adherence to comprehensivism or bureau-professional modes of operation within the SMTs generally is combined with a grudging acceptance of market imperatives. The managers of these schools appear to display what Clarke and Newman (1992: 10–11) describe as 'a complex sense of dislocation and uncertainty about the possibilities and prospects of becoming a new manager combined with a sense of confusion and loss about old certainties'. The following quotes do not do justice to the complexity of that sense of dislocation but capture something of the discomfort felt:

'The idea of . . . using terms like "marketplace", people are absolutely horrified by that. I don't think any of us are embracing that willingly but in the knowledge that . . . if we don't ensure that we're successful we simply won't survive.
(Deputy headteacher, Milton school, 17 July 1991)

'The idea of letting and all that sort of thing has very much come to the fore and it seems a terrible waste of the amount of time we have to spend actually, headteacher's time . . . and having this commercial base that wasn't there four years ago [1988], but has to be there now. You know, the joy and bliss when we got a Greek wedding . . . with the marquee and we got loads of money for it, and I thought, what am I doing sitting here celebrating the fact that people are going to have a wedding in the grounds? It didn't really have anything to do with what we were there for, but yet we couldn't help celebrating the fact.'
(Headteacher, Overbury school, 1 August 1992)

'I don't think you can have a premise that you have winners and losers in education. I don't think society can afford to run on those sort of principles . . . and I think this sort of, this marketplace business is potentially very dangerous. I mean we have to respond to it, that's the problem, that's why we're sort of running round in circles at the moment, because we can't just take the moral high ground and say, "We will have nothing to do with that"; we have to be part and parcel of it. But I just think it's a very bad thing . . . I don't think you've got any choice but to join in the game, you can't just stand back and wring your hands.'
(Deputy headteacher, Northwark Park school, 10 June 1992)

There are a number of ways in which senior managers attempt to resolve their sense of dislocation. One method involves a kind of role distancing, a degree of cynicism in 'acting out' but not taking seriously a position or perspective. For example, at Milton the language of the market and finance is evident in the school, but it is talked about

'with a wry smile . . . It's something we reluctantly deal with, I don't say we accept it . . . I don't think of the head as a chief executive, I think of the head as a teacher concerned with teaching kids, and I think . . . of governors as a way of enabling and helping the head to bring about the condition necessary for the most effective form of teaching. Financial aspects and all this form of competition, I look upon it as something we have to deal with, but not something which is going to change our way of viewing education.'

(Chair of governors, Milton school, 9 June 1992)

Such 'distancing' techniques are evident elsewhere. At Overbury,

'every time a word like "marketing" has been used, not every time, lots of times, there's an apology, somebody will say, "Well if we've got to market – sorry!" . . . because there is discomfort with the use of the word.'

(Parent governor, Overbury school, 4 July 1992)

'Marketing gets mentioned and it always gets mentioned with inverted commas round it. You know, we are "marketing", as [if] it's somehow a dirty trade to be doing, it's not what we're here for. But obviously there's a recognition that if you don't market, if you don't sell what's good about your school, you're not going to actually fill your school.'

(Deputy head, Overbury school, 2 November 1992)

Another strategy adopted by reluctant bilinguals is to carve out a space within the new discourse in which to pursue traditional professional concerns. This involves arguing that market-related activities can have a duality of purposes, where one set of purposes is commercial, and the other educational, and that, approached in the 'right' way, the two can be reconciled. Thus a number of senior managers talked about the 'positive' side of marketing:

'I don't like education in the marketplace, I don't like it at all, I find it all extremely uncomfortable . . . I think it subtly alters the agenda about what schools are about really. I think we should be talking about education and pupils and not about selling the school. Having said that, I think there are some benefits that have come out of having to look very carefully at your – . . . People feel marketing is a rather dirty word, and I know that if you read marketing books, there is actually a very good side to marketing because it actually makes you look at your own practice, and actually deliver what you say you're selling, you actually have to do it, so in that way it does improve practice in the schools, so I think some of the things – because we have to write documentation about what we're doing, and we have to promote ourselves, we actually have to make sure we damn well do it, and I think that's good. But I just feel slightly uncomfortable about it.'

(Senior teacher, Martineau school, 16 July 1992)

Linked to this is a tendency for senior managers (and indeed staff) to distinguish between *acceptable* forms of marketing which do not involve compromising traditionally-held educational values and principles and unacceptable forms of marketing, which do. Thus Mrs Alison, the headteacher of Overbury, distinguishes between marketing with a small 'm' which is muted and gentle and marketing with a big 'M' which is glossy, aggressive and relatively expensive. One of the Parkside deputy headteachers makes a distinction between 'positive marketing' and 'pure publicity':

> 'I think the marketing is much more concerned with the quality of the product you put out at the end of the day, at the end of the year, your relationships which are reported outside, so the quality of what you do is constantly demonstrated. That's what I call real positive marketing because the children go out every day and . . . then tell parents what you're doing . . . The other thing is preparing expensive glossy things which have a lot of photographs in them but not much text, which are then set out as pure publicity and I'm not sure that I embrace the publicity aspect very much at all. It's part of my style, quite honestly, to be a fairly quiet effective worker, doing what I call a good job, simply and successfully for parents, and I'm not someone who jumps up and down on a soap box with a microphone and says "Come and do this." So the head is much more involved with the publicists, and I'm much more involved with the strategists, if you like. So I find it quite difficult to come to terms with. I find it difficult as well to sometimes agree to the amount of money which is spent on it.'
>
> (Deputy headteacher, Parkside school, 3 June 1992)

The headteacher of Fletcher, Mr Edison, expresses his bilingualism in a slightly different way. He is what the deputy at Parkside would call 'a publicist' but suggests it is possible to accommodate a high-profile marketing strategy to the existing values and qualities of the school.

> 'We have a clear view on what we are, what we stand for, what we're trying to achieve and let's bring the two together, let's bring our value system as a school together with the realities of the market-place, so that we are saying to parents, "This is what we do stand for, this is what we do achieve," so that the messages coming out in PR [public relations] are actually based on a sort of genuine vision . . . and I think it's quite crucial, to get those two together because I think schools which haven't thought through their value position, will do all sorts of somersaults in order to catch up with what they perceive to be the latest trends in the marketplace.'
>
> (Headteacher, Fletcher school, 6 January 1992)

The headteacher of Goddard, Mr Framling, offered a similar formulation but also brings another perspective to bear on the values dilemma confronting schools: the question of what you can get away with.

'I don't think you can market, in the sense of brochures and me standing up and doing my bit, unless there is some reality behind it, because you get sussed very quickly because there's 900 families experiencing this school every day of the week, so if the messages that you give out are at variance with that . . . then it just becomes marketing, and I think the key thinking for us to do as senior managers in this school is to give the school a sense of direction and purpose.

(Headteacher, Goddard school, 7 June 1992)

Other headteachers, however, find the stance of presenting the school's values in a way which is consistent with what consumers are looking for far more problematic than Mr Edison or Mr Framling suggest.

'Parents have a more simplistic view of learning and teaching than is actually a reality of school [and she talks about the three Rs, SATs and GCSEs]. There is clearly a great deal of pressure for us to achieve on the academic front . . . Other skills, other aspects of achievement, may have to go down the plughole to satisfy the main one. As I say, it's our job as professionals to see that they don't entirely go down the plughole.'

(Headteacher, Parsons school, 12 January 1993)

In Chapter 5 we will explore in some depth the tension which the headteacher of Parsons has identified here – the tension between market pressures and traditionally held 'professional' values. We will explore how schools are presenting themselves to parents, and the extent to which these representations indicate a shift in the dominant values of comprehensive schooling as commercial considerations become increasingly influential in school decision-making.

The ability of headteachers to resist the pressures of the market is heavily dependent on the market position of their schools. The head of Overbury, for instance, felt able to comment that

'on the one hand, it would be very naive not to be aware of [marketing] and that you need to do X, Y and Z. But, on the other hand, I think that I really do feel now, even more than I did before, that you do what's right for your school, that you shove things forward, that you sell what there is and that's that.'

(Headteacher, Overbury school, 1 August 1992)

But this stance is clearly related in her own mind to her school being oversubscribed. She admits 'that if things were different' the luxury of integrity would be lost. Integrity is conditional.

> 'If we were in that tight corner, fighting for survival, then I think probably you do, rightly or wrongly, put money into glossy marketing, which is just more down the end of marketing with a capital "M" rather than a small "m". Can you understand the shorthand? But we're not in that situation and so we can continue keeping our integrity.'
>
> (Headteacher, Overbury school, 1 October 1992)

The head of Pankhurst adopts a similar stance. The school's secure recruitment base is derived from the perception of parents that it offers a grammar-school type of education, the fact that it is the only (state) girls' school in the authority and the fact that the school performs well in local league tables. This allows for considerable freedom of manoeuvre.

> 'It's easy in a way for me to sit here and say I'm untouched by these filthy market forces, as long as we have more girls wanting to come here than there are places for them, which is the position we've been in for two years, the last two years.'
>
> (Headteacher, Pankhurst school, 17 June 1993)

However, in schools like Northwark Park, Milton and Parsons, where the market positions of the schools are a good deal more fragile, managers find it far more difficult to keep hold of their integrity. In addition, management stances are not static but shift according to the vagaries of local conditions and the actions of other schools, as the headteacher of Overbury pointed out: 'Your marketing isn't just what's happening in your own school, it's what's happening in other schools, because if other people are doing things and you're not then that gives a message about you, that you didn't create, but it's there.' In particular, Mrs Alison's SMT is very aware of, and quick to react to, the activities of its nearest competitor, Lockmere school.

> 'Well they're the school that is more aggressive than other schools. We feel it quite keenly, because we, because of our position and so on, are in competition perhaps with Lockmere [school] whereas we're not with Fletcher [school], for example. They are more aggressive, and it is felt that there is more of a "sell" rather than a reflection of the truth. Now I think that's partly wrong, actually, but that is the perception and . . . I will alter some of the things that I say and do when I go out to schools, knowing that Lockmere has spoken to various junior schools that I have. I mean last year at this time, and it happens in the autumn term is when all the aggro comes out really,

because that's when people are panicking about not going to have enough kids for the following year, when it's all happening, Lockmere had a policy of going into schools and doing a very hard sell. They went into a school that we always traditionally went in to. And people referred to it as the "Lockmere Road Show".

(Headteacher, Overbury school, 1 August 1992)

The case of Milton illustrates very powerfully how management positions can shift in response to external pressures. In an earlier publication (written at the beginning of 1993) we characterized the headteacher of Milton, Mr Bracewell, as a 'dove' in the marketplace (Ball *et al.*, 1994). Mr Bracewell was attempting, we suggested 'to articulate a language of ethics, of principles, and to relate his practice, albeit hesitantly, to those principles' (1994: 355). We noted a 'relative absence of changes in policy or practice [in the school] that seem to be market-related' (1994: 362). Although the school had opted out it had done so as a tactical move to escape from the anticomprehensive policies of the LEA. We observed that what distinguished Mr Bracewell's school from other grant-maintained schools was its new school title (1994: 362).

It calls itself a 'Grant-Maintained Comprehensive School'. Whatever market advantage that could accrue from being grant-maintained might well be cancelled out by the highlighting of *comprehensive*.

Mr Bracewell's position was captured in the following interview extract.

'We have the notion in school, I hope it's in the school, it's certainly in the senior team, in planning and so on, which we call issues of principle and value. It's partly ironic, but even though you can be ironic about it, what it means is that you don't rush in to do ten ton of glossy – you do a good, you do the best possible open evening that you can do, I take a lot of care about it. But that's one of our issues of principle and value. I don't want to run into glossy stuff. I say to the parents, the prospectus is not posh . . . I think what the school is saying to itself is, "How do we do it within the principles and values of the school?" Also in terms of pragmatism, you don't want any kind of balloon business, you don't want to suddenly go up market, and bombard people with mailshots and who knows what else. I mean we do a reasonable prospectus, we do what I take to be quite a nice little simple foldover thing – what we stand for. We advertise in the local press, we advertise our sixth form in the local press, a discreet advert, yes we do that.'

(Mr Bracewell, headteacher, Milton school, 25 June 1992)

Since then, some dramatic and rapid shifts have occurred at Milton. The school has now produced a glossy prospectus from which all references to the school's distinctive egalitarian comprehensive ethos have been re-moved, as has the title 'Grant-Maintained Comprehensive School' from the front cover. In addition, the school has begun to circulate a glossy mailshot to homes in the surrounding area. (We describe some of these shifts in greater detail in Chapter 5.) Thus Mr Bracewell has become in-creasingly implicated in the market, despite his deep hostility to, and dis-comfort with, the values he is being forced effectively to embrace. (It should be noted however that, currently, Milton school still remains non-uniform, and it is the only school in Northwark LEA which has not ap-plied to become selective.)

A 'critical event' which brought home to Mr Bracewell the reality of his new managerial role was a financial crisis which hit the school during the first year of LMS. The crisis was generated by an announcement (later withdrawn) by Northwark Council that the LEA would be making sig-nificant reductions in its education budget which would have necessitated redundancies at a number of schools including Milton. Mr Bracewell and the governors quickly responded by nominating several named members of staff for redundancy without consulting the staff. As it turned out, the strength of local opposition to the cuts influenced the council to restore the full budget (the 1992 General Election was imminent), but the event gave rise to a great deal of ill-feeling amongst the staff at Milton and rep-resented a turning point for the head in terms of his role in the school and his relationships with staff. The headteacher had had previous experience of *passing on* redundancies made by the LEA, but under LMS it was Mr Bracewell himself and the governors who were *making* staff redundant.

> 'It was clear to me that I could no longer be the person who had you in and told you the bad news and mopped it up and was rotten about the Authority and then did what I could for you, and then I was the good guy. I was clearly going to be the bad guy and there was no way round that.'
>
> (Headteacher, Milton school, 25 June 1992)

Whilst virtually all school managers are being inducted into what Plant (1992: 87) calls a *culture of self-interest*, the responses of schools do appear to be distinct. Pankhurst, Overbury, Northwark Park, and arguably still Milton and Fletcher, represent examples of what Mclaughlin (1991: 38) calls 'reorientation change' which involves 'absorption of the language of the market but in such a way that it would make little or no impact on the dominant culture and core working arrangements of the organization'. Martineau, Parsons, Lymethorpe, Parkside, Trumpton and Flightpath are much closer to what he calls *colonisation change* which 'involves major shifts in the cultural core of the organization and all its existing forms of actions and activities' (1991: 38). This kind of change is associated with, and facilitated by, the development of a managerialist style of organizational control and relationships, that is by the assertion of *technical rationality* over and against *substantive rationality*.

Something of the sort of shift involved here is evident from Mrs Davenport's account of the new managerial culture at Parsons and the tensions which have developed between some of the staff and the senior managers. The stress on the language of management and the work that this language does in changing working practices and working relationships is important.

'A whole new vocabulary has entered into schools, particularly the management of schools, to do with LMS, in a way that didn't happen before. We did not use the same vocabulary that we're now using under local management. We're having to relate the management decisions that we make to the use of the resources available in the school, and it doesn't matter whether they're human resources or physical resources or equipment resources or whatever. We have to take account of whether they are used in the most effective, cost-effective, and other aspects effective, ways. So we do talk about cost-effectiveness, about accountability, we talk about quality control of various kinds of expenditure, we talk about budgetary control and we talk about each department having delegated financial and other managerial responsibilities, in a way we never did before. I think it still is the province of the most senior managers in the school principally, but it's increasingly being used throughout the school. The culture is changing, all levels are aware that its not just money, it is about "management" and everybody is a manager. So the culture is changing, the language is changing and we are using the language of the marketplace more and more. You hear people talking about "cornering the market in this particular aspect of school work" or "where is our market?", "who are our customers?", "who are out clients?". And some people object very strongly and feel this is not the way in which they as professionals think teachers should be operating but that tends to be the old, rather patronising left [-wing] attitude which is gradually growing out.'
(Mrs Davenport, Parsons school, 20 November 1993)

We were able to identify degrees of tension if not always outright conflict between managers and teachers over this issue of changing culture and of 'cost' versus 'professional' decision-making in almost every one of the case study schools. Such tensions and conflicts were often grounded in longer institutional histories and older sets of relationships within the schools but were brought into new focus by the pressures of the education market. Trumpton school provides perhaps the most pointed and dramatic of these conflicts and we now want to give some more detailed attention to this example.

New managerialism – the case of Trumpton

Trumpton is by no means a typical school, whatever that might mean, but it is very much a critical case in the education marketplace. It is a well-established, mixed comprehensive school which developed out of a secondary modern. It is located within a highly competitive market setting, a setting which, as a result of the combination of Government and LEA policies, is increasingly diverse and competitively highly charged. It is also a setting which by virtue of history, demography and LEA policies, has a significant surplus of school places. Trumpton occupies a specific reputational/status position in the local market arena (Ball *et al.*, 1995) which imposes considerable limitations upon the room for manoeuvre of the school in the changing competitive context, and the senior management are fearful about the school's future recruitment in this context. The senior management are both reactive and proactive in accommodating to the pressures and demands of this competition.

The case of Trumpton serves three related purposes here. First, it encapsulates in heightened form, some of the pressures and effects on schools of the policies of parental choice and formula funding which are represented in the Education Acts of 1988 and 1993. Second, it serves as a way of exploring some of the relationships between these policies and the changing and enhanced role of forms of business management in schools. Third, it highlights the struggles over policies – the micropolitics of change – which ensue when policies are 're-created' or attempted within institutions. General legal frameworks and policy imperatives are inserted into idiosyncratic institutional settings by specific actors. They enter and interact with a particular history and a particular set of institutional conditions. As a result, policies need to be understood as much in terms of what is enacted as what is intended. They are always partial in relation to the complex whole of organizational life. Policies are inevitably crude and simple. Practice is typically sophisticated, contingent and unstable. The assertion of, and resistance to, policy is always hedged around with some degree of chaos/freedom.

The ongoing micropolitical struggles at Trumpton, between what could be called the 'old guard comprehensivists', who are firmly rooted within the discourse of bureau-professionalism, and the 'new managerialists', is a struggle over both form and content: that is, the substance of several key decisions taken or initiated by the senior management team were challenged or resented by 'old guard' staff; but, in addition, these staff objected to the manner of decision-making and the management style adopted by the senior management team. Increasingly, this produced a polarization between management and staff, a 'them and us' relationship between the managers and the managed (see Bowe *et al.*, 1992).

'There was a bit of a crisis really last summer, in that there was a huge amount of concern over the way in which management decisions were being taken, so much so that the head felt the need to almost apologize for it at the beginning of term, because there was a real rift between the staff and the senior management team, and the governors sort of caught wind of this through the teacher governors. It's certainly been quite a painful period for a lot of people, the transition to GM status.'

(NUT representative, Trumpton school, 1 February 1994)

For example, there was 'reaction' in the school to a speedily implemented programme of minor works and refurbishment (£300 000 spent in five months) which was implemented to use up pre-grant-maintained budget savings. This programme was animated and organized by the newly appointed senior finance and administrative officer, Mr Norris, and one of the deputies, Mr Mann, who were regarded with suspicion by some staff.

Mr Mann: John [Norris] became for a while the focus of a good deal of resentment really, from staff.

Mr Norris: Yes, I think so. It was summed up by a teacher governor who said to me – and it was with a tone of complaint – he said, "I don't know, there's been more change in the two months you've been here than in the last twenty years," and I said, "Well it's about time then, really." And that's the backdrop to it. I mean it's change of any sort I suppose – teachers' experience of change since the Tory government of 1979. I mean any change I think now is anathema to them and upsets them and puts them on edge, because these are clearly good changes, and anybody coming in could see that.

(Interview, 20 May 1993)

Apart from the redesignation of 'space' involved here, an important part of the resentment among staff was focused upon the nature and style of the decision-making involved, which might be seen as 'business-like'. The method of decision-making was taken as symbolic of a new managerial regime.

'Things [were] being done that weren't discussed, weren't discussed in depth and over a long period of time [which] staff themselves found quite disturbing, not all staff. I mean I have to keep on reminding myself because there are a small number of quite vocal, long-standing members of staff who were a bit concerned, it upset them somewhat, their equilibrium was undermined and they didn't like it, and they made a bit of a noise about it . . . In any building works there are going to be problems, and . . . they suddenly leaped to the attack, saying, "Here's another example of something we don't know about." Blah, blah, all the rest of it. It was just symptomatic of their refusal to kind of move, they were clinging on to the past . . . My view – I can't substantiate it – . . . is that they were used to the feeling that . . . Trumpton was a secondary modern, works for principally working-class kids from the various estates in Carbridge, second class, we'll put up, make do, and that's the way it's always been and there was that philosophy behind that attitude.'

(Deputy headteacher, Trumpton school, 20 May 1993)

An important element of the new management at Trumpton is the shift of emphasis from consultation or participation to 'speed of decision-making'. In a sense there is now a mismatch between the internal and external expectations concerning the timescale of decision-making. The senior management team are determined to adjust their practice to the external timescale. Indeed, the need for swift action is used as an argument for avoiding or limiting internal debate and thus extending the scope of managerial discretion.

'There was quite a lot of democracy in the way that the school worked in that there were various forums and the senior management team would bring up things and they would use staff meetings as a sort of debating forum and there were working parties that would work on something and put it forward, and I think that in the late eighties, that was thought to be a lumbering and rather overly liberal style of management, in that it meant accepting things that came from working groups, and I think the old style of management wanted to let things – alright, if people came up with ideas, just to let them through, rather than feeling that they needed to sort of take the helm. They weren't so paralysed that they couldn't let ideas come from teachers, and increasingly, as line management has taken over, there's sort of an industrial parallel, they feel as if they need to control the direction that the school is moving in and that consultation is often perceived to be the time to talk about something, but we end up going back to what they wanted to do in the first place. Or you're given restricted choice, a working paper is given [with] four models to choose from, and . . . the initial premise that you're going to move in a particular way has already been taken. And there's been a very significant change along those lines and a sort of paternalism, if you like, that there's no time to give people time to think and to work on ideas and then bring them back and have a structure where ideas move backwards and forwards . . . It moves very rapidly and you're

given restricted choices which to some extent people like because it means that they don't have to be involved so much. It's quite a clever trick because it means that people have to put less time in and I suppose accept it because it provides them with a warm and cosy framework, even though they don't have a lot of say in it.'
                    (NUT representative, Trumpton school, 1 February 1994)

'New managerialism', as noted by Clarke and Newman (1992:15), 'presents an approach to managing which offers to "fill the gap" created by the dismantling of other forms of organisational power, especially the limitations imposed by organised labour'.[1]

Thus, while the staff see the SMT as 'gung-ho' and unaccountable, the SMT see the staff as living in the past and as unreasonably unwilling to change. However, this is not simply a mindless opposition of wills or simply the disruptive effects of change in a previously stable system. It is also a power struggle. Here we see management as a 'transformational force' (Clarke and Newman, 1992:6) set over and against the 'old regime'. To reiterate, change is only part of the problem here. What are also at stake are the methods and locus of organizational control, although the NUT representative also recognized that school managers now face new problems requiring new methods of working.

'I think that's the difference, they have a clear agenda now, and I suppose . . . you have to give them credit for what they've done, the school is more clearly managed than it was in the past . . . Schools . . . used to basically run themselves and management systems used to operate, but they didn't necessarily achieve a great deal. There was a huge amount of inertia built in just through custom and practice and it's probably very difficult for headteachers.'
                    (NUT representative, Trumpton school, 1 February 1994)

Nonetheless, the 'old guard' staff were particularly disturbed by the appointment and key role in the management team of the administrative officer (or bursar). The role and influence of the administrative officer seemed indicative of new forms of decision-making and a new set of institutional priorities.

'We've also got a bursar now which is an entirely new role, and there was no real consultation about what his job represented, but he sort of slipped mysteriously into the senior management team . . . He's got no educational role at all. His role is, he oversees the finances of the school and he's the line manager of all the non-teaching staff, but he's also on the senior management team, so he helps formulate policy, and that change was resented by a lot of people, because there was no real announcement, he just sort of appeared on the senior management team, and it was assumed that that was it and it was okay for him to do that.'

(NUT representative, Trumpton school, 1 February 1994)

The NUT representative saw several existing members of the management team as representing a new kind of educational manager.

'A lot of people who've moved into schools . . . that have become grant-maintained are part of . . . a new school of management, that . . . use industry-related jargon. You know, they talk about marketing and they talk about clients, and I just think that they're the new breed of school managers . . . They enjoy the cut and thrust of this new type of job, and although they might say that it's not their fault, that they're having to pass on the economies that have been handed down to them, I think really they quite enjoy the challenge of that . . . They've actually come in around the same time, they were all appointed fairly recently.'

(NUT representative, Trumpton school, 1 February 1994)

The chair of governors also saw the SMT as newly animated and excited by the apparent freedoms of GM status and the demands of competition. As we noted above, LMS and GM status are, in education, the particular forms of the rhetoric of 'liberation' which ran through and underpinned the resurgence of management theory in the 1980s and which linked new managerialism to economic recovery and national interest.

'It's lovely watching Louise [headteacher] and John [administrative officer] and a couple of other members of the senior management team really sitting there and working out new plans, new ideas . . . what will be good for the school, what would be a better selling point for the school, and being excited about it, yes, because now it's their business; the buck stops here.'

(Chair of governors, Trumpton school, 15 June 1993)

This may be a good public sector example of what management guru Peters has termed 'thriving on chaos' (Peters, 1989). There is certainly little evidence here of what Clarke and Newman (1992: 10) talk about when they describe 'how uncomfortable the process of transformation has proved to be' for public-sector managers.

It is interesting to consider the careers and perspectives of the key members of the Trumpton senior management team in the light of the above. The headteacher, Mrs Grange, a home economics teacher, spent six years as a deputy headteacher before working for two years as an LEA inspector. This offered a very particular kind of preparation for head-teachership set within a strong interventionist, management culture.

'There was the actual practical work that we were supposed to be doing, which was going into the schools and . . . creating insti-tutional intervention that would alter them, but I think the thing that interested me the most . . . was what we could find out that would enable us to actually pull out indicators, behaviour – call it whatever you will – that will tell you what kinds of interventions you should make, that would help all schools to improve. If you want to prepare headteachers, if you want to train headteachers, then that's the way to do it.'

(Headteacher, Trumpton school, 22 May 1992)

Mr Mann, the deputy headteacher with responsibility for public relations also came to the school by an unorthodox route, again via an LEA appointment but in his case having been an education officer. And the senior administrative and finance officer was also appointed from an LEA, in this case Northwark itself. He was a capital development officer, and again imbued in a particular managerial culture. This generated a specific interpretation of the market and of the necessities of the school's response, and this was undoubtedly influential within the SMT.

'We're not commercial in that way, it's just that . . . it's all been laid out for us, and somebody has got to accept that that is the case, and that if you don't swing with it, you're going to go under. It's as simple as that in my view . . . The one thing Northwark LEA did in particular . . . was allow people to use their imaginations and come up with schemes and plans . . . – "Do we really need that block over there; why don't we think of another use for that block, take the income, and use it for the education of the kids?". Now there's nothing intrinsically wrong with that I don't think.'

(Senior administrative officer, Trumpton school, 15 June 1993)

The senior managers are particularly oriented to issues related to recruitment, marketing, income generation and cost-saving. The career histories of Trumpton's senior managers, together with their orientation to recruitment and income, their concern to relate recruitment to 'output', and the staff's view of their language and decision making as 'non-educational', strongly suggest they are operating within a new managerial mode of power which is set over and against the old 'bureau-professional' regime of welfare schooling. As Clarke and Newman (1992: 6) put it,

Management . . . is the force elected by the New Right to carry through the restructuring of the welfare state. It is the agency which inherits the dismantling of old regimes and provides a new regime (a new mode of power) around which organisations can be structured.

As indicated already, the result of this shift and the polarization it has produced has been a series of confrontations of various degrees of seriousness between the SMT and the staff. The forthright responses of some of the staff has led to some backing down or change of tactics by the SMT but, as the NUT representative sees it, the outcome of these has been minor changes of style and method rather than any significant change in overall direction or purpose:

> 'So although there have been some small compromises – there were some large compromises in certain areas, but generally speaking I think that they're learning to manage more subtly rather than back down. I mean, I'm not blind enough to think that we've achieved that much particularly in changing their minds about the direction the school's going in.'
>
> (NUT representative, Trumpton school, 1 February 1994)

Underlying these events we can see a more fundamental struggle underway: a struggle the senior deputy headteacher, Mr Mann, was clearly only too aware of – a struggle between what the school was and what it might become, between an ILEA culture and a competitive culture. The first sees the school as serving its local 'community', while the second sees the school as set in an open and fluid market place. The first, paradoxically perhaps, is seen by senior management as stultifying and rooted in entrenched and out-moded ideas. The staff who inhabit this culture are seen as 'captured' by the school's history. The second is seen as dynamic and innovative. It is a culture which is driven by expediency rather than by principle and oriented to financial rather than educational priorities. Interestingly, both camps see themselves as defending comprehensive education. The 'old guard' see comprehensivism as rooted in a particular set of practices and commitments. The new management see the future of comprehensivism at Trumpton as resting on the achievement of an intake comprised of a cross-section of student abilities. Here, then, we see market policies being struggled over within the micro politics of the institution.

All of this, set within the broader context of changes stemming from the Education Reform Act 1988 and changes in teachers' pay and conditions of employment, means that the relations between teachers and management are under strain. In the interview extract we cite below, the headteacher talks about senior managers becoming the teachers' 'enemy', in place of LEAs, because they are now 'the employer' and must take the difficult decisions. Mrs Grange recognizes that there are potential difficulties here but argues that these are well managed by maintaining openness with staff. Clearly, however, there is a tension between openness and speed of decision-making.

'The various authorities, particularly Northwark, have provided for schools a very useful enemy which enables you all to feel nice and cosy and loving towards one another, . . . and there's the thought that the dynamics could alter and you could turn into the enemy yourself. As the senior management team . . . we will have to be careful to maintain our close brief on the school. You have to continuously feel its temperature as it were. The initial analysis goes on, "You don't just do it once, you keep on with it." What you have to do, I think, and it's what we've tried to do here, is determine management principles, and we've done that, and one of them is honesty with our staff . . . And it means never fiddling things, being straightforward and stating everything, not hiding things behind closed doors or anything like that, all out in the open, and we will continue to do that. Now by doing so we've built up quite a body of trust . . . and I think that that will continue, I think it will stand us in good stead, but it will only continue . . . One of the difficulties with schools is that headteachers and senior management teams were mistrusted because it was thought that they were doing naughty things behind closed doors. The staff here don't think that because we don't have have a history for doing that, and it's important.'

(Headteacher, Trumpton school, 22 May 1992)

The teacher governor, Mr Holloway, is less sanguine about the success of the management balancing act.

'I think that another side of the marketing is that it – well it's not just marketing, but it's part of the . . . ethos of the school, the public or community view of the school that the deputy headteachers and the head get very much involved in that side of it, and . . . people feel that they're not addressing the needs of the school, because their perception of the needs of the school are different to the perception of deputy headteachers, and there becomes a void between what management want and what classroom teachers want and I think that's a dangerous situation, very dangerous situation. And I mean, I don't think it's the fault of management, I think it's the fault of the system . . . and I think it's also the fault that people don't understand the system. And . . . I mean you don't need discontentment in an institution . . . when there's enormous discontentment going around outside. It's like . . . a cancer . . . it's alright as long as you can keep the cancer outside the gates. Once the cancer gets in the gates there's problems, and I think it's getting into this school now.'

(Teacher governor, Trumpton school, 16 March 1992)

The market is meant to encourage self-interest and discourage principled responses. Individual motivations and commitments are muddied by the pressures of survival. As a result, individuals are sometimes unclear in their own minds as to why they are doing certain things or acquiescing to certain things. There are new 'off-the-peg' vocabularies of motive which service and legitimate the 'new realism' but which sit uneasily alongside the professional socialization experienced by most incumbent senior managers in schools. However, in the future, that socialization itself may be different and some of the tensions outlined here will slip away. Second, the public image of the school or the concerns of certain groups of parents easily become mixed up with educational decision-making so that the reasons for decisions become unclear at the level of policy. All this is meant to mean that schools are more responsive and are more concerned to maximize 'output' performance. As we have tried to stress, it would be wrong to see the senior managers at Trumpton and elsewhere as simply unprincipled.

Conclusion

As a 'critical case', Trumpton school illustrates many aspects of the market and management as the twin dynamics for public-sector change. In the local marketplace, Trumpton is under pressure from all sides and the senior staff are in the position of casting around for a future for the school, or, to be more precise, a future that does not carry with it the stigma of 'sink' or 'SEN' (special educational needs) or 'vocational school'. The outcome of recent deliberations has been the decision taken by governors, at the behest of the head, to try for Technology College status – with a focus on Science, Maths and Technology – what might be seen as an 'up-market' but 'realistic' response to the position the school finds itself in (an ironic decision given the history of resistance to Northwark's attempt to make Trumpton into a 'magnet school').

'The Technology College initiative was entirely motivated by the fear that we were going to become the secondary modern of Northwark and they wanted something that they thought would attract parents, however spurious it is, . . . and they were really quite honest about that, they were saying that, in general, schools who've

changed their names to Technology College, attract more people
. . . just because of the name alone.'
(NUT representative, Trumpton school, 1 February 1994)

One interpretation of such a move is that it will allow the school to
reinforce its appeal to its traditional constituency, while providing scope
for attracting other parents who might be interested in such specialization. The senior administrative officer had indicated this line of thinking
in an earlier interview.

'But as for our intake, we take largely working-class kids . . . from
central Northwark, Carbridge, Bridgeside and we've just got to
work on that . . . and maybe start applying some of the management's thoughts about what is going to work for these kids, what is
going to appeal, and try and concentrate some resources.'
(Senior administrative officer, Trumpton school, 15 June 1993)

In other words, Trumpton is seeking a niche in the market, but a niche
that does not condemn the school to a second-class future. The market in
which the school is operating is 'cut-throat' *and* rigged. The Trumpton
staff, the senior teachers in particular, face the full forcefulness of
education market forces. Other schools, with different settings and
histories and possibilities do not, or at least not to the same degree. The
case of Trumpton thereby conveys some important conceptual as well as
substantive messages about education policy. While, in general terms,
events at Trumpton are framed and driven by external policy requirements, the press of policy is mediated by the conditions of the 'lived'
market within which the school operates – demography, geography,
class and ethnic context. The LEA's interpretation of national policies and
the pursuit of its own ideological agendas are also a part of the particular
local conditions with which the school must come to terms. These are
points made previously. In addition, however, the realization of policy,
in terms of its first-order effects on and in the school, is also affected and
inflected by the perspectives, commitments, histories and careers of the
staff and managers of the school and the outcomes of various struggles
and confrontations between them. In the longer term, the combination of
these requirements, conditions, mediations and struggles will determine
the second order effects of policy as regards educational standards and
social equity. We cannot simply 'read off' or generalize the impact of
policy from either policy-makers intentions or theoretical predelictions.

One consequence of the interrelated Education Reform Acts of 1988
and 1993 however is a refocusing and concentration of key conflicts inside
the school. That is not to say that schools were not previously sites of
conflict and struggle; this is patently not the case. A degree of conflict,
sometimes deep and pointed, is normal in 'value-organizations'. But the

scope and nature of conflict (and potential conflict) is now changed and has a double frame. On the one hand, there is the struggle for survival, the 'them and us' of competition between schools, of suspicion and rivalry, and the antagonisms and competition for preferment that this sets up within the school – SEN versus technology, pastoral versus academic, etc. On the other hand, there are the struggles over the costs and exigencies of survival, a different kind of 'them and us', the tensions of purpose and commitment between management and teachers. In both cases, management is crucial in the mediation, deflection and channelling of conflict. Importantly in this, attempts may be made to 'play-off' the internal and external rivalries against one another to provide a basis of shared purpose. The Trumpton case also underlies the need for a 'diachronic' perspective in the analysis of reform and change. The forces of the education market unfold over time, conditions change, policy emphases shift, opportunities arise. The internal dynamics of struggle and adaptation take place against and in relation to the trajectory of the local market over time.

Notes

1 It is important to note that we are referring here to the assertion of the managerial prerogative or the 'right to manage' in general terms rather than the use of the rhetoric or practices of the 'loose–tight' organizational structure (Peters and Waterman, 1982) or the creation of a 'transparent' organization where everyone is responsible for achieving corporate objectives. As Clarke and Newman (1992: 16) suggest

> 'there are problems about taking [this version] of new managerialism too seriously . . . It may be practised rhetorically even though forms of control being exercised change superficially or do not change at all . . . It is more likely that many organisations are relatively untouched by the new managerialism, even though they are exercising the manager's "right to manage" in other ways'.

5

SCHOOLING IN THE MARKETPLACE:
A SEMIOLOGICAL ANALYSIS

Introduction

This chapter will be organized around an analysis of the semiotic systems which schools communicate to the 'outside world'. Semiotics is an important and fruitful area of analysis in the new market context for at least three reasons. First, what we refer to as new semiologies of schooling appear to constitute a major cultural transformation within education, with concerns about self-presentation, surface appearance and image increasingly becoming a main preoccupation for school managers. This has implications for the amount of energy, attention and resources which can be devoted to other aspects of schooling. It also has potential consequences for the nature and integrity of the relationships which constitute schooling – relationships between teachers and parents, teachers and children, management and staff, primary and secondary schools and between secondary schools themselves. Second, semiotic shifts are worthy of exploration because to a significant extent they are rooted within and have implications for a whole range of school practices, processes and values which are evolving in response to the 1988 and 1993 legislation. Third, semiotic analysis is helpful in illuminating the way in which the incentive structure of the market operates in practice, that is the way in which the various layers of influence identified in Chapter 3 impinge upon and shape school cultures and values.

We begin by pointing to the growing significance of symbolic production for schools operating in the new market environment. We then go on to explore changes in the form and content of school imagery and the effects of these changes. Our concern throughout is to identify common trends, whilst not losing sight of complexity, nuance and exception.

The enhanced significance of signs

Image production cannot be divorced from the 'substance' of school practice; nor can it be narrowly confined to the domain of 'promotional activity'. Messages about the ethos, culture, values, priorities and 'quality' of educational provision are inescapably conveyed by the following:

- school practices and policies;
- the language and format of school documentation and activities;
- the age, fabric and design of school grounds and buildings, facilities and furbishings;
- styles of management and headship;
- school designations (whether church or county, single-sex or co-educational, or whether comprehensive, grammar or secondary modern);
- the socio-economic characteristics of catchment areas; and
- the size and nature of student compositions.

This means that with varying degrees of intentionality schools have always been engaged in producing images which carry messages about themselves as institutions, messages to which some parents are acutely attuned (see Chapter 2).

Many schools have, moreover, for some years and for a variety of reasons been conscious of operating within a market. Martineau school, from its inception as an amalgamation of two low-recruiting girls' comprehensives in 1986, has been highly attuned to the necessity and techniques of marketing.

> 'From the beginning, simply because it was a new school, we had to talk about image, so we were much more conscious of image here, because we'd got two amalgamated schools, we had to get rid of that, we had to have a new image. So maybe for this particular exercise [marketing post-Education Reform Act] we were well placed by accident. And so we did go in for fancy logos and flags and daffodils.'
> (Deputy headteacher, Martineau school, 16 July 1992)

The logo and other symbols were attempts to invent traditions. Pankhurst and Lymethorpe were also the product of amalgamations of schools with histories of poor recruitment and they faced similar challenges of having to establish favourable local reputations. Trumpton, Lymethorpe, Overbury and Parsons were secondary moderns in previous incarnations which meant they had to work hard at image management to counter the negativity associated with the secondary modern school in popular consciousness. Fletcher's 'market awareness' originated in the early 1980s when the gentrification of the school's immediate environs meant that many local children were 'lost' to the private sector, and the school had to recruit from further afield. The school's position on the edge of the authority and the growing reputation of Fletcher's traditional competitors in Pendry and Misslethwaite accentuated the need for an active marketing policy (see Chapter 3).

'Without a . . . relatively secure catchment area, we've always had to go out recruiting . . . We've always been very conscious of the fact that there is no guarantee at all every year that our numbers will be as they were before.'

(Headteacher, Fletcher school, 6 July 1992)

Power (1994) has pointed out that: 'The education market is not the result of recent policy, but stems from the long-standing relationship between education and a stratified social structure.' Certainly, many middle-class parents have always effectively acted as consumers of education, schools have always competed for their custom and local school systems have always been organized hierarchically, reflecting and reinforcing social stratification more generally. Differentiation has been the historical 'hallmark' of English education. However, whilst competition between schools was not invented or initiated by the Education Reform Act, the policies of open enrolment and per capita funding have given school markets a decisive new edge to them. The financial consequences of poor recruitment are now far more immediate.

'Whereas a few years ago, we were worried about our numbers in terms of not being able to get staffing and so on, we had time to pick that up and over a couple of years we became stronger, and it was fine, but . . . our finances are not so healthy that we can afford in September, to take less children and still be very solvent. I mean if we take ten less Year 7 than we need, we're talking about ten times £1500 or whatever, and instantly we have less money and you've got to look at losing staff, and schools will be pushed very quickly into a downward spiral, through LMS [local management of schools]. You can't sort of say, "Well next year we'll do this, this and this." So you can't afford to sit back, really, and say, "Over the year let's see how it goes, we'll keep our fingers crossed." Instantly you've really got to start worrying.'

(Headteacher, Overbury school, 17 June 1991)

Schools can no longer appeal to their LEAs to help them over 'lean periods'.

> 'Now the money is more difficult to come by and consequently, if you want to educate the kids properly, you've got to get up and look for it rather than say to ILEA, we need it for these kids, they're not getting [enough] textbooks, or they have social handicaps . . . we want more teachers. Now we have to get the money to do that, and we can't get it from the local education authority.'
>
> (Chair of governors, Milton school, 9 June 1992)

A deputy headteacher at Parsons made a similar point, commenting that in the past, if there was a need for increased staffing,

> 'we'd just go and bang on the LEA's door and make a case for it, and sometimes we won and sometimes we didn't, but by and large we won here which meant that in 1989 we'd got a very healthy staff:pupil ratio and the formula under LMS [local management of schools] said that that had to change drastically . . . There's a much greater . . . financial awareness now than there's ever been, and that's being seen in the fact that the staffing is much tighter.'
>
> (Deputy headteacher, Parsons school, 13 July 1992)

Responding to the market is for many schools now a question of survival. A school with subscription levels too far below its standard number is in danger of being unviable and/or of having to make large-scale redundancies. Most of our case-study schools have already used redundancies or 'natural wastage' to 'downsize'. There is a persistent fear in low-recruiting schools of being caught within an irreversible cycle of decline. To avoid this situation, such schools need to enhance subscription. Yet, as we saw in Chapter 3, many of the factors which influence recruitment, particularly those associated with demography and geography and the general socio-economic environment, are beyond the control of schools. Image, on the other hand, is something schools can *attempt* to manage even if they do not have ultimate control over how they are seen. The Education Reform Act has, therefore, generated a much stronger link between school image and school viability than existed previously.

> 'The amount of money you get for the school depends on the number of pupils you have, so therefore if you want money for the school, you've got to get more pupils, and you can only get them at the expense of other schools, so we will have to compete more with

other schools, we have to advertise, we have to put ourselves about, we have to make sure everyone knows what a good school Milton is . . . Instead of being happy about it, we have to tell everyone now, we will have to go out and make sure that we recruit sufficient kids to enable the school to continue on its present sort of level. So I mean we are becoming more and more conscious of this situation and it will certainly more and more affect the use of the energies of the staff.'

(Chair of governors, Milton school, 9 June 1992)

'Whereas we were aware [in the past] of staffing capitation being linked to the total population of a school, the school's viability was never in question; whereas now, if you don't recruit and if you don't bring in an appropriate number of children under LMS [local management of schools], there comes a point of no return. As the income goes down and as the standing costs go across, there comes a point at which the school is non-viable in financial terms. It has been the province of all managers in this school to get that message across loud and clear – you recruit or you die, and you are attractive to your parent population in order to do so. That has meant, as far as I am concerned, that we pay much much more attention to getting our message across.'

(Headteacher, Parsons school, 20 May 1991)

Even oversubscribed schools feel there is little room for 'complacency' (a number of schools used that term) and there is a perception of volatility and fashion in parental choice.

'I think that [the school] is thinking more about the way it presents itself to parents, and it does definitely think more in a . . . commercialist way. We do know that we need to have parents, so we are looking at our literature, looking at the way we do parents' evenings, looking at the physical aspect of the site . . . thinking about how we present ourselves to the press. We're doing things that I think . . . we did do before, but we're doing more of it and in a more systematic sort of way because we know that we've got to keep the number of children that we've got in the school, if we want to offer a first class education to the children who are coming, because you get much more flexibility in a school with 1050 than we used to when we had 900 . . . It's not an overwhelming change in ethos but it's a sort of change in emphasis.'

(Chair of governors, Fletcher school, 13 May 1993)

'It only takes one or two parents from a certain school to think this is the school to now go to, and they're influential, so everyone else comes. And then in two or three years time another school uses

yellow pencil sharpeners and that's the thing. I mean it's not quite as fickle as that, but it by no means reflects always what a school is like, I think, and things certainly shift about in this borough.'
(Headteacher, Overbury school, 17 June 1991)

Whatever their market position, then, schools generally feel a need to try to make themselves more attractive to consumers, to be reflexive about the messages they communicate to the 'outside world' and to cultivate images that will appeal to parents generally and especially to *particular sorts of parents*. In the new policy environment of market forces and local management of schools (LMS), the production of signs assumes an enhanced significance. This is reflected in the fact that increasingly headteachers appear to be taking more control over the processes of semiotic production. For example, in Martineau, in the past the writing of the prospectus (which had consisted of a spirally bound series of photocopied sheets) had been a collaborative exercise. But

'after the principal saw the Cardinal Heenan [school] prospectus, [the old prospectus] was put in the bin [and replaced by a professionally produced glossy brochure] written from beginning to end by the principal . . . There's a whole team of people now that are reading it, to get the style right, to get the grammar right, to see there are no mistakes, and is it sending the right message?'
(Deputy headteacher, Martineau school, 16 July 1992)

'At Lymethorpe, now all publications and letters and so on are vetted really strictly by the head. Nothing goes out of the school into the community unless it's absolutely right . . . even letters that the students . . . write off to companies. If they use headed notepaper from the school the head wants to see it, wants to see everything, and he'll want to see a draft, then it's got to be corrected, the grammar's got to be absolutely right. The image that we create outside in the community is one of the number one priorities of the school.'
(Teacher, Lymethorpe school, 3 February 1994)

The concentration of decision-making about image in the hands of senior managers and particularly headteachers may well be seen to reflect the kinds of broader transformations in styles of management, in the respective roles of senior managers and staff, and in staff–management relations discussed in Chapter 4.

New semiologies

Not only is imagery becoming more important to schools, but the form and content of imagery is being transformed in the process, creating new semiologies of schooling. We will now analyse some of the key elements of these changes. In doing so, we will explore the material implications of the new semiologies, their relationship to the incentive structure of the market and some of their potential consequences for relationships and values within schools. Our analysis is organized around an exploration of what we have identified as three overlapping sets of developments:

- the use of more sophisticated production techniques and the resulting 'glossification' of school imagery;
- the commercialization of texts and an associated focus on 'visual images' and explicit indicators of 'quality'; and
- a growing emphasis on middle-class symbolism.

Glossification

Image management in most schools seems to be focused around a number of 'core' activities: the refurbishment and decoration of school buildings; the production of publicity materials; communication with the press; 'liaison' with primary schools; and a variety of public events (e.g. open evenings, open days, student productions, consultation evenings and governors' annual meetings for parents). We focus here on three of these areas – buildings, promotional events and prospectuses – in order to convey something of the flavour of the changes taking place more generally within school semiologies.

Buildings

The CTC is in some senses at the leading edge of a new approach to school building. Established as part of a 'movement' designed to forge closer links between business and education (Whitty *et al.*, 1993), the business orientation is very evident in the decor of the school as well as in its language and organization. Parents are referred to as 'customers' and the 'customer – provider' relationship is reflected in, and enhanced by, the reception area which is organized and furnished like an open-plan building society office. The long low-level reception desk is run by business-dressed young women, visitors wait sitting on expensive-looking sofas amid potted plants and displays by local artists, looking at the clocks on the wall behind the desk which show the time in London, New York, Tokyo and Frankfurt. All of this is reinforced by the state-of-the-art equipment in the college, much of it provided by industrial sponsors. The corporate decor is particularly striking at the CTC, but it is a style to which other schools would appear to aspire. Milton, Martineau and Pankhurst have all revamped their reception areas over the last two years. Milton has purchased new zebra logo carpets to enliven its reception area and develop the school's 'corporate image'. Martineau, like the CTC, has installed a building society-type desk and the headteacher's concern that the 'corporate colours' be used consistently throughout the school extended to an insistence on maroon gas taps in the refurbished science laboratories. Pankhurst's iconography, as expressed in the physical fabric of the school, was previously that of an old-fashioned grammar school. It has been totally overhauled:

> The situation used to be a rather dark corridor at the entrance where you had to find your way somewhat labyrinth-like to the head's office. Now there's a painted reception area, immediately inside the main entrance, a sliding glass panel and one signs in the visitors' book and wears a visitors' badge. Very like visiting a large multi-national company . . .
>
> (Observation notes, Pankhurst school, 17 June 1993)

Promotional events

A parallel set of changes are apparent in open days and evenings. On the whole, these are becoming slicker and are geared towards selling the school in a far more thrusting way than was previously the norm in schools. This was our perception but also that of many of the teachers we interviewed. The following observation was fairly typical:

> 'When I used to go to open evenings at my old school, I used to help out in the chemistry department or whatever, everyone just seemed to be very jovial and they were just showing you round and everyone was very relaxed, it was very informal . . . Perhaps it's because I'm on the other side of it now, and I'm actually the teacher rather than the pupil, but I did notice for the first time that everyone, the senior management were very concerned, and very worried and very stressed and . . . there were . . . two members of staff walking in front of a group of people, about twenty foot in front, just to make sure everything was going okay. So yes, it made me realize, . . . when I saw these people running around, that they were just there to get these people in. They weren't there to show them the school so much as grab them.'
>
> (Newly qualified teacher, Trumpton school, 20 March 1991).

Milton's 1992 open evening was, according to one of the deputies, 'more tightly run' than on previous occasions: departmental displays around the school were 'unified', that is 'done in a particular typeface . . . with everything looking the same around the school . . . whereas previously . . . departments [did] their own thing'. Fletcher has also revamped its open days. Parents are now shown round by a senior member of staff rather than a pupil so that parents' questions can be answered, senior teachers are 'primed' with the sorts of questions parents ask, there is a more systematic and organized programme, and class teachers are under strict instructions not to send students 'out' as a disciplinary measure. A newly qualified teacher remarked that 'there's an active policy during the open week . . . for you not to put pupils outside the classroom, because it's a bad image.'

> 'So the whole thing has become much more professional and I think that's very important. You know, you don't want parents to have a view that the school is incompetently run. I mean they might go round the school and see lots of very good teaching, lots of classes working, but then there is something out of order which takes place which, had a senior member of staff been there, they might have dealt with or been able to explain.'
> (Headteacher, Fletcher school, 6 July 1992)

The 1993 open day at Martineau resembled a business fair, with all teachers and sixth-formers wearing yellow daffodils, the 'school flower'. The school symbol, the cedar tree, was very prominent everywhere. In general, a sense of corporate image was strongly evident. At Trumpton's open evenings, the deputy headteacher indicated that staff are 'encouraged' to dress appropriately, which means 'quite traditional in their appearance'. The hall is arranged formally, and the senior staff and governors are lined up on the stage. In the words of the deputy headteacher, this is 'purely for image, because I think that's what people want to see'.

> 'One of the staff . . . said he didn't particularly like the "Tory Party Conference set-up" at the end . . . and my view is, well look at any party conference now and see the same thing, which is stage-managed, which is sensible.
> (Deputy headteacher, Trumpton school, 20 November 1991)

Part of the stage management at Trumpton involved the senior team collectively drafting the headteacher's speech for the open evening.

> 'Well we sat down beforehand . . . It's a corporate, senior management affair, as it were, so we actually sat down and said, "Well what do we want the head to say?" And basically it was . . . appear traditional, . . . conservative with a small "c", emphasize traditional things, like hard work and discipline, emphasize the fact that the [LEA] don't particularly like the fact that we exclude a significant number of pupils, we exclude more than they would like us to exclude, not permanently, but for various things, particularly for fighting, and particularly for bullying, emphasize that, emphasize the fact that our examination results, in terms of numbers of GCSEs

has improved by 25 per cent over the last three years, which is not bad. We've played about with statistics a bit, everybody does . . . keep it fairly short, sharp and to those areas.'

    (Deputy headteacher, Trumpton school, 20 November 1991)

In both Martineau and Trumpton senior management would like to establish a staff dress code to be 'encouraged' throughout the school year, not solely at formal events.

'Teachers should be expected to wear a sort of uniform which is expected of a professional.'

    (Deputy headteacher, Trumpton school, 20 May 1993)

Prospectuses

As far as school brochures are concerned, the 'home-spun' stapled-together (often poorly) duplicated black-and-white sheets have been largely consigned to the wastepaper basket or recycling bin. Promotional materials have rapidly assumed an increasingly glossy, colourful guise, with schools taking advantage of the latest desk-top publishing technology in their communications with parents and with home-grown prospectuses giving way to professionally produced ones. In most of our case-study schools, brochures are still being designed in-house but printed externally. In Riverway LEA, the prospectuses are written in a common format and designed and produced centrally by the LEA in order to preserve the authority's corporate image. In 1994, the common Riverway style was up-dated and made more glossy in order to discourage schools producing individual brochures and to avoid a consequent demise of the corporate front. Nevertheless, Parsons school has produced its own brochure as a supplement to the Riverway LEA one and Fletcher school produces a glossy annual magazine which is distributed to prospective consumers. Lymethorpe school's 'visual image' was created by a local printing firm which is represented on the school's governing body. Parkside school drew on the expertise of Sunstar, the local bread factory, for the design and production of its brochure. Flightpath school's prospectus and a series of glossy fliers were designed by a professional advertising company. A number of schools are now also producing promotional videos for use at open days and to show to children at local primary schools.

The developments we have described in this section are, we suggest, significant for two reasons. First, the material implications should not be underestimated. The work of image production whether in the form of press releases, brochures, open evenings or primary 'liaison' absorbs significant quantities of teacher time, emotional energy and financial resources which could have been spent on enhancing the educational experiences of children in the school. Competition between schools means that the costs are likely to continue to rise, as the commercialization of image production takes on a momentum of its own. The production of a glossy brochure by one school is matched or up-staged by the prospectus of another and the process may well continue to escalate as the aesthetic expectations of consumers continue to rise. The headteacher of Overbury reflected the position of a number of headteachers when she expressed considerable unease with the amount of time spent on recruitment: it 'disadvantages what you might want to do in your own school, the kids in your own school'. She distinguished between marketing with a small 'm' which is muted and gentle and marketing with a capital 'M', a more aggressive approach

'where you actually say, Well . . . it's no good just doing this and this, we have to spend money on something that looks glossy— and you're spending money on that instead of on the textbooks. And that kind of thing is for me the line between what I've found acceptable in the past and what I would like to have always said I would find unacceptable.'

(Headteacher, Overbury school, 17 June 1991)

'We've said, "Well yes, we'll put £1000 more into the publicity budget, because, yes, we do need little leaflets that fold over as well as the prospectus," but at the same time two years ago we'd have been agonizing and saying that £1000 would buy a computer for the geography department or whatever, whereas now we don't have those discussions, [we] just do it.'

(Headteacher, Overbury school, 1 August 1992)

The head is here articulating what we have observed in many of our schools – a shifting of the boundaries of what is defined as acceptable, a constant process of squaring and re-squaring uncomfortable decisions with individual consciences. She is engaged in the process of *values drift* (see below). The investment in marketing tends to be justified by school managers on the grounds that the financial cost will be recouped if the school succeeds in attracting extra students. An annual marketing bill of £2000–3000 is seen as a drop in the ocean compared to the money such an investment can bring in. Each Year 7 student attracted to a Northwark LEA school, for example, will be worth more than £10 000 over five years in the school and if the student stays on in the sixth form, will be worth an additional £6000 (or thereabouts) over two years (on 1993–4 figures; see Table 3.3). But whilst a £2000–3000 investment in marketing might make economic sense for individual schools, when these sums are added up across the system as a whole, it becomes apparent that *significant amounts of money which could be spent on teachers and textbooks are being diverted to meet the costs of publicity and presentation.* If every school were to spend 'only' £1000 per year on marketing, that would amount to a total annual marketing bill for the UK as a whole of £28 million.

There is, however, a second less tangible but nonetheless important significance of these developments. It is that the new glossiness may well result in a fundamental transformation of some aspects of the character of schooling. This is something which has positive as well as negative dimensions. On the positive side, newly painted and carpeted classrooms and corridors and attractive publicity may serve to raise the self-esteem of students and teachers, and redecoration and refurbishment may help to create a calmer, brighter and more pleasant learning environment. But on the negative side, the cultural cost of glossification in some areas, together with the tighter control by headteachers over imagery, may be a loss of the kind of individuality, friendliness and student input which may be associated with more primitive production techniques. A primary liaison teacher makes precisely this point in relation to the welcome booklet for new students.

'Things have changed, like the nature of the booklet that they get. We hope [it] has become more kind of . . . child-friendly towards them. I mean it has always intended to be. In fact, I'm not sure that computers don't take that away a little bit, because when we used to have to Banda everything or run it off, we used to include the children's own handwriting sometimes. We had a page in it called First Impressions and they'd write about what it was like to come to the new school, but now it's all done on the computer, perhaps it's lost a little bit of the character of the kids.'
(Primary liaison teacher, Parkside school, 11 May 1992)

The semiotics of 'suit-wearing' are also of interest in relation to change in character. Suit-wearing by teachers is designed in part to convey, both internally and to the 'outside world', a business-like, formal efficiency and a number of teachers expressed a sense of loss associated with the spread of more formal teacher dress. Some of the objections made by teachers were practical but others concerned the implications of suit-wearing for staff–management and teacher–student relations:

'There's certain people in the school who are like – do you know what I mean by "suits"? There are people in this school that . . . always wear a suit and . . . they seem very detached, whereas . . . in my view of schools and schooling, you actually can't be. I'd hate to dress in a suit to come to teach, because I wouldn't feel relaxed, because I want to relax in the classroom, yes, and they teach from a sort of lead position, and I don't really think you can teach from a distant position.'

(Newly qualified teacher, Fletcher school, 17 November 1992)

This teacher refers to 'the suits' as a 'business faction who want to see an efficient machine'. They are contrasted with 'the other side . . . who are very . . . child-centred, who want to just look at the individual and special needs and this type of thing'. The association between teacher dress and pedagogic style is probably not as clear-cut as she suggests, but certainly the business connotations of suit-wearing taken together with a whole range of other developments, like building-society style reception areas, do at least superficially seem to generate a more formal atmosphere and a more formal and distant set of relationships than was previously evident particularly in many London comprehensives.

Commercialization of texts

Where detailed and informative descriptions of school policies and organization, and of curricular and extracurricular activities were once the norm in school brochures, now shorter, 'punchier', less-informative and more promotional texts are becoming commonplace and a greater proportion of space is devoted to photographs. This development is consistent with the exhortations of marketing experts.

> The value of good design lies in its ability to convey a message succinctly and clearly to the reader; one image can be worth pages of copy . . . The copy should be written to reinforce images; concentrating on benefits not provision, it should seek to convert the initial attention and interest into a desire for the product and thus to action. Fewer words are always better; shorter sentences rather than long; and simple language rather than obscure terminology and complexity.
>
> (Pardey 1991)

The new Martineau brochure, like a number of others, looks and reads more like a company prospectus than a traditional school brochure. It even 'shares' the advertising slogan of one of the major high street banks – Martineau is a 'listening' school. The old Martineau duplicated prospectus was essentially an information-giving document containing a great deal of factual detail about the school which has been edited out of the revised version. The deputy head acknowledges that whereas the original brochure 'was quite useful in the school for visitors and useful for new staff', the new one, 'is market-oriented, [oriented] to selling the school'. Flightpath's prospectus, designed by a professional advertising firm, resembles a travel brochure with its effusive tones and generous use of superlatives:

> Our modern, spacious campus is one of the finest . . . Bright, light teaching blocks are arranged round tree-lined courtyards . . . Our brand new Sports Centre comes complete with 14 station weight training, cafe-bar and conference centre . . . surrounded by 20 acres of playing fields and flood-lit all-weather pitches . . . Our nationally award winning curriculum ensures that students are taught a comprehensive range of basic skills, while creativity and initiative are nurtured through investigation and problem-solving . . .

Additionally,

> [The heads of year at Flightpath are] highly experienced. [There is a] superb range of clubs. [The school has a] growing national and international reputation [and enjoys] dynamic community success, . . . excellent facilities and modern resources. [In the sixth form] our relevant and challenging curriculum provides outstanding opportunities for academic achievement and personal development . . . Our reputation for technological excellence has resulted in several leading computer companies choosing Flightpath to showcase their latest systems.
>
> (Flightpath school prospectus)

This is perhaps one of the more extreme examples of the commercialization of the language of school – home communication, but it is an extreme example of a general trend. This trend is associated with a perception that the judgements that many parents make about schools are based on superficial indicators of schooling rather than on any knowledge or understanding of the processes and practices which lie behind them. Martineau's approach is quite clearly founded on such an analysis.

> 'I have problems about the consumer. I certainly think when choosing a school that they know what they want actually, but . . . in a way [parental choices are] patently uninformed. I expect that sounds patronizing, but I think . . . that many parents are rather uninformed about what schools are offering, so [we] therefore go for rather overt things like uniform . . . We go very much on outward symbols. In fact we now have a flags policy where we fly a lot of flags in the school [of the nations] of our children. So a lot happens actually in ritualistic, overt symbols of what the school is.'
>
> (Headteacher, Martineau school, 30 June 1992)

Flightpath's headteacher explains that his school's use of commercial advertising techniques was in response to the general impact of the contemporary semiotics of commerce on 'the public':

'I suspect that in a generation that is bombarded by the media and by advertising in particular, that education needs to be presented in a similar form because if it's not, it doesn't impinge upon the minds of the public, the parents and so on . . . they respond to the spirit of the age in an advertising-marketing sense and I think that we have got to try and address that.'

(Headteacher, Flightpath school, 11 June 1992)

The head of Lymethorpe takes a similar view. Drawing on the expertise of one of his business governors, and citing the example of Guinness, he has set about cultivating a 'visual image', using specific colours and logos which people will automatically associate with Lymethorpe.

All of this suggests that schools are increasingly concerned to *attract* rather than *inform* parents. *Whilst schools could play a role in facilitating and enhancing parental understanding of the processes and practices of schooling which lie behind the 'visual images', the market inhibits such an approach by putting pressure on schools to focus on what is visible (and/or measurable) rather than what is important.* Of course the visible/measurable and the important are not necessarily mutually exclusive. Many of the more conspicuous and quantifiable aspects of schooling are educationally neither unimportant nor counterproductive. Children's educational experiences may be greatly enhanced by improvements in the physical environment, as we have already noted. Literature which is attractively presented and simply written may be more accessible to parents and children. Success in examinations enhances the self-esteem of students and extends further education and career opportunities. And what is conspicuous and measurable can carry messages about the less visible and less tangible dimensions of schooling – the quality of relationships and of teaching and learning. Favourable levels of punctuality and attendance, for instance, may be indicators of an enjoyable and stimulating curriculum. Promotional materials and other concrete symbols of schooling, however, do not necessarily provide an accurate reflection of what is happening in schools. What is conspicuous and measurable may be misleading. An obvious example is raw examination results, which tell us more about the socio-economic composition of student bodies than they do about the quality of teaching and learning in schools. A litter-free school might be filled with students who find the curriculum unstimulating, unchallenging and unenjoyable. As far as open evenings and days are concerned, there are many aspects of quality which cannot be easily seen on a fleeting visit to a school where events can be stage-managed and lessons rehearsed. And glossy brochures and stylized promotional events often convey idealized images of school processes and practices which do not always accurately describe what actually happens in schools.

Student uniform is an especially good example of how simple and overt images may conceal the more complex and covert processes and relationships of schooling. There is a commonly held belief in schools that, on the whole, middle class parents favour uniform because they view it as an indicator of 'discipline'. Therefore, in an effort to boost recruitment and attract those consumers deemed to be desirable, non-uniform schools such as Northwark Park have introduced uniform and uniform schools like Parsons, Fletcher and Trumpton are applying their uniform rules more stringently. Yet most teachers we interviewed were sceptical about the relationship between uniform and discipline. They believed that, in essence, discipline is constituted by the quality of relationships between students and between students and staff. (Trumpton's senior management were an exception, believing that a strictly enforced uniform policy can help to foster a hard-working ethos.) Many teachers felt that uniform can in fact be detrimental to staff – student relationships, in part because the enforcement of uniform rules means that teachers are drawn into a series of confrontations with students when there would otherwise have been no conflict. But for parents, the quality of relationships is difficult to see and evaluate; uniform and other explicit indicators of 'quality' are, by contrast (and definition), highly visible.

Despite the idealized images of schools' public portrayals of themselves, this does not mean they are generally dishonest. However, there is inevitably some manipulation of the truth. In some senses the new semiologies resemble a simulational hyperreality, an 'aesthetic hallucination of reality' (Baudrillard, 1983), or a collection of free-floating signs which appear to be only weakly associated with the actuality of school provision. Of course, it would be romantic to suggest that prior to 1988 the accounts schools gave of their activities in their literature and at their open days were accurate representations of the reality they purported to describe. Whilst the old-style duplicated prospectuses might have been more informational than the new-style glossies, they were still designed to convey particular images and often what they described were policies and intentions rather than really-enacted practices. The noise and semiology of equal opportunities in particular were often far divorced from school practices as they were experienced by students and teachers. However, our evidence suggests, first, that image management is now far more conscious and deliberate than it was prior to 1988 and, second, that this is because *the market is providing a far greater incentive than existed previously for schools to manipulate images rather than genuinely inform parents and children.* This has implications for the integrity of relationships between schools, on the one hand, and parents and children on the other. Our evidence from parental interviews suggests that, increasingly, there is a considerable degree of scepticism amongst parents, particularly 'insiders' – those who work in, or in relation to, education themselves – about the accuracy of claims made and of images presented by schools.

Middle-class symbolism

Not only are the messages embedded in school communications becoming simpler, they are also becoming more uniform and somewhat formulaic. Generally, school marketing texts, whether in the form of mottos, glossy publications or headteachers' speeches at open evenings, appear to be constituted by a series of generic, double-coded signals: an increasingly muted language of equality and access, 'caringness' and friendliness operates alongside a more strident language of achievement, performance, results and discipline; aspects of progressivism feature alongside re-invigorated traditionalism. Northwark Park's motto tells us that the school is committed to 'traditional values in a modern context'. Parkside is the 'Urban village school where achievement matters'; it is also a 'caring' school, but as in other schools, 'caring' is a carefully qualified term. According to a primary liaison teacher at Parkside, 'When I say caring, that's not meant to be in a soppy sense, it's an overall care for their academic progress as well as anything else.' The headteacher's speech to parents at Overbury's open evening typifies the double-coded approach.

> The school was proud of the two students who gained nine grade A GSCEs, and the ones who got into Oxford and Cambridge, but they were also proud of other pupils who achieved 'their own best'; there is liaison between subjects, but the school refuses to dilute subjects by offering them in neat packages like Humanities and Creative Arts; they believe in students sitting in absolute silence in rows, learning things by heart, but they also believe in children learning by doing or thinking; extra curricular activities range from highly competitive, to not competitive at all; the school has good facilities, but facilities aren't everything – the key thing is the staff and the pupils; there is strong discipline but it is not heavy or repressive but giving children clear parameters to enable learning . . .
> (Observation notes, Overbury school open evening, Autumn 1991)

This kind of dual imagery serves to generate the appearance of institutions able to offer all things to all people: schools are concerned about the academic and the pastoral; they are traditional and modern, conservative and progressive, disciplined but caring; and they cater for the most able and the least able. The aim is to ensure that schools maintain as wide an appeal as possible.

Beneath the double-coded 'veneer' of school imagery, however, a careful analysis of promotional materials and events over the four years from 1990 to 1994 suggests that, on the whole, particular themes are increasingly being played down and others played up. In general, schools are drawing more attention to those 'overt symbols' which denote academicism, performance and discipline. There is therefore an emphasis on examination results, Oxbridge entry successes, Latin, setting, provision for 'gifted' students, uniform and exclusions. Fitz *et al.* (1993) and Woods (1992) noted a similar set of traditionalist emphases in the schools they researched. There is also an emphasis on hardware and facilities in our case-study schools, in particular computer technology. In addition, opportunities for girls are advertised and 'girl-friendly' subjects such as Drama, Art and Music given a high profile. There is less emphasis generally on schools as friendly and caring institutions, on the processes of teaching and learning, on provision for children with special needs and bilingual students. Symbols of multiculturalism continue to be utilized in school publicity (like Martineau's flags policy, referred to above). Antiracist discourses, on the other hand, appear on the whole to be more muted, although there are exceptions (see below).

These patterns of emphasis are very clearly rooted in the incentive structure of the market. They emanate from two related concerns within schools. One is to attract those students who will enhance *at lowest cost* schools' positions in the league tables of examination results, attendance levels and school-leaver destinations. The other concern is to retain (or create) what is often referred to as a 'balanced' intake. This latter concern is predicated on the belief that a properly comprehensive education requires a properly comprehensive intake. The following view was typical of those articulated to us in schools:

> 'I think what people here would say is that every school should take its share of problem families, problem children, children with special educational needs, we don't not want those children at all, but a school which is full of children like that, very easily becomes a sink school, because nobody puts the resources in that you need to deal – that's why secondary modern schools didn't work, and a true comprehensive must have its share of the motivated parents who are going to work with the schools, and then you can distribute your resources so that you can cope with and help and bring up . . . those children who don't have those kinds of motivated parents.'
>   (Headteacher, Northwark Park school, 5 February 1992)

Thus, school marketing strategies are increasingly being founded upon a crude two fold categorization of consumers. In the first category are those families which schools desire to attract because they are viewed as an asset to the school. In the second are those which are considered 'undesirable' because they are seen as a liability.

The former category consists of children of a high measured ability, those who are committed to education and those with supportive parents. *Such children are likely to enhance a school's league table performance with minimal investment.* They are also viewed as contributing to a 'balanced' intake. A range of descriptors is used to categorize this group. A head of department at Northwark Park defines 'the sort of parent that the school wants' as 'a fairly well-educated parent who will support you in the majority of things that you do'. The head of Lymethorpe refers to the school's recent success in attracting more of 'the rather more discriminating parents' and one of the Lymethorpe teachers refers to a need to appeal to 'the discerning sort of parents' whose children are 'the brighter pupils'. A teacher governor at Flightpath identifies as 'one of the unspoken aims of the school' the desire to attract 'middle-class, high-achieving children.' According to a senior teacher at Flightpath this aim derives in part from a desire to expand the sixth form because of the additional money which sixth formers are worth and in part from a realization that children with special needs, of whom the school has many, take up 'a lot of extra time'. A senior teacher at Martineau points to an

> 'enormous divide between the kind of enabling parent who insists that homework is done and helps with homework too, makes sure there are books in the home to the other end where perhaps they haven't got room, they haven't got the time, they haven't got the ability – just not enabling at all.'
> (Senior teacher, Martineau school, 9 March 1992)

The chair of governors at Martineau, Mrs Thomas, is upfront about wanting to attract more 'able' children into the school, partly in order to preserve a comprehensive intake, but also because it is seen to be important for the survival of the school in an environment where so much stress is placed on exam results.

> *Researcher*: And how do you explain the concern to attract more able children to the school?
> *Mrs Thomas*: Well . . . because . . . now that . . . all one's results have to be published in newspapers and so on and so forth, in a sense, given that [we] were pushed into what's called a market, it isn't surprising that people say, "Well we want to actually make it look as though [the results] we produce are good, are quality," so I think that is . . . one of the aims. On the other hand, . . . with all the schools there are in Northwark, you can do your best to attract as many able children as you can, but in fact your school is going to be very comprehensive, because if you're going to survive

financially you've got to have a school of about 1300 to 1500 children or you can't survive. You need that number of children economically, so I mean you've got to have a comprehensive intake, you can't just survive on having able children, but you'll jolly well compete with other schools to get those that there are. I think that probably sums it up.'

(Interview, 7 May 1993)

She went on to cite two examples of things the school was doing to attract more 'able' children. One was a stricter insistence on uniform and the other was an increase in exclusions.

A particularly desirable category of children are girls who are perceived as behaviourally more amenable than boys and academically more highly achieving. In order to attract more girls, the headteacher at Northwark Park is concerned to combat the rough, tough, macho image of the school fostered by the numerical dominance of boys in the school. Girls can also be strategically deployed in school documents and events to this end.

'We've always been aware of wanting to attract girls, but we've never really gone out of our way. But this year we will have to put that as a significant factor, so that I would want departments to be having more – to make certain that it is the girls showing the technology.'

(Deputy headteacher, Trumpton school, 18 January 1991)

Further,

'The thing about boys is that they do less well in GCSEs . . . that's why we want more girls. . . . You actually can't go out, because it's against all the Equal Opportunity thing, to try and increase the number of girls as an objective. You can actually go out and say we're very good for Art and Music, which may have the same effect.'

(Chair of governors, Fletcher school, 13 May 1993)

Music in particular conveys subtle messages about social class as well as gender. Martineau's headteacher alluded to an association between music and social class when she expressed concern about the possibility of St Stephen's (a Church of England school located in an adjacent authority) moving to Northwark (see Chapter 3) and its plans to select for a music specialism: 'What you're really choosing [when you select for musical aptitude] is, in the main, children from supportive . . . homes'. She is keen for Music to have a high profile in her own school.

'I am a firm believer that parents, a lot of parents, care about Music . . . I think it's a good seller really that we do have two choirs here,

that we do have an orchestra. That's rather traditional stuff, but I'm happy to have that.'
(Headteacher, Martineau school, 30 June 1992)

A number of schools have started to use musical performance at their open evenings to signify 'quality':

'This time with the Music in the foyer, that was deliberately to say, "We have Music going here" . . . music of all sorts is taught, learnt and enjoyed in this school, to get that message across, because we think it's a very powerful performance indicator.'
(Headteacher, Parsons school, 12 November 1993)

Some groups of South-Asian students are also treated as valuable 'commodities' in the marketplace. A parent governor at Parkside refers to the possibility of the school shaping its curriculum in order to appeal to the perceived proclivities of students with a South-Asian background: 'the Asians tend to be very strong on Science subjects and that is bringing good results for the school, which is ideal'. The headteacher of Northwark Park told us, 'I think that we have not tried very hard to get into the Asian community. It's an area we ought to do some more work on.' South-Asian girls are perhaps the most prized category of student. Thus Martineau is grateful for its

'captive market [of] Muslim girls [who] of course . . . want single-sex education. That's a great bonus for us to start with, and we build on that.'
(Chair of governors, Martineau school, 7 May 1993)

The second category of consumers, the 'undesirables', consists of the less 'able', children who have emotional problems or who are behaviourally disruptive, working-class children whose parents are viewed as not valuing education, who 'just' send their children to the school because it is local, and children with learning difficulties and other special needs (although there are some exceptions) who are expensive to educate and who threaten 'balanced' intakes. Schools with strong special needs departments are concerned about the messages that strength in this area conveys as well as the financial consequences of having large numbers of children with learning difficulties. The following sentiment, articulated by a teacher governor at Trumpton, was shared by all the schools in our sample with good reputations for special needs provision:

'The school has an enormous intake of SEN [special education needs] kids, an enormous intake of statemented kids. But that's another thing; you work hard, you develop an area, you get known as a good

school for SEN and so what happens? – you're flooded with SEN
kids which don't drag the resources with them that they need and so
disproportionately affect the resourcing of that school.'
                    (Teacher governor, Trumpton school, 16 March 92)

At Northwark Park the prospect of accepting two new Year 7 children
with severe learning difficulties was viewed with concern by management because of the image that might create. The school was relieved that
one of the families chose another school.

'Luckily, the parents have decided to go elsewhere . . . But we were
beginning to think, "Oh my gosh, are we going to start getting a
reputation? – ah yes, Northwark Park, they integrate students with
these difficulties," and then, you know, what effect does that have on
the perception of parents [of] that school? When they come to want a
school for their Band 1 kid, do they send them to that school?'
                    (Head of SEN, Northwark Park school, 17 March 1992)

Martineau's decision not to 'advertise itself as being a school with SEN
children' is informed by a similar perspective.

'I think the school would like to see itself as a school with a good
academic reputation and I think that there is almost a fear that [if the
school has] got SEN children, with a good SEN department, that
parents might think, they can't be good academically if they've got
those children there.'
                    (Chair of governors, Martineau school, 7 May 1993)

We have no direct evidence which suggests that schools are identifying
particular ethnic groups within the 'undesirables' category, but national
statistics on exclusions do suggest that Afro-Caribbean boys are at least
covertly being assigned to this group (Bourne *et al.*, 1994).

*The new symbolism is important because it carries messages about what and
who is valued in schools* and because, as we shall see in Chapter 6, it has
implications for, and is rooted within, policies and processes which have
practical consequences for children. Through the symbolism and associated policies and practices the market valorizes certain kinds of success,
activities, behaviour, *and children*, and devalorizes others.

It is important to note, however, that the binary distinction between
'desirables' and 'undesirables' has not been entirely shaped by and
imposed upon schools by the new structure of provision. The division of
children, and indeed whole classes and year groups, into 'good' and
'problem' is deeply sedimented within the everyday discourse of many
teachers and operates alongside more empathetic and progressive versions of the needs and desires of children and their parents. The point is,
however, that whilst individual teachers and managers might retain their

own more sophisticated and sensitive readings of consumers and their preferences, when it comes to image-making (and other school practices, as we shall see) these tend to be 'squeezed out' leaving the more simplistic representations dominant. *The market provides little space for subtle and sympathetic understandings and analyses of the heterogeneity, complexity and depth of consumer needs and preferences.* Whilst the market might foster a greater degree of responsiveness to parental desires and preferences, it is only the preferences of particular groups of parents which effectively 'count'. We will pursue this point more substantially in the following chapter when we look at the consequences of this kind of responsiveness for internal school practices.

Variation and nuance

One conclusion that may be drawn from our observations is that although the market is supposed to promote diversity of provision, it appears to be having the opposite effect: being too distinctive in the marketplace is risky because significant groups of potential customers may be alienated. The market seems to be generating what might be termed a *fear of exceptionalism*. Having said that, we want now to introduce some messiness and complexity into the picture. While there is a very definite semiotic shift in schooling, we do not want to give the impression that in schools' communications with the outside world an 'old' language based on a set of concepts relating to comprehensive education is in any *simple* sense being superseded by a 'new' less complex, more uniform, performance-oriented commercial language. The bilingualism which Clarke and Newman (1992) note in the internal language of educational institutions (see Chapter 4) is replicated in the external language. Educational and market discourses co-exist to different extents and in different ways in different schools. We want here to focus on the semiotic responses of two schools, Fletcher and Milton, in order to illustrate, in some depth, the kinds of shifts which are occurring in the external languages of schooling and to provide a sense of the sorts of variations which exist in the precise nature and pace of change in different schools.

Fletcher school

In Fletcher's semiotic system, the language and practices of marketing are being grafted onto a liberal humanist progressive comprehensivism, which is possibly being transformed in the process. The headteacher, Mr Edison, makes no attempt to disguise his hostility to various aspects of the Government's policy; in fact he positively parades his antipathy, writing impassioned critiques in *Fletcher Voice*, the school's annual magazine for parents. In the 1991 edition, Kenneth Clarke's 'frontal attack on the teaching of contemporary issues' was dismissed as 'dangerous nonsense'.

> Humanities have a vital role to play in enabling young people to use knowledge critically, to explore values and examine issues in any society past or present. That is their function in a democratic, pluralist society and that is how Humanities teachers will continue to teach regardless of the political posturing of the latest Secretary of State.
>
> (Headteacher, Fletcher school)

At the same time the headteacher is keen to monitor market trends, to conduct market research and to promote the school. The school's publications have become increasingly glossy, slick and more pro-fessional with lively up-beat graphics of the kind used in the tabloid section of *The Guardian* newspaper. Fletcher's 1993 prospectus contains less information than previous versions, reflecting the general trend identified above and the text is punchier. It briefly signals the school's pedagogical approach.

> Sparking off curiosity and challenging students to think for them-selves are at the centre of Fletcher's approach to the curriculum. We promote this . . . by encouraging the students to be actively involved in their learning [and] by providing opportunities for the students to research issues, discuss topics in class and work together in small groups. We build on the best primary school practice whilst preparing the students from the start for GCSE and beyond.

Also mentioned is 'the importance of homework in each child's programme of learning [where] [e]ach student records the homework in their Diary which we ask parents to check weekly'. We are told that 'the curriculum [is matched] to the ability of the students' and that the school has 'an exciting extra-curricular programme'. The very brief run through in the prospectus of the school's pedagogical approach conveys the image of a school which is progressive (cf. 'active involvement', 'group work', 'primary school practice'), caters for children of all abilities by providing individualized programmes of learning, and values non-academic as well as academic activity (cf. extracurricular programme). Yet at the same time the brochure reassures the reader that the school is rigorous (cf. homework policy) and disciplined ('The school has in place a variety of sanctions which are used to deal with any unacceptable behaviour'). The modern – traditional dyad, designed to appeal to a broad spectrum of parents, is thus clearly in evidence here as it is in all of our case-study schools.

Enblazoned on the shiny wallet folder, which holds Fletcher's brochure and other documents and is distributed to prospective parents, are the school's four newly-formulated 'core values' – 'self-reliance', 'team-work', 'improvement' and 'achievement'. These values and their definitions were drawn up by Mr Edison. The staff, the PTA and the Student Council were 'involved' as part of the 'consultation process'. The headteacher indicated in interview that the identification and defining of core values was in large part a marketing exercise and essentially represented a re-articulation of the school's existing values. The perceived status of the core values document as a marketing ploy is captured by a comment made by a newly qualified teacher, interviewed at the time of the 'consultation' process. Trying to recall what the values were, she commented, 'I mean it was just basically one of those bits of bumph, do you know what I mean, which you get to say how good Fletcher is'. It would therefore seem that in the new market environment, morality itself is being commodified: values are now treated as products to be packaged, marketed and sold.

Fletcher's 'core values' are not incompatible with 'a commitment to the broad-based humanistic view of education' (*Fletcher Voice*, 1992), with 'a caring supportive community where life is enjoyable and where there is equal provision regardless of gender, race or culture', with a curricular approach concerned with 'sparking off curiosity and challenging students to think for themselves', or with a school which is 'participative and collaborative and . . . very child-centred' (1993–4 prospectus). Yet at the same time, the concepts of 'self-reliance' and 'improvement' are in keeping with the individualism and work-ethic philosophy associated with the neo-Victorian moral vocabulary of contemporary tabloids and mainstream political parties. In the full statement of core values, under the heading of 'self-reliance' is the mention of 'a vigorous equal opportunities policy'. However, that phrase does not appear in the summarized version presented to parents in the brochure, and it may be significant that 'equality' was not selected as a core value in its own right.

Fletcher is a school still very much rooted in a liberal humanist progressive version of comprehensivism, and the 'new' core values may simply represent a repackaging of the school's existing values in a more populist form, which is the head's intention. Alternatively, the way in which the core values are presented and the processes by which they were formulated may be viewed as embryonic signals of a subtle shift both in values and in the culture of management.

Milton

In Milton the shift is less ambiguous. The school's publicity indicates a substantial retreat from a proud celebration of comprehensivism in 1992 towards an affirmation of performance-oriented goals a year later. Up until 1993, the school's comprehensivism was central to the way it presented itself.

> 'Because we've chosen to be, and the governors are unanimous on this, we have chosen to be a comprehensive school, . . . we have actually got to use that as our major selling point.'
> (Parent governor, 21 October 1992)

The headteacher was extremely sceptical about marketing and the notion of consumer gullibility: 'people sending their children to schools are not as foolish and as easily duped by gloss or pork pies [lies] or whatever'. In small print on the front cover of the 1992 prospectus, Milton was described as 'A Grant-Maintained Comprehensive School'. In the text, examination results were not mentioned. Emphasis was on the social values and social climate of the school and the processes of teaching and learning. The aims of the school were clearly set out. They were 'to create a vigorous, cooperative community where students can learn happily and well'. The school was 'committed to valuing all members of the school equally and to equal opportunities for all'. It sought 'to build on the strengths and contributions of all groups in the school'. The school believed 'that all students are entitled to a broad and balanced curriculum'. It aimed 'to offer students a rich school experience which will lay the foundations for confident, tolerant active citizenship in our changing society'. These themes provided the organizing concepts of the whole prospectus and were used as subheadings for the remainder of the text. Although the prospectus was glossy, the emphasis was on the philosophy and values of the school which were described in detail, and the language was egalitarian comprehensive school language.

The description of the sixth form was emblematic of the approach and tone of the whole prospectus. The academic content was not discussed. Where learning was referred to, the emphasis again was on process rather than content. But the main emphasis was on the social and personal development aims of the sixth form:

> The sixth form aims to be comprehensive in practice. It sets up structures to bring students from all backgrounds together in fruitful activity so that they learn from and contribute to each other. All tutor groups are mixed ability, mixed course and mixed age. They have a pastoral curriculum to follow . . .
> The sixth form aims to be intellectually exciting and socially

challenging. Apart from the lessons, the aim is to create a variety of activities which make intellectual, social and moral demands on the students . . . The sixth formers are . . . challenged to contribute to the community of the sixth form, the school and the local area and to take responsibility for organising this contribution.

In the 1992 edition of the prospectus in the section on special needs, a sentence which did not appear in the 1991 version was inserted, referring to the existence of 'special provision for students of marked ability'. With the advantage of hindsight it is possible to view this added sentence as a foretaste of more extensive changes to follow – in form, tone and content.

In 1993, the school prospectus was radically overhauled. It moved to an A5 from its A4 format, a wallet was introduced at the back for inserting additional information and the prospectus contained colour instead of black-and-white photographs. As in the revamped brochures of other schools, the detail was removed so that it is more of an advertising than an information-giving document. There were also small but significant additions to the text and alterations of order which subtly reflect a shift in priorities. The introductory letter from the head, whilst following roughly the same format, was in 1993 amended in significant ways. It is worth reproducing the two letters in full:

Prospectus, 1992

Dear Parent

Moving to a secondary school is an important event in your child's life. This booklet is written to give you a clear idea of how the school works, what we believe and what we expect of pupils.

Milton is a friendly place, where you will always be made welcome. We are a happy and hardworking community and expect a positive contribution from all our pupils. We believe that a close relationship between home and school is vital in ensuring a good, well-ordered school where children learn effectively and happily and where teachers enjoy teaching. We aim to provide a lively, happy and thriving educational community which is both stimulating and vigorous. We trust that you will find this a useful guide and one which gives you and your child some idea of the character of the school.

Yours . . .

Prospectus, 1993

Dear Parent

At Milton we offer the opportunity for girls and boys to develop to their full potential in a caring, structured environment.

Milton has Grant Maintained status and a dedicated staff who value each child's unique characteristics. We are committed to providing the very best education for each student. We believe that a close relationship between home and school is vital in ensuring a good, well-ordered school, where children learn effectively and teachers enjoy teaching.

I trust that you will find this a useful guide, which gives you and your child a clear idea of the character of the school.

Yours . . .

The emphasis in the first letter is on the friendliness and happiness of the school and on the school as a community. The word happy and its cognates were used three times. In the 1993 version all references to friendliness and happiness have been removed. Instead of children learning 'happily', the school aims to be a place where students learn 'effectively'. The collectivist emphasis in the first letter shifts to a more individualized emphasis in the second. The revised letter is not anti-comprehensive but it demonstrates a subtle discursive shift. One of the aims of the revised text appears to be to present the school as purposeful and the headteacher as decisive. Thus the collective 'we' in the last paragraph of the 1992 version has been replaced by the more authoratative 'I' in the 1993 prospectus and 'some idea of the character of the school' in the 1992 version by 'a clear idea of the character of the school' in the 1993 one. The contrast in tone between the two opening letters is symptomatic of differences between the prospectuses as a whole.

The strong statement of aims and values in the 1992 and previous prospectuses is in 1993 reduced to two fairly generalized and tame sentences about the intended 'promotion to the full' in the school of 'the intellectual, physical and moral development of all its students'. Gone are the references to the 'cooperative community where students can learn happily and well', to the commitment 'to valuing all members of the school equally and to equal opportunities for all', to the 'rich school experience' and to 'active citizenship'. The section on the comprehensiveness of the sixth form has been omitted as well. In addition, the headings in the 1993 version have been changed to appear more value-neutral than before. The new headings include the 'National Curriculum', 'Students' Progress', 'Personal and Social Education', 'Discipline' and 'Rewards and Responsibility'. The text beneath these headings is divest of any references to the values of comprehensivism. In the 1993 version, the site, staffing and facilities are amongst the first aspects of the school described and precede the two sentences on the aims of the school, so that the material qualities of the school appear to be given greater prominence than fundamental values and relationships. Also prominent is the claim that the school has 'an excellent record of academic success and a strong record of cultural, artistic and sporting achievement'. In the section on Sport in the 1993 version, a sentence has been added referring to the school's 'record of success at local, regional and national levels'. The passage on Music also has an additional sentence, drawing attention to the existence of bursaries 'for our most able musicians'. Perhaps most significantly, on the cover of the 1993 prospectus, the words 'A Grant-Maintained Comprehensive School' no longer appear.

These textual changes reflect an overall shift in the Milton prospectuses between 1992 and 1993 from an emphasis on the *quality of relationships and processes of learning to academic results*, from cultural *activities* to cultural *achievements*, from a concern about *equality of access and treatment* to a concern about *the most able*. The 1992 school prospectus was original and distinctive and paraded comprehensive values. In the new brochure comprehensive values are understated and the format and text appear tame, formulaic and emulative of the publicity of other schools.

Values drift

We now want to set the developments described in this chapter within an analytical framework which gives emphasis to, and provides one way of conceptualizing the value effects of marketization. The examples of Fletcher and Milton schools illustrate the complex and varied forms of interaction between two very different discourses. Both schools are still drawing on a traditional comprehensive school vocabulary which gives particular emphasis to the needs of the less 'able', to equality of access and the quality of relationships, and to processes of teaching and learning. However, this vocabulary and its associated values are increasingly being combined with a market-oriented lexicon which gives emphasis to what is easily visible and can be quantified, in particular student performance and examination results. This discursive shift is part of a process of *values drift* which the market appears to be effecting in schools. We use the term to refer to movement across a series of continua which combine to form a *values spectrum*, represented in Figure 5.1.

The two sets of values, as summarized here, represent two largely oppositional conceptions of the nature and purposes of schooling. The values on the extreme ends of the continua are ideal types and we want to emphasize that, in practice, schools can only rarely – if ever – be described as conforming to these in their pure forms. Moreover, the two sets of values are not always necessarily mutually exclusive. The semiotic responses of schools (and indeed the internal practices which we consider in Chapter 6) indicate, however, that on the whole, school value systems

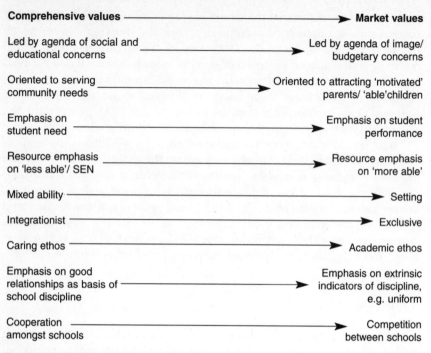

Figure 5.1 Values drift.

are 'drifting' from the left to right along the continua, crudely speaking, from 'comprehensive' values to 'market' values.

Schools have different starting points, however, and they are moving at different degrees and at varying rates, as the cases of Milton and Fletcher indicate. In Fletcher, the semiotic shift is subtle and ambiguous. At Milton, it has been swift and dramatic. In trying to make sense of these differences in rate and degree of change it is useful to return to the concentric circles model explicated in Chapter 3. The differences cannot be explained in terms of contrasting individual value–stances of the two headteachers. For such an explanation to 'fit' Fletcher's headteacher would have to be more deeply entrenched within a comprehensive values paradigm than Milton's. Our data do not suggest this is the case. If anything Mr Edison's use of language in his interviews with us suggests that he may be personally, if reluctantly, more comfortable with an 'agnostic' response to market forces than the 'dovish' Mr Bracewell (Ball *et al.*, 1994). Rather, it appears to be the very different local market contexts of the schools which is the crucial explanatory feature here. Although Fletcher's market position is considered by its management to be fragile, it is nevertheless more secure than Milton's. Whilst Fletcher has been oversubscribed in recent years, Milton is heavily under-subscribed. Fletcher is, therefore, relatively insulated from the pressures imposed by the new legislative framework. The school is by no means completely immune, hence the shifts described, but the degree of insulation Fletcher is experiencing allows for a relatively muted semiological response. Milton's more precarious market position seems to have generated a more rapid and acute semiotic shift.

Exceptions to the comprehensive – market trend

In a few cases, and along particular continua, schools are moving against the general trend, that is away from 'market' values towards 'comprehensive' ones. The explanation for such exceptions often lies in the particular local market context within which the school operates. We look here at the cases of Trumpton and Lymethorpe.

Trumpton

Whilst, in general, antiracist discourses appear to have been muted in school publicity in recent years, Trumpton *introduced* in its 1992 prospectus a *new* section drawing attention to its antiracist policy. In addition, its 1993–4 prospectus included an expanded passage on language support, drawing attention to:

> a number of specialist teachers whose aim is to promote the achievements of pupils of New Commonwealth origins. This includes bilingual pupils and pupils of Caribbean descent. These teachers work within mainstream classrooms, alongside class teachers, helping to ensure there is equal access and progress through the National Curriculum.

This specific example provides a sense of the complex way the market impacts upon schools. As we have already observed, Trumpton's senior management are highly semiologically conscious. They have conducted questionnaire surveys of Year 7 parents to inform their promotional activities and the headteacher's open evening speech was carefully constructed by the senior management team to appeal to the 'right kinds' of parents. The head of SEN at Trumpton told us that a member of senior management encouraged her to 'keep a very low profile' when she visited primary schools because the SMT are concerned about the growing proportion of SEN children attending the school. We have identified in Chapter 4 a willingness by the senior management of the school to compromise certain well-entrenched commitments in order to secure a more 'balanced' intake and to ensure the school's survival. Yet an emphasis on provision for Black and bilingual students carries with it a risk of alienating many of those middle-class families who are valued in the market place by schools generally and by Trumpton specifically. Thus, superficially at least, the utilization of antiracist discourses in Trumpton's publicity appears to be inconsistent with the SMT's stridently pragmatic response to market forces. However, a closer look indicates that there may be good commercial reasons for the emphasis. By drawing attention to its antiracist policy and its support for 'pupils of Caribbean descent' in recent brochures, alongside policies and practices which signify traditionalism, academicism and discipline, Trumpton appears to be trying to 'capture' a particular market segment – local Afro-Caribbean families whom the school clearly feels it cannot afford to alienate. Here the impact of the legislative framework on the school is being mediated by the effects of the ethnic make-up of the school's immediate social environs. Similarly Parkside's emphasis on the teaching of Punjabi in its publicity is presumably designed to attract and retain students from Punjabi-speaking families who constitute a significant proportion of the local population.

Lymethorpe school

Like most schools, Lymethorpe's semiological response to market forces is constituted by a series of double-coded symbols and the 'not-only-but-also' syndrome to suit everyone is clearly in evidence. In his 1992 open evening speech, the headteacher informed his audience that Lymethorpe was:

> 'a growing school . . . but . . . isn't going to become a huge school . . . We are a very caring school and you'll always receive a warm welcome [but] I should say that I can be jolly strict and stern . . . On the other hand, we do like to ensure we can build up good relationships with the children . . . What's special about this school is our concentration on how individual children achieve . . . There is a potential high achievers group that we identify early on . . . Those with learning difficulties are also identified early on and we have an outstanding special needs department.'
>
> (Observation notes, Lymethorpe school open evening,
> Autumn 1992)

However, as in other schools, beneath the double-coding it is possible to detect a number of important shifts in emphasis which suggest that the school is trying to attract a more 'balanced' intake. There has been a stricter insistence on uniform-wearing and a 'tightening up' of home-work setting. There are concerns about the perceived negative effects of the school's good reputation for special needs provision on its intake and a consequent effort, according to a senior teacher, 'to stress other things' such as 'the excellent Music and Drama facilities' and the potential high achievers group. In these ways the school's semiotic response conforms to the general trends described above. At the same time, however, results are hardly mentioned in the school's publicity and the main semiotic emphasis is increasingly on the school as *the* local, neighbourhood, community, family school.

> Generations of families have been educated at Lymethorpe and we have a number of former students on our teaching staff . . . Lymethorpe in the 1990s is a thriving community school accessible to all people in the area, providing education from the cradle to the grave . . . At any one time you may have the pleasure of meeting people aged from two weeks to 99 years old, all enjoying the benefits of education at Lymethorpe.
> (Promotional booklet, Lymethorpe school, 1993)

The message is reinforced in the booklet with a map in which the school is labelled 'Lymethorpe: your local school' and by one of the 'checklist' questions that parents choosing a school are encouraged to ask: 'Are the closest friends of my child also choosing the school we, as parents, are choosing for our child?' The booklet also advertises Lymethorpe as 'a beacon school for open learning'. These emphases can be clearly linked to the socio-geographical characteristics of the school's immediate locale. We described these features in Chapter 3, but, to reiterate, Westway's south side is made up of a number of localized, distinctive social communities or 'urban villages'. A weakly integrated transport system and a network of major roads which forms barriers around the 'villages' creates a series of 'natural' catchments. Lymethorpe's marketing strategy is therefore geared towards preventing 'leakage' from the school's 'natural' constituency by promoting itself as a vibrant cultural focal point for the local community. The strategy is based on a realistic assessment of what is possible: the school is near the bottom of the league tables and given the socio-economic nature of the catchment area and the association between social class and examination performance, this is likely to remain the case. We have seen that the tendency is for the legislative framework of the market to encourage an emphasis on student performance and to discourage neighbourhood, community comprehensive schooling through its abolition of catchment areas and its promotion of competition. However, Lymethorpe's local market context functions to 'distort' these legislative effects to the extent that the school's 'community-ness' has become, according to its headteacher, its 'main selling point'.

Conclusion

In this chapter we have been concerned to perform a delicate balancing act. On the one hand we have isolated and described some important general semiological trends brought about by the new legislative framework, and we have suggested that these are part of a broader process of *values drift* occurring within schools. In broad terms, we described the shift as a movement away from a set of values which we refer to as 'comprehensive' to a competing set of values which we have termed 'market' values. At the same time we have tried to avoid over simplification by building on our analysis in Chapter 3 in order to demonstrate how specific local market contexts can mediate and refract the effects of the national policy framework. The result of these processes of mediation and refraction are variety, unevenness and sometimes apparent inconsistency both within the responses of individual schools and across the school system as a whole. However, there is always a danger that in trying to capture faithfully the complexity and depth of social processes as they are experienced on the ground, one over emphasizes difference and apparent indeterminacy at the expense of vital overarching effects (Gewirtz, 1994). We want, therefore, to underline the point that although local markets are complex and varied, the general trends we have identified are striking. What the changes we have described amount to is a significant cultural transformation within schooling. To summarize our arguments, that transformation has at least four dimensions: first, significant quantities of financial resources and teachers' time and energy are being diverted from educational to marketing activities; second, the cultural transformation may well involve a shift in the nature of relationships between parents and schools as the latter are increasingly engaged in the manipulation of images to attract parents rather than inform them; third, what is visible and quantifiable is effectively being given more weight than processes and practices which are more intrinsically important but cannot be easily seen; fourth, by emphasizing such things as examination results and student performance to attract the more 'able' children, schools are sending out messages about what and who is valued in schools and ultimately about the purposes of schooling. This is one of the ways in which the market valorizes certain kinds of success, activities, behaviour, and therefore children, and devalorizes others. Thus although the focus of this chapter has been on image production and symbolism, we have already begun to demonstrate that semiotic shifts have important consequences for the processes and relationships which constitute schooling. In Chapter 6 we want to take that argument further by focusing specifically on *internal* school practices and their social and educational consequences.

6

INTERNAL PRACTICES: INSTITUTIONAL RESPONSES TO COMPETITION

Introduction

In Chapter 5, we were concerned primarily with how schools are representing themselves to the outside world. We demonstrated that a key element within what we referred to as 'new semiologies of schooling' is a shifting pattern of emphasis, with symbols of academic performance, discipline and girl-friendliness increasingly being highlighted. In this chapter we want to look more closely at some of the policies being enacted *within* schools in the new market context and to look at some of the systemic consequences of these policies with a particular, but not exclusive, focus on issues of equity. We identify and explore a number of key interrelated trends. First, we argue that concerns about image are driving schools in some instances to adopt short-term and superficial solutions to deep-seated problems which ideally require a significant investment of time and resources to resolve. Second, we argue that the market is encouraging schools to pass the buck of responsibility for the most socially and educationally vulnerable students and that this appears to be leading to an intensification of segregation across local school systems. Third, we argue that schools are introducing practices which are likely to result in increased social segregation and provisional differentiation within institutions. Fourth, we argue that the market appears to be effecting a redefinition and a narrowing of scope of schooling to exclude the social dimensions of education. Finally, we suggest that by promoting a view of schooling and children as commodities, the market may be generating a new 'hidden curriculum' of the school.

Short-termism

In Chapter 5 we suggested that the market encourages schools in their external communications to focus on what is visible and quantifiable rather than what is important (although we acknowledged that the two were not always mutually exclusive). However, the emphasis on the visible and the quantifiable is not restricted to schools' promotional activities. Our evidence suggests that in schools which feel they are vulnerable to market forces (and that category includes some oversubscribed as well as undersubscribed schools) *the new preoccupation with image is leading managers to adopt apparently superficial and short-term solutions to problems even when, in the longer term, such strategies may be socially and educationally unhelpful or even counterproductive.* The new structure of funding introduced by the Education Reform Act 1988 means that the financial impact of poor recruitment is immediate (see Chapter 5). That immediacy appears to be leading to a perception in many schools that any perceived 'weakness' which may damage an institution's reputation must be rectified as swiftly and demonstrably as possible. Yet some 'problems' – such as poor levels of attendance and student behaviour – are not ideally suited to what might be called 'quick fixes'. Uniform policy is one example of a quick fix. We have already argued (in Chapter 5) that a strictly enforced dress code for students might give the appearance of discipline but, in practice, may lead to a deterioration of student – teacher relationships within schools or at least fail to contribute to the establishment of positive relationships. Our evidence suggests that school approaches to truancy are also subject to the quick-fix mentality. With the introduction of attendance league tables, a number of schools are increasingly investing energy into telephoning and writing to parents of absentee children and/or publicizing the fact that they are 'clamping down' on poor attendance and/or adopting computerized registration schemes. This kind of high-profile, and in some cases hi-tech, response allows schools to demonstrate fairly quickly and publicly that they are 'doing something' about truancy. In addition, such campaigns might well be successful in encouraging some parents to ensure that their children attend school more regularly. But there are concerns within schools that the strategy is being pursued at the expense of addressing the *causes* of absenteeism. As one of the teacher governors at Flightpath school put it: 'it takes the focus off what we should really be doing [which is looking for a] positive way of getting children in'.

Permanent exclusions can also be used as a quick fix and they are on the increase: 'in the autumn term alone of 1993 there were 3671 permanent exclusions in England and Wales. This is only 200 less than the number officially recorded for the whole of 1992' (Williams, 1994: 13). The rise may partly be accounted for by the existence of a perception in schools that exclusions figures (as long as they are not overly high) are viewed by parents as an explicit indicator of good discipline (see also Woods, 1993). Exclusions can also help to enhance a school's league table position by removing from its roll children who are persistently late, absent or who might perform poorly in exams and not continue into further education. In some cases, children may be threatened with exclusion as a means of 'persuading' their parents to 'voluntarily' withdraw them from the school, although the unofficial nature of this strategy means that it is difficult to ascertain the extent to which it is being used. One education welfare officer explains how it operates:

'If you have a school that has a high profile, who wants to be . . . at the top of the league of achievement, at the end of the day, they don't necessarily have to go through the official . . . procedure for getting the child to move. If you were a working-class single-parent mum and, you know, Black or White but particularly if you're a Black, working-class, single-parent mum, who's called to the school and you are faced with a whole little row of people . . . who have got suits on who are White men who know it all who tell you that your child isn't coping [in] that school and would be better off in another school, then . . . the odds are you're going to move the child, and find another school. Now, that parent might not know that they don't have to, there is no way they have to, unless that child is permanently excluded though the proper system, and I think that happens quite a lot . . . So then the child moves as a transfer.'
(Education welfare officer, Northwark Park school, 10 June 1992)

This tactic, which might be termed 'constructive exclusion', may be what one school governor is describing in the following extract:

'In extreme cases somebody could be excluded on academic grounds, if they were actually wasting their time and everybody else's – not because they're dim, but because they're just . . . wasting a place and wasting resources. It hasn't happened yet, but certainly some students and their parents have been interviewed and the situation has been put to them, if there isn't an improvement,

then there is very little option but to ask you to take your daughter away.'
(Chair of governors, Martineau school, 19 August 1992)

Constructive exclusion enables the child involved to leave the school without the stigma of being labelled an 'excluded student'. In addition, it enables the school to remove unwanted children without having to go through any formal process, and it means that the exclusions figures can be kept at an 'acceptable' level. Oversubscribed schools can also use the existence of waiting lists to take a hard line with 'troublesome' students. 'Difficult' students are told that

'"if you continue to behave like this . . . we don't need you here, we've got people queueing up to get in, and if you don't want to stay here and abide by our rules, then you can go somewhere else, and we'll have somebody who does." I mean, that does come into play, yes. But then in any oversubscribed school at any time that is used . . . It's not a new thing . . . It's certainly been used time and time again – "We don't need you personally here . . . you're just a body here"'.
(Newly qualified teacher, Martineau school, 14 June 1993)

Exclusion, particularly constructive exclusion, is a relatively quick and easy way for a school to manage 'problem' children. However, whilst the strategy might solve the *school's* problem, exclusion is rarely of assistance to the *child* involved, and the school to which the excluded child transfers is left to pick up the pieces. Because Northwark Park, as an undersubscribed school, is subject to a high number of casual admissions, the EWO at the school has had a great deal of experience of trying to settle in children who have been permanently excluded from other schools.

'If the child is behaving incredibly badly at one school, moving him to another without addressing the reasons why they behave badly is not going to solve it, because if they've got a problem with authority or they've got a problem with relationships or they're bullies or whatever, they're going to be a bully somewhere else, because you've not looked at the reasons why they're doing it, and it makes it worse, because they've just got a whole new lot of people to bully . . . I can't think of any [circumstance when transferring a student] in the second or third or fourth year of secondary school will solve any child's problem, because you're creating another one, you're giving them an environment they don't know, a whole peer group

they don't know . . . structures that they're not sure of, you're making a problem worse for them.'
    (Education welfare officer, Northwark Park school, 10 June 1992)

What the EWO is pointing to is the fact that behaviour which most schools find unacceptable (like bullying or persistent truancy) is often an external manifestation of more deep-seated problems experienced by the child. To address the latter would demand a far greater investment in time and resources than is involved in the quick-fix approach. Viewed in more general terms, this kind of adaptive response to the education market is symptomatic of the narrowing down of 'education' to exclude social aspects of children's learning and development (see below).

Passing the 'buck'

The examples of exclusion and attendance policies illustrate how concerns about image are in a number of respects encouraging schools to focus on the *symptoms* of problems rather than on their *causes*. Relatedly, in a market-led system it is in the self-interest of schools to pass the buck. Whilst schools could play a role alongside and in collaboration with other agencies in supporting children with emotional, behavioural or learning difficulties, the incentive structure of the market encourages oversubscribed schools to shift the burden of responsibility elsewhere. Exclusion, whether 'constructive' or formal, is one mechanism for passing the 'buck', often leading to 'cost-shunting within and between uncoordinated agencies' (Williams, 1994: 11). The strategy means that *undersubscribed schools, which are forced to accept as casual admissions pupils excluded from other schools, are faced with having to support disproportionate numbers of socially and educationally vulnerable children without the resources necessary to do so properly.* (Some schools in this position are also losing support and specialist staff for other reasons, for example the phasing out of Section 11 funding and the closure of programmes like Urban Aid.) Not only does 'cost shunting' have negative consequences for equity in provision but it may also be untenable on economic grounds. A recent report on exclusions from primary schools (Parsons *et al.*, 1994) 'shows that it is far more cost-efficient and "20 times" more effective to support the child within the school, than it is to exclude them and bring other agencies into play' (Williams 1994: 11).

In addition to exclusion, some oversubscribed schools are using other sorting practices to raise the raw-score potential of their intakes and to create an image of exclusivity designed to appeal to middle-class parents. There is evidence of an increase in both *formal* and *informal selection* in schools. By 'formal selection' we mean admissions procedures which are overtly designed to select children according to specific published criteria, such as 'ability', 'aptitude' or 'motivation'. Such formal selection practices may often covertly discriminate against particular groups, as we discuss below. By 'informal selection' we mean the covert 'management' of admissions processes which effectively discriminates between more and less 'valued' applicants. Informal selection might include admissions procedures which, by design or default, lead to what Bourdieu and Passeron (1990) refer to as 'self-exclusion'.

The evidence suggests that nationally informal selection is on the increase, with interviews being conducted prior to places being offered in order to assess 'suitability' (Bush *et al.*, 1993). We want to illustrate the various mechanisms which schools have at their disposal for informally selecting students by focusing on the case of Martineau, which is accused by its competitors of practising subtle forms of selection, but we want to emphasize that Martineau is by no means untypical of many oversubscribed London schools. Informal selection is, of course, not a new phenomenon. However, our evidence suggests that the market is increasing the potential for it to occur. In Chapter 2 we argued that the education market constitutes a specific cultural arbitrary which privileges those parents who have the appropriate cultural resources for decoding 'the objects displayed' (Bourdieu and Passeron 1990: 51–2). This is perhaps particularly the case in the kind of local market which operates in Northwark where school admissions have been wholly deregulated; that is, all the schools are now responsible for organizing their own admissions which means that parents apply directly to the schools and not to a central admissions bank run by the LEA. To decode a complex deregulated admissions system like this one demands particular skills, knowledge and confidence and can therefore result in informal selection through *self-selection* and *self-exclusion*.

'People who were keen to get their children in here, put us as first choice, they understood they had to do that, and appealed if they couldn't get a place, filled in the forms for appeal. People who were unclear about the entry procedures, maybe didn't put us as first choice so they didn't get a place . . . and may not have appealed. Then they end up somewhere else . . . What's happened is the onus is much, much more on parents . . . finding out about schools and getting their child into the school they want. I mean that's always been the case to some extent, but there has been a bit of protection within an LEA system – coordination of admissions, and that's all gone and it's going to go. I mean, next year parents who want their children to come here, have to come to the school, will have to get themselves an application form and fill it in, whereas previously if you applied for an LEA school, maintained school, you'd do that with the headteacher of your daughter's primary school, so . . . it's sort of done for you, really, and it's all explained for you, whereas . . . we will send out application forms to primary schools for people to pick up, but it's really up to parents to get. And also people who get the forms in first, I mean by [the] deadline, will be at an advantage. It does subtly operate against people who . . . maybe English isn't their first language, [people who] don't understand the system.'

(Senior teacher, Martineau school, 16 July 1992)

Application forms can also informally discriminate by discouraging particular groups of parents from applying. In the Martineau form, parents are asked to include the following information: their places of work and occupations; the subjects the child is 'best at'; any special talents or achievements; subjects they find difficult; details of special help given, e.g. SEN or English for Speakers of Other Languages (ESOL) support; number of days absent during the last three months; sporting interests and abilities; musical instruments played and examinations taken, including grades; details of performances in concerts and exhibitions; other interests; and reasons for applying to Martineau. A form like this gives the *appearance* of selectivity and might inhibit some parents from applying to a school by giving them the impression, that if they did apply, their application would be rejected. This might be because the parents are unemployed and do not have a place of work or occupation to put down on the form, because they might feel their child lacks appropriate 'talents and achievements', because their child does not play a musical instrument, because he or she has been frequently absent in recent months, or because the child receives some kind of learning or language support. This kind of self-exclusion works also in relation to the construction of waiting lists and the use of appeals procedures (Adler *et al.*, 1989).

'We operate it fairly on a waiting list, but if you've got a waiting list, the sort of kids who get on the waiting list quick, they're middle-class people who know the system. They write in early, get their forms in early, they're sort of self-selected in a way. I mean . . . if you're out of school for some reason, like you've been excluded from another school, half-way through the year you need to find a school place. Places that don't have waiting lists are the schools that are less subscribed and therefore seen as less good and have less money and don't keep the same . . . quality of teachers. So it's not a deliberate ploy on the part of this school, it's . . . the overall education policy on admissions which means we're going to end up with some schools which are oversubscribed and sink schools.'

(Senior teacher, Martineau school, 16 July 1992)

Another practice which may be interpreted as constituting informal selection is the home–school 'contract' which parents and children are required to sign before they are offered a place. These are becoming increasingly common in schools but vary in the nature, specificity and in the quantity of expectations stipulated. The Martineau contract is particularly demanding of parents. They have to agree to ensure attendance and punctuality, encourage and support their daughter with her work, supervise her homework, attend parents' evenings and school functions in which their daughter is involved, keep her in the correct uniform, provide her with a well-stocked pencil-case, a calculator, dictionary and recorder, pay for the replacement of damaged or lost books, and support the policies of the school. The agreement includes a warning (in bold print):

Failure to keep to this agreement may result in disciplinary action. Serious cases may be taken to the governors.

The headteacher cites a governor who welcomed the agreement as 'something that will really be influential in bringing the *right sort of parents* into this school' (our emphasis). The introduction of the agreement certainly has the potential to encourage a greater degree of self-selection and exclusion, a point made by a senior teacher.

'Although it doesn't have a legal basis, . . . it's an agreement about what they can expect of us and what we expect of them. Now that . . . I think will have an effect because obviously with open enrolment you've got this enormous oversubscription. People knowing about this [the agreement], . . . if they're in the least bit worried about being able to keep their part in that deal, they're not going to put their kids forward . . . What we're hoping to attract is a wide mixture. We're also hoping to attract, by the way our agreement is set out, people who are committed to education.'

(Senior teacher, Martineau school, 16 July 1992)

Fletcher also uses a 'voluntary agreement' which is 'designed to establish the relationship between home and school on a basis of mutual trust and openness'. This is signed by the student, their parents, their form tutor and head of year and specifies obligations for each party including, for parents, attendance at 'parent – teacher meetings to discuss my child's progress'. Flightpath's contract is more general and is one-way. Parents are asked to sign a document indicating their agreement to 'support the school in all matters relating to Attendance, School Rules, Uniform . . .

Equal Opportunities'. It seems realistic to suggest that the more secure a school's enrolment, the more demanding its contract can be. Flightpath cannot 'afford' to discourage any parents from applying for admission. The agreement at Martineau is also associated with attempts within the school to effectively redefine comprehensivism to include an element of exclusivity.

> 'The school will continue to be comprehensive. But I think we're thinking of all sorts of ways – how do we enhance the comprehensive image, the image that anyone could get into it and therefore they could do what they like, basically, when they get here? And we have to fight, I think . . . against that all the time.'
> (Headteacher, Martineau school, 30 June 1992)

A small and growing number of schools, including Martineau, are now seeking and being given permission by the Secretary of State under the terms of the Education Act 1993 to introduce *formally* selective admissions policies. In May 1995, 57 schools had applied to the DFE for permission to change their admissions criteria to include some form of selection. By September 1995, five of the nine state secondary schools in Northwark had introduced some kind of selection of their Year 7 intakes on the basis of 'ability' and/or 'aptitude'.[1]

The practice, manifested in the selective and exclusionary policies of oversubscribed schools, of displacing responsibility for the more vulnerable children in society has serious implications for equity in school provision, because the inevitable corollary of these policies is differentiated provision and increased social segregation. Working-class children, who, on the evidence of previous research, are most likely to fail the covert and overt tests of 'ability' and 'motivation', and children with emotional, behavioural, language or learning difficulties, are on the whole likely to be increasingly 'ghetto-ized' in undersubscribed, under-resourced, understaffed, low-status 'local' schools. At the same time, middle-class parents are most likely to apply and have their children selected for the oversubscribed, favourably-resourced, favourably-staffed, high-status 'cosmopolitan' schools. Statistical data compiled by Northwark LEA indicate that these processes are already occurring. A report by the LEA published in October 1994 concludes from an analysis of school intakes based on the results of the London Reading Test that

> the trend over the last three years indicates the selective loss of the more able pupils [to private schools and to schools in other LEAs] at secondary transfer is increasing in magnitude. [And that] overall the

grant maintained schools and the CTC received a higher proportion of the top performance groups than the LEA schools.

Given the relative poor resourcing of undersubscribed schools and the effects of socio-economic context on student performance (Coleman *et al.*, 1966; Bridge *et al.*, 1979, McPherson and Willms, 1987), segregation, whilst possibly raising the achievement of children in the cosmopolitan schools (see Chapter 2), is likely to be detrimental to the performance of children in the local ones. This is not to denigrate the commitment and quality of staff in local undersubscribed schools, but such schools acknowledge themselves that they lack the resources necessary to effectively meet the high levels of student need with which they are faced.

There is a racial dimension to the segregatory effects of the market as well. Because ethnic-minority children are disproportionately represented amongst the most economically disadvantaged sections of the population (e.g. the homeless, travellers, refugees; Commission for Racial Equality (CRE), 1993) they are more likely also to be disproportionately represented in the undersubscribed schools (although that is not likely to be the case for particular groups of South Asian girls who are valued in the marketplace). It is not simply their socio-economic location, however, that makes ethnic-minority children vulnerable. The CRE (1993) have voiced concerns about admissions processes which are potentially indirectly racist for other reasons. The particular examples they cite are the use in selection procedures of reports from primary schools and of interviews with parents and children. Both of these techniques might leave students exposed to cultural or racial stereotyping. There is a specific worry (CRE, 1993: 7–8) that the use of admissions criteria which include aptitude, motivation and commitment are particularly difficult to apply objectively and fairly.

> Such factors as demonstrating a suitability for, or a commitment to, a school may be difficult to measure accurately when parents and/or pupils are from cultural groups different from the interviewer. The language of the interview may also disadvantage a parent who is unfamiliar with English, however competent his or her child is in English.

A paucity of admissions information in community languages can also discriminate against ethnic-minority families as can a failure to circulate application forms in languages other than English. The CRE (1993: 16–17) have also noted the potentially racially discriminatory effects of waiting lists:

> If there is any requirement or condition to have a child's name placed on a waiting list by a certain age this may discriminate, on racial

grounds, against those who are unfamiliar with the concept of such lists, who do not know of the existence of such lists because they are advertised in places and in languages with which they are unfamiliar, or who are recently arrived.

Afro-Caribbean boys who are being excluded from schools in disproportionate numbers (Bourne *et al.*, 1994) are likely to be the most disadvantaged in the marketplace. In Northwark in 1990–91 Afro-Caribbean students constituted 45 per cent of all indefinite exclusions from secondary schools and 56 per cent of all permanent exclusions. Afro-Caribbean *boys* made up 31 per cent of all boys excluded indefinitely and 42 per cent of those excluded permanently (Northwark Statistical Report). The 1991 Census indicates that only 6.1 per cent of Northwark's total population were Afro-Caribbean.

Studies of market policies in other countries report similar increases in provisional segregation and inequality. For example, Moore and Davenport (1990: 201) in their study of magnet programmes in four U.S. cities found that

> [G]iven the discretion exercised in recruitment, screening, and selection, there was an overwhelming bias toward establishing procedures and standards at each step in the admissions process that screened out 'problem' students and admitted the 'best' students, with 'best' being defined as students with good academic records, good attendance, good behaviour, a mastery of English, and no special learning problems.

Chenoweth (1987) found similar processes at work in San Francisco's magnet programme (see also Blank, 1990). Goldring and Shapira (1993) reporting on four elementary 'schools of choice' in Tel Aviv, Israel, note the unrepresentatively high socio–economic status (SES) composition of the schools. Hershkoff and Cohen (1992: 25) conclude from a review of research in the USA that 'any educational improvement that a market approach might bring comes at a price: the creation of an underclass of disfavoured and underfunded schools'.

Internal provisional differentiation

We have already described how image–related and financial concerns are driving policies on attendance, exclusions and admissions and how the latter two practices are leading to provisional differentiation and segregation between schools. We now want to explore the processes of provisional differentiation and segregation *within* schools which are being generated by the market. In particular, we want to focus on SEN provision and the grouping of students.

We observed in Chapter 5 that some schools are concerned about the financial consequences of gaining a good reputation for special needs. In short, children with special needs are on the whole viewed as a liability in the marketplace: they demand a high level of investment whilst producing little 'return' in terms of examination league table performance (Housden, 1993). One of the practical consequences of this concern has been, as we saw in Chapter 5, the down-playing of special needs in school publicity. Another consequence of market forces has been a redistribution of resources within schools away from provision for children with learning difficulties. Pressure on resources combined with a concern to avoid job losses is leading some managers to adopt what are euphemistically termed more 'flexible' staffing structures in which teachers are used to teach subjects they were not trained to teach (Spalding, 1993; Sinclair *et al.,* 1993). Learning support teachers, in particular, are being redeployed to other departments. Where redundancies do have to be made, special needs teachers are amongst the most vulnerable. In part, this is because they are viewed as less economical than subject teachers as they do not teach whole classes and because some special needs teachers are employed on a more casual basis than specialist subject teachers. However, it can be argued that an additional reason why learning support is being singled out as a particular casualty of 'budgetary flexibility' is the 'logic' of the market which suggests that resources are better invested in those children likely to get five or more grades A–C in the GCSE examinations taken at 16 years, so that within schools' spending priorities, special needs provision becomes a less worthwhile investment and is thus devalorized. As a deputy headteacher at Northwark Park explained, 'SEN provision is expensive, so it's eating up your money and your time and if you're being asked to produce a good set of examination results, then you want as much of your resourcing to be directed at that'.

It is important to note that the impact of the market on SEN provision is felt unevenly amongst schools. Perversely, it is provision in those schools which have greater numbers of children *requiring* learning support which is most vulnerable because such schools tend to be the ones which are undersubscribed and so financially less secure. At Trumpton the special needs department shrank in the three years from 1989 to 1992 from six to three full-time teachers whilst the numbers of children requiring support have increased. In Pankhurst, on the other hand, there is a perception that special needs are adequately supported in the school. The school has only one full-time SEN teacher but that is seen to be appropriate for the level of need in the school. However, in considering the relative effects of the market on schools of different kinds, it is difficult to make precise comparisons since each school has its own criteria for assessing 'learning difficulties'. In Pankhurst, for example, 120–130 out of a total of 850 students are defined as having learning difficulties (approximately 15 per cent), whereas in Trumpton the figure is 159 out of 1250 students (8 per cent). Pankhurst (which is well-subscribed and predominantly middle class) can clearly afford to have a more liberal definition of what constitutes a learning difficulty than Trumpton (which has traditionally been undersubscribed and is predominantly working class). Students who are in receipt of additional support at Pankhurst would not be defined as requiring such support at Trumpton, or would not fall within the scope of the support available. In schools where there is most pressure on resources, the criteria for 'needing' learning support are narrower

> 'when we had six full-time SEN teachers, we could help all pupils throughout the whole school. Now we actually concentrate, apart from statemented children, on Years 7, 8 and 9. We just haven't got the staff.'
>
> (Head of SEN, Trumpton school, 20 March 1992)

> 'Here there are lots of kids who we don't work with [and] who we should be working with because our cut off is just so much lower.'
>
> (Head of SEN, Flightpath school, 3 July 1992)

> 'We do have to keep on lowering our baseline because of the staffing situation, because of the fact that we've been cut. We've only got two members of staff now, we can't help as many kids . . . We keep on having to bring the line down to help really the ones that are at the very bottom, the desperate ones, whereas when we had five members of staff we probably would have had the cut off point much higher.'
>
> (Head of SEN, Northwark Park school, 26 June 1992)

Whilst the introduction of the new Special Needs Code of Practice is generally welcomed in schools there are concerns about how effectively it can be implemented within a context of diminishing resources. Reductions in specialist learning support effects all children, not just those with special needs, as the loss of additional staff in classrooms means that 'mainstream' teachers have to spread their attention more thinly. Again the loss of Section 11 staff and other teachers funded by external projects exacerbate the trends noted here.

Whilst provision for children with learning difficulties is being reduced, many schools are developing policies for, and some are channelling extra money into, provision for 'gifted' students. Whilst there are good educational grounds for schools developing and improving provision for 'able' children, the main driving force behind such developments appears to be *commercial* rather than *educational*.

'I have introduced an able pupils' policy because parents with able children are often those who are most anxious about sending their children to a comprehensive school. Now, all the research, I believe, bears out that able children will do as well in a comprehensive as they would elsewhere, but people need convincing of that and if we have a policy that we can explain and offer to parents of what we do to enable them, to ensure they are stretched and they are taught extremely well, [we] will reassure them. And that policy will be new for September.'

(Headteacher, Parsons school, 20 May 1991)

'It's seen as a good marketing tool. I mean when Fiona was acting head last term and she had a bit of extra cash . . . it was quite a controversial decision within the school and within the staff, that she put the money into an able pupils' project . . . I mean she gave a bit of extra staffing to me, and as far as I was concerned that was complete marketing, because as a Humanities teacher there's not very much more that we can do for our students than we actually do in the lessons apart from laying on enrichment, but I think just to be able to say, "We do things for able pupils," will appeal to perhaps those parents . . . who think their daughters should be in private schools, but perhaps they're not able enough to get there or the parents can't afford the place or whatever.'

(Head of department, Pankhurst school, 18 March 1992)

'There was a definite push towards having children of a higher ability doing, rewarding those kids, not ignoring them, making them feel worth something within the school, and making sure that parents understood that.'

(Deputy headteacher, Trumpton school, 9 June 1993)

Similar considerations are also leading many schools to review their student-grouping arrangements. We have already observed (in Chapter 5) that schools are increasingly highlighting setting in their promotional literature and activities, but as is the case with the down-playing of SEN provision, it is not simply a rhetorical shift which is involved here. A marked shift away from mixed-ability grouping towards setting is evident in virtually all of our case-study schools, although there are exceptions within individual subject areas; for example, at Fletcher the Science department has over the last five years moved away from setting towards mixed-ability grouping in all years. Mrs Farthing, the headteacher of Pankhurst, was one headteacher in our case-study schools to hold on to some kind of position of principle on mixed-ability grouping.

> 'I don't have a sort of, if it's not in mixed ability groups, then it's not comprehensive view . . . I think the subjects are different and I do think that the nature of their subject and the way they manage their teaching, affects the kind of groups that they can handle, or that they work with. I'd be very disappointed if the teaching staff, as a group, wanted to move to a sort of wholesale either streaming or banding in the school.'
>
> (Headteacher, Pankhurst school, 17 June 1993)

She is not reluctant to make the school's practice clear to parents: 'Oh parents have asked me about streaming, and I've said we don't, we certainly don't stream them'. In September 1993, Martineau moved 'from almost totally mixed-ability teaching . . . to almost none' (chair of governors). This was despite opposition from staff in some subject areas:

> 'We don't agree with streaming in the Humanities cluster at all and we've sort of held out against it. It now looks like we're going to have a directive to stream.'
>
> (NUT representative, Martineau school, 18 June 1993)

There are a combination of factors at work in the re-examination of grouping. There is a 'climate of concern' about grouping which has been fuelled by Ministerial comment. In addition the differentiation of national curriculum programmes of study in some subjects is creating new difficulties for teachers of mixed-ability groups within a context of reduced funding. At Northwark Park,

> '[the staff are] finding it more and more difficult, you see, resources have been cut, there's no doubt about it, we have fewer resources for special needs help, for example, and the ability range in this school is very, very broad. Our bright children are very bright, and our less able in some cases are very less able, and I think that with the national curriculum coming in, there are more and more subjects which are saying, "Coping with that ability range within the classroom without the kind of support that you need is very difficult," so I mean . . . I am about to review mixed ability.'
>
> (Headteacher, Northwark Park school, 5 February 1992)

> 'The cheapest way to teach kids is to put them in a room with seventy and to impose discipline. I mean that's cheap, it's not necessarily effective but . . . that becomes the thing which your resources dictate to you and the question is not whether you can do it better or whether

more kids would benefit, and I think what's happened in Northwark Park is that as teaching resources have quite dramatically reduced, over the years, they are being forced into bigger groups . . . and those resources again start to direct the methods that you have to use. So the new development plan involved a review of mixed ability teaching.'
(Chair of governors, Northwark Park school, 9 November 1992)

The re-introduction of setting in schools which previously taught mixed-ability classes is also partly a response to pressure from school inspectors. There is, additionally, however, a very strong perception in schools that middle-class parents with 'able' children have a preference for setting. Our own evidence suggests that mixed ability is indeed still regarded sceptically by some parents (see Chapter 2) and at least one question about grouping was asked at the majority of open evenings we attended. In relation to this, school managers are concerned about the image-related consequences of being seen as a school committed to mixed ability. The chair of governors at Martineau, Mrs Thomas, was quite candid on this issue:

Mrs Thomas: I think there were . . . two forces really. One was the whole business of inspectors saying . . . "Actually you need more differentiation in the school." So that was one pressure I think, to go for setting, and then I think without any question the other pressure was that the school be perceived as being able to cope better with more academically able children . . . I'm not sure that was actually said as explicitly as I'm putting it now but it was certainly said explicitly to me . . .

Researcher: Right, but that was in response to, I mean, how does that link up with parental choice?

Mrs Thomas: Well I think it links up with the perception that parents want to choose a school that has a good academic record. Whether that's true or not is quite immaterial. That is the perception . . . of the school, they think that's parents' perception. They may . . . be totally wrong but I think all that adds fuel to the need to say, don't think [if you send] your child here that they'll get shoved into a class and just messed around, not know what they're doing, you know, we like bright children and we make provision for them.

Researcher: So is part of that wanting to attract more bright children?

Mrs Thomas: Yes, without any question.
(Interview, 7 May 1993)

The solution, arrived at in many schools, has been to create a timetable structure which will allow individual departments to make their own decisions about grouping. Cynically, in micropolitical terms, one might suggest that this also creates a situation within which pressure can be brought to bear on individual departments separately while avoiding open, general discussion of the issues of principle. Some staff at Trumpton, including the deputy headteacher, were certainly suspicious when the SMT introduced a system of 'voluntary setting' that there was a 'hidden agenda to reintroduce streaming'. Individual departments, who continue with mixed ability, whose GCSE results in any one year are relatively poor, when compared with other departments, may also find themselves under pressure to 'reconsider' their grouping arrangements. A 'flexible' approach to setting can, in some instances, lead to covert setting, where formally 'unsetted' subjects are timetabled at the same time as 'setted' subjects for the same year group. The formally 'unsetted' subjects are then 'setted' by default.

Whilst setting might benefit – or certainly not disadvantage – the 'able' middle-class child, there is also some awareness in schools of the potentially damaging effects of setting regimes on student morale and behaviour and its implications for equity.

> 'I know even from my experience of ILEA . . . when you look[ed] at
> the bottom set and the bottom band they were uniformly Black. When
> you looked at the top sets . . . they were always uniformly White.'
> (Headteacher, Parsons school, 20 May 1991)

Martineau had had a good record of achievement under mixed ability and concerns were expressed about the possibly detrimental effects of 'setted' teaching on 'lower ability' students and the concentration of Afro-Caribbean students in bottom sets across subjects.

> 'It has to be said that our Band 3 exam results were pretty good, so with
> a mind to that we have to make sure that setting will . . . include the
> educational experience of all pupils.'
> (Head of SEN, Martineau school, 16 July 1992)

A head of SEN talked about the danger of 'labelling' and its consequences for those children who are placed in the bottom sets.

> '. . . and the self-fulfilling [prophecy] bit, that it's quite likely that
> students who'll be set and who might be in the bottom set in Science,
> once Maths starts setting, and Modern Languages start setting, and it
> starts spreading, so it's quite likely that it's the same kids who will be in
> the bottom set across the board and you then get this sort of, the
> development of the, you know, D-stream culture and the label of
> failure, and . . . the sort of movement which is there, in-built in a
> mixed-ability class, is lost because the gap gets wider. Your A stream
> goes shooting off and the C stream is down there still messing around
> at Level 2 . . . and so you can't transfer a child from the bottom

stream . . . further up because they're just not covering the same work any more.'

(Head of SEN, Northwark Park school, 26 June 1992)

Indeed, these perspectives are supported by a significant body of research which has shown that setting regimes discriminate against those placed in the lowest groupings who are more likely to be from working-class and Black families (Hargreaves, 1967; Lacey, 1970; Troyna, 1978; Ball, 1981). As Tomlinson (1987: 106) has observed, 'ability is an ambiguous concept and school conceptions of ability can be affected by perceptions that pupils are members of particular social and ethnic groups and by the behaviour of individual pupils'.

Whilst many of the changes taking place in schools in the context of marketization appear to be retrogressive in terms of ensuring equality of opportunity, where girls are concerned the market seems to be having the opposite effect. Attempts to make schools attractive to girls are not limited to tokenistic references in open evenings to girl-friendly subject areas and to gender equality policies or to photographs of girls in Science laboratories. A number of our case study schools are making some practical attempts to support girls. Milton for instance, is attempting to implement policies which will enable girls to feel 'safe' in traditionally non-female areas such as Design and Technology and Computing. Northwark Park has introduced some all-boys groups 'so that girls' experience of the classroom would not be that they were swamped' and times are set aside when only girls can use the library.

The additional emphasis on Drama, Music and Arts which the market appears to be effecting in a number of schools might also in some senses be viewed as a positive outcome of market forces. There was, however, a current of feeling in some of our schools that it was children from middle-class families who were disproportionately benefiting from the energy schools are investing in raising their Arts profiles. At Martineau, the headteacher has been concerned about the quality of recent school productions and has asked the head of Performing Arts to ensure that in future only the 'more accomplished' students appear in public perform-ances. Martineau productions, she insisted in a paper prepared for staff, must always be 'stylish'. This is yet another example of how image-related concerns are leading schools to increasingly channel teacher time and resources into provision for the most able. A head of department at Northwark Park observed that those students taking up the school's recently expanded range of enrichment activities are predominantly middle-class:

'The children that come along to these extra classes are those sorts of children. Because the other children have to go home and look after brothers and sisters, . . . [or] because their mum wants them to go to the shops or they have to go home because their travel pass finishes at a certain time. You know, all the sort of social, financial constraints that their parents have got, these children have got as well. So really we are just catering for the middle-class children who would have ended up with them anyway.'

(Head of department, Northwark Park school, 2 February 1994)

A similar view is expressed by the NUT representative at Fletcher, who refers to a small group of middle-class parents who he feels are exerting an undue influence on the curriculum by putting pressure on the school to offer extra Music classes at the expense of the majority of children in the school.

'We have a very strong Music group and a lot of activity after school, and a lot of the children that have these lessons are from that group of parents and they will fight like hell to keep that going . . . There is a small charge now, a small charge levied, but nothing like having to pay for private lessons and . . . children that are learning Music, a musical instrument, are withdrawn from their lessons and are taught individually. Now I'm not saying that's wrong. I'm just saying that will be fought tooth and nail to be kept, even maybe at the expense of a teacher, and put the class ratio up.'

(Teacher, Fletcher school, 17 November 1992)

Narrowing of scope

A persistent theme of our analysis has been that, effectively and increasingly, particular groups of students are being valued in the marketplace more than others. Linked to this is an apparent tendency within the school system for greater value to be placed on particular kinds of activities than on others. What we appear to be seeing is an effective narrowing of scope in the role and purposes of schooling. The policy orientation of the English market puts almost exclusive emphasis upon instrumental, academic and cognitive goals. For example, there is no requirement for schools to publish information on the expressive, cooperative and community aspects of schooling, on levels of enjoyment, happiness, stimulation and challenge for teachers and students, on degrees of innovation and creativity in school approaches to teaching and learning, nor on the quality of special needs provision (although a new code of practice for special needs has been introduced). This narrowing process has its concomitants in other aspects of reform (as, for example, in the restructuring of teacher education courses) and is part of the

discursive shift discussed in Chapter 4. That the 'parap'
market in conjunction with the statutory requirement'
curriculum and a harder-edged system of school inspec
very significant impact on the discourse and structu
organization is particularly evident in the installation of variou
performance monitoring into the day-to-day practices of schools. 1.
targetting of resources in relation to performance measurement and
outcome enhancement is facilitated by the budgetary virement provided
by LMS and is given increased urgency by the decline in real terms in school
budgets. One illustration of this in practice is Fletcher's '42/92 Campaign'.
This was an attempt, which was successful as it turned out, to ensure that at
least 42 per cent of GCSE students obtained five or more grades A to C and
that 92 per cent obtained one or more A to G grades. The governing body
allocated £7000 to the campaign which was aimed at those students who
were considered to be functioning just below the target thresholds.
Various inputs and support activities were aimed at this group.

It is perhaps perverse to wish to be critical of changes produced by
market policies which lead to more careful monitoring of activity and use
of resources, and which offer teachers evaluation and feedback on their
work with students. However, the re-orientations in priorities, institutional cultures, and in resource distribution merit careful attention. The
use of prescribed operational indicators is one mechanism by which the
scope of 'valued' activity is limited within schools and it reinforces a
narrow, commodified perception of students. As the techniques of
monitoring and costing are refined, in a situation of continuing reduction
in resources, then the pressure and temptation is for schools to reduce or
dispense with those activities and curricula which are not directly
prescribed or which do not contribute directly to market indicators or
image formation. Logically, those schools which are worst off under
formula funding will be under most pressure to plan their activities and
their curriculum most directly by targeting and costing methods.[2]
Another example of this narrowing of scope is the restructuring of year
teams at Martineau. The heads of teams are no longer called 'Year Heads'
whose main role was to oversee the *pastoral* care of students. They are now
Year Curriculum Coordinators whose primary responsibility is for the
academic progress of students, and no alternative pastoral structure has been
created to fill the gap.

Commodification of schooling and the child

Our analysis so far has demonstrated that within the education
marketplace, not only schools or school services but also children

memselves are coming to be viewed as commodities, some of whom are more valuable than others. *The emphasis seems increasingly to be not on what the school can do for the child but on what the child can do for the school.* Without more intensive research it is difficult to assess how far this changed cultural regime is affecting students directly. We do have evidence which suggests that, in some schools, students are being made very aware of their value as commodities in the new environment, particularly at sixth-form level because of the extra funding attached to them.

'Increasingly, the students are aware of their worth and I think that's quite an interesting development . . . "I'm worth £2200 to this school," is a phrase that I've known a Year 11 student say to me, as if it was a bargaining [ploy] and there was one lady [to whom] I retorted that . . . "£2200? You know, you're not worth the trouble, go to Riverway, we don't need £2200 of your trouble, or whatever it is".'

(Head of sixth form, Flightpath school, 1 July 1993)

The fact that the commodification of students has so readily permeated relationships in Flightpath may indicate more about the nature of pre-existing relations between some members of staff and students than about the effects of marketization. A more widespread feature is students being encouraged to stay on in the sixth form, at least until enumeration day in January, when it may not be in the student's best interests to do so.

'One student is worth so many pounds. There's a very strong pressure, therefore, to accept students who would be better advised to go elsewhere. I mean we've tried to be honest, I think we've got to be honest. There are Year 11 students who are just finishing their GCSEs, who come to me for advice and I feel I have to tell them what the full range of options is. I think it's only fair to tell them that such and such a college exists, that does such and such a course or in some cases even, and I'm not sure the headteacher would be too happy about this, but it has happened where we have had the course that the particular student is interested in, but both the student and I have felt that they needed a change and would be better going to a college. And I think that's only fair. It's a somewhat unfair pressure on me I think, to say that we've got to recruit everybody regardless of what's in their best interests. So that's an unfair pressure. And sometimes we have truthfully, we have had one or two in the sixth form who perhaps should not have been in the sixth form, but they were here because they wanted to be and it was very useful to have them to boost the numbers, and boost our income. We still don't do it as much as some institutions I won't name, but there are local places that will take anybody. It's not quite as easy as that, there are enumeration days during the year so it's not quite who you've got on roll for the first day of the year and after that you can say, "Goodbye," and get the money, but nevertheless there is an element of creative accounting, if you like.'

(Head of sixth form, Northwark Park school, 10 June 1992)

All of this may also have 'learning outcomes' through a new 'hidden curriculum' of the school. With the creation of the education market, school students are located within and subjects of a new educational and moral environment; they are exposed to, and educated within, a new values set. The sense of what education is and is for, the nature of the social relationships of schooling, teacher–student and student–student relationships are potentially all changed by the forces and micro-practices of the market.

The process of commodification and the conflicts between the educational and the commercial is also evident in the ambiguous nature of primary 'liaison'. The boundary between establishing contact with primary schools to facilitate a smooth educational transfer of students as against 'selling' the school to potential customers is now distinctly blurred.

'The job that I've got has changed very subtly . . . over the last two to three years really, as the general climate has changed and I think because we've become GM and I think you need to be very clear and have a very clear understanding about what we're actually doing because I feel very uncomfortable going to a school to promote Martineau in a sort of hard-sell way, either to teachers or to pupils, I wouldn't want to do that. But at the same time I feel very strongly that we have got a lot to offer and I genuinely believe that so I'm sort of tied in between the two . . . I think what's changed is that liaison previously was more closely tied to sort of curricular links, and transfer links, about getting the best for children as they crossed schools and also looking at how the curriculum changes between Year 6 and Year 7, where they cross over but that hasn't happened so much recently . . . [I find it] difficult on a moral front if you see what I mean. I find that quite difficult. I don't want to sit in front of a load of children in a primary school and . . . market the school in a hard-sell kind of way. I find the two things very difficult . . . Because if I'm selling, it's not like selling a product like toothpaste . . . It may be the right school for some pupils and not for others. I mean you sometimes get two children in a family that need very different kinds of schools, so I feel a bit uncomfortable about pushing it in that sense, particularly to children. They tend to listen to the last person they've spoken to, and if you're a convincing person, good at talking to children, I mean I can talk to 10, 15, kids about Martineau and they all want to come to Martineau when I've walked out of the room and I think that's a bit difficult. The other aspect of it is that we then become oversubscribed, which is good, which is what we need because we need money to keep the school going, but what happens to the kids we don't accept?'

(Senior teacher, Martineau school, 16 July 1992)

Conclusion

The many and various Conservative Secretaries of State for Education since 1979 have made no secret of their antipathy towards the idea and practices of comprehensive education, and the Education Acts 1988 and 1993 contain various provisions and requirements which directly or indirectly work against comprehensivism. In particular, the form taken by the market in education, created by these Acts, is producing attritive change in the culture, structure and practices of education. The effect of this is to replace attempts at comprehensivism with a system that is increasingly differentiated and stratified. The principle of equal value, however weakly and unevenly articulated and practised, is now being systematically displaced by commercially-based decision making driven by competition. We are not suggesting that a simple and wholesale abandonment of comprehensive values is occurring within schools: for many teachers comprehensivism remains a cherished point of principle. It is, however, possible to identify a whole range of shifts and changes in school practices which sit uneasily with or operate against comprehensivism, and the market rewards shrewdness rather than principles. As we have tried to indicate elsewhere in this account of our research, it is both values and language and organization and practice that are being altered by the policy complex of the market.

In the struggle for survival in the market, senior managers are confronted with two decisive sets of pressures generated by the combined effects of open enrolment, formula funding and the publication of specific performance indicators as market information. One set of pressures revolves around the need to attend to the academic performance and behaviour of students on roll. In particular, there is pressure on schools to ensure the best attainments from those students who are able to register levels of performance which will contribute to the local reputation and overall comparative position of the school in relation to its rivals. The other set of pressures revolves around the need to attend to, and if necessary and possible alter, the social composition of schools in order to raise the raw-score potential of student bodies. Our research suggests that the material outcomes of these twin pressures in schools are:

- increased differentiation and segregation, both within and between schools;
- a redistribution of resources away from those with greatest learning difficulties, both within and between schools;
- the commodification of education and the student;
- the re-orientation, redefinition, and narrowing in scope of schooling; and
- the establishment of methods, structures and values of organization and management 'borrowed' from industry and commerce.

Notes

1 The schools' reasons for doing so vary. Northwark Park, for example, agreed to select part of its intake in return for the LEA providing a much-needed building programme. Martineau justifies its application to become selective on the grounds that it will enable the school to retain a 'balanced' comprehensive intake. See Chapter 3
2 The use of such methods of school management is the focus of our current research: ESRC funded project no. 235544

7

CHOICE, EQUITY AND CONTROL

Introduction

Thorough analysis of public service markets can never be easy or straightforward. Such markets are diverse, complex and unstable. As we have demonstrated, in practice, education markets are also highly localized. They display the effects of both planning and chance, and they have their own histories and idiosyncracies. Nonetheless, the importance of the specifics of local circumstances should not be allowed to obscure general patterns and trends that are evident across settings. In designing the study reported here, we deliberately sought out settings in which the dynamics of the market – choice and competition – would be to the fore. From observation of these settings over three years, we have identified some key, general features and trends at work in the operation and effects of market forces in education. Our analytical focus has been throughout, not so much on the schools and parents we have researched as *market players* but on the *policies and the market complex within which they function.* Nevertheless, we see school teachers, managers and parents as bringing different priorities, values and skills into play within the particular structures and disciplines of the market in which they find themselves located.

Two main research concerns underpinned this account of our study. One was to identify, unpack and examine the main features of the workings of local education markets, to begin to make some sense of, to describe and conceptualize, choice and competition in practice. The other was to tease out some of the implications and effects of the operation of local markets for equity and the distribution of access to educational resources. As regards the latter in particular, there is further work needing to be done, but we feel confident that we have captured some of the key aspects of the consequences of the education market in terms of inequalities.

We have identified two competing definitions of equity implicit in the arguments advanced in favour of choice in education. One definition conceptualizes equity in desert-based terms. The contention here is that goods should be distributed according to merit or desert where the 'deserving' are defined as those families motivated to take advantage of the policy of open enrolment. The other definition views equity in needs-based terms – meaning that educational resourcing should favour those with greater educational need and those with fewer private resources in the home and community to be able to meet educational needs (Levin, 1990). In what follows we will tease out and pull together the central threads of our argument to evaluate the market in terms of these two definitions of equity. Our emphasis is primarily upon the needs-based conception.

The main findings of the study can be simply summarized in four general statements:

1 The market is a middle-class mode of social engagement.
2 Parental choice of school is class- and 'race'-informed.
3 Schools are increasingly oriented towards meeting the perceived demands of middle-class parents.
4 The cumulative impact of findings 1–3 is the 'decomprehensivization' of secondary schooling.

The market as a middle-class mode of social engagement

Our interviews with parents indicate very striking class-based differences in family orientations to the market both in terms of parental *inclination* to engage with it and their *capacity* to exploit the market to their children's advantage. These differences are starkly represented by the three types of parents which emerged from our coding of the data – the privileged/skilled choosers, the semi-skilled choosers and the disconnected.

The *privileged/skilled choosers*, who are almost exclusively professional middle class, have always been advantaged in terms of access to educational resources. They were well-placed to get their children into schools of their choice prior to the Education Reform Act 1988 but we argue they occupy an even more favourable position post-1988. The privileged/skilled choosers are inclined to a consumerist approach to choice of school, that is, the idea and worth of having a choice between schools is valued and there is a concern to examine what is on offer and seek out 'the best'. These choosers demonstrate a marked capacity to engage with and utilize the possibilities of choice. Their economic, social and cultural capital enable them to 'decode' and operate to their children's advantage school systems and organizations. In making their choice of school, they are engaged in a process of child-matching. The privileged/skilled choosers are oriented to high profile, élite, often selective, cosmopolitan maintained schools which recruit some or often many of their students from outside of their immediate locale. These schools are usually oversubscribed and are often considered by privileged/skilled choosers alongside the 'local' system of private day schools. Some are more committed to the state sector, others express serious doubts about state schools and some waver uneasily between the two systems. Despite this, choice of secondary school is typically linked to long-term educational and career planning.

The *semi-skilled choosers* tend to emanate from a variety of class backgrounds, but most importantly for the purposes of the current discussion, this group is likely to include those families which we suggest are targeted by Conservative education policy – working-class families, disadvantaged by the system of 'selection by mortgage', who are strongly motivated to make the most of the 'opportunities' for choice afforded to them by open enrolment. Semi-skilled choosers are strongly inclined to engage with the market, but they do not have the appropriate skills to exploit it to maximize their children's advantage. These families talk about potential school choices as outsiders, often relying, at least in part, on the comments and perceptions of others. Recently – immigrant families are among those who fit this profile. Their lack of direct experience and knowledge of the English school system and/or lack of necessary cultural or linguistic resources inhibit them in the fulfillment of their aspirations for their children. Semi-skilled choosers may also be hampered by finance-related considerations including time and transport constraints. The mismatch between inclination and capacity amongst the semi-skilled may mean that these families are frustrated in the marketplace. Some semi-skilled choosers are oriented to the cosmopolitan maintained schools but may have to 'settle' for the local, community, comprehensive schools.

The *disconnected choosers* are almost exclusively working class. The market is of limited relevance to this group because they tend not to be inclined to participate. Disconnected choosers are primarily oriented to the local comprehensive schools, partly as a result of a positive attachment to the locality and to going to school with friends and family. In addition, school has to be 'fitted into' a set of constraints and expectations related to the demands of work and household organization. For low-income families on time-constrained budgets, the limitations of private and public transport play a key role in decision-making. Such choosers have limited capacity for participation in the education market but they are making active and positive choices. However, these are not made in ways that reflect the primary values of competitive consumerism which are embedded in the English market complex.

The three 'types' of chooser illustrate two ways in which families may be privileged or disadvantaged in the market. First, competition between parents for schools disadvantages those families who are inclined to enter the competition but who are not well placed to exploit the market to their advantage, either because of insufficient finances or inappropriate cultural and social capital. Second, choice has different meanings in different class and cultural contexts; it is a socially and culturally constructed phenomenon; and families are disadvantaged or privileged as a consequence of the values which inform their conceptions of choice-making. The model of choice-making advocated by the government and encapsulated in the *Parent's Charter* (DES, 1991; DFE 1994) represents only one model, i.e. the consumerist version so comfortably embraced by the privileged/ skilled choosers and perhaps less comfortably – if equally enthusiastically – by the semi-skilled choosers. However, this particular construction of choice making is much less relevant to the disconnected or local choosers. Because they value locality over and above other considerations when it comes to choosing a school, they are not inclined to spend time immersing themselves in consumerist activity and agonizing over a range of possible options. There is, therefore, a mismatch between the culture of consumption of the local school choosers and the culture of provision. The culture of provision is much more closely matched to the culture of consumption of the privileged chooser. To use Williamson's (1981) terminology, the market form of school provision reflects the 'ideal of cultivation' of the dominant group. Or in Bourdieuian terms, the dominant class possesses the necessary cultural code for decoding the cultural arbitrary of the market. Here we can see the actual realization of social advantage through effective activation of cultural resources (Lareau, 1989: 178). Because schools are funded on the basis of how many students they have, 'locality' is not a value which the market system rewards. The high-profile, élite, cosmopolitan, maintained schools to which the skilled and some semi-skilled choosers orient themselves, are likely to be oversubscribed and therefore favourably staffed and re-sourced. Such schools can benefit from the economies of scale that being full offers them. The local, community, comprehensive schools, on the other hand, may be – although will not necessarily be – undersubscribed. They will have similar overheads in terms of building maintenance, fuel bills, etc. as the oversubscribed schools and have to offer the same range of courses but to student bodies which may have higher levels of need (because of their socio-economic profiles, families histories, linguistic backgrounds). However, undersubscribed schools will have less money to work with and are therefore likely to be underresourced and understaffed. This will make it extremely difficult for local schools to match the perceived quality of service of the cosmopolitan schools. By the linking of biography to social structure, our analysis of school choice in relation to class and capital illuminates the reproduction of class position and class divisions and points up the changing form and processes of class struggle in and over the social field of school choice. As we argue, viewed in these terms, the market and parental choice is a class strategy.

> The definition of the legitimate means and stakes of struggle is in fact one of the stakes of the struggle, and the relative efficacy of the means of controlling the game (the different sorts of capital) is itself at stake, and therefore subject to variations in the course of the game.
>
> (Bourdieu 1986: 246)

The political and social construction and maintenance of the educational field (of parental choice and diversity of schools in this instance) is the outcome of political and class struggles. Its operation, via processes of individualization (choice) and the characteristics of the requisite cultural and social capital (how and what to choose and who and what you know), are classic examples of Bourdieu's notion of symbolic violence: 'the violence which is exercised upon a social agent with his or her complicity' (Bourdieu and Wacquant 1992: 167).

Class- and 'race'-informed choosing

A further aspect of choice-making which tends to be neglected in the literature on parental choice but which emerges from our own data is that parents seem to make choices on the basis of the perceived class and in some instances racial composition of schools. There would appear to be at least two reasons for the invisibility of class- and 'race'-informed choosing in the literature. First, parents in interview, on the whole, are reluctant to offer class and 'race' as factors influencing their choice of school since in the English 'public domain' these are neither 'accepted' nor 'acceptable' reasons for choosing a school – although euphemisms are employed, e.g. references to 'rougher elements'. Second, attitudes to class and 'race' are deeply ingrained and may 'function below the level of consciousness and language' (Bourdieu, 1986: 466) so that parents may not directly recognize or acknowledge that they are making class-or 'racially'-informed choices.

Despite the difficulties of accessing data on 'race'- and class-informed choosing, our research methods have enabled us to gain some insight into these aspects of school choice. In talking about their reasons for choosing particular schools, parents commonly referred to the 'intuitiveness' of school choice and to 'gut feelings'. Such replies may indicate a 'substructure' of thinking about school choice underlying and informing a 'superstructure' of commonly proffered reasons – discipline, uniform, facilities, ethos, results, teaching styles, etc. A fine-grained analysis of the parental interviews indicates that there are subtle class-related messages/signs to be read off from the school setting, the demeanour of students and the attitude of staff in the process of choice-making and, in evaluating these, parents may be seen as seeking a match between family habitus and school habitus. 'Racially'-informed choosing is particularly prominent in south Westway LEA, with many White working-class parents rejecting Gorse school because of its high intake of pupils with a South Asian background and some South Asian parents choosing that school because it is regarded as 'safe' and because of its singular emphasis on educational traditionalism and academic achievement.

Segregation by class and 'race' within the English education system is not new. The system of assigning children to schools on the basis of catchment areas which operated prior to the Education Reform Act 1988 meant that schools have always been socially and 'racially' segregated *to the extent that residential segregation exists*. The policy of choice in education is unlikely to reduce such segregation, if parental choices continue to be informed both by class and and often by 'race'. If anything, choice may well exacerbate segregation by extending it to previously integrated schools serving socially and 'racially' mixed geographical areas. Furthermore, processes of segregation are likely to be enhanced because of the premium being placed by schools on 'able' children.

Schools and the perceived demands of middle-class parents

In the English education marketplace, schools have a primary incentive to maximize their examination league table performance at minimum cost. Because the bulk of school funding is allocated by formula on the basis of pupil numbers and not need, those children designated as more 'able' are worth more to schools than those with learning difficulties. Filling up a school with 'able' children and keeping children with SEN to a minimum is the cheapest and most labour-efficient way of enhancing league-table performance. Critical commentators have suggested that the logic of the market implies that children with SEN will increasingly be viewed as a liability in the marketplace and that resources will flow to the most 'able' (Willey, 1989; Lee, 1992; Housden, 1993). That is the 'logic' of the market, but what is the practice?

As we have indicated, within our case-study schools, particularly undersubscribed ones, it was firmly believed that survival in the marketplace makes it necessary not only to fill the school to capacity but also to retain or create 'balanced' intakes and to raise the raw-score performance potential of student bodies. School managers and staff typically speak about the need to target those sections of the population likely to enhance their league-table performance in various ways. Some refer to the need to attract more 'able' pupils and others, because of the association between measured ability and social class, talk about a desire to appeal to more middle-class families. Others, more reticent about using the language of class, speak euphemistically about targetting more 'motivated' parents. However, whatever the language employed, schools are adopting a number of strategies in order to raise the raw-score performance potential of their intakes, and, because of the correlation between measured ability and social class, school policies on a variety of issues are being increasingly influenced by a desire to attract more middle-class and, in some cases, aspiring working-class parents. Although the desire to appeal to the middle-class parent is usually only one amongst several rationales for the development of such policies. Some examples of policies designed, at least in part, to make school more attractive to middle-class parents include the re-introduction of setting, the devalorization of SEN and the increasing use of selection and exclusions. Developments in Northwark are of particular interest because the authority is attempting to put into practice the policies of selection and specialization which the Education Act 1993 appears designed to promote. The selective and exclusionary practices of schools, working in association with the class-biased nature of the market as a form of social engagement, and the selection of schools by parents according to class-and 'racially'-based criteria, appear likely to intensify the social segregation of schooling.

The re-orientation of schooling towards the interests and preferences of middle-class parents and the accommodation and response of schools to the market and competition are evident in the ways in which they are changing the form and content of their communications with parents and potential parents. The semiologies of market schooling are beginning to borrow heavily from both the techniques and the actual messages of commercial marketing.

Many teachers and school managers now find themselves caught in value and ethical dilemmas, between personal principles and institutional survival at any cost. The personal and institutional struggles to which these dilemmas give rise often result in *values contortions* and a process of *values drift* (Gewirtz *et al.*, 1993b). While no school is immune to the disciplines of the market, some are more subtly *re-oriented* by the language and culture of the market and others are thoroughly *colonised* (Mclaughlin, 1991). In many cases, such values tensions in schools emphasize the 'gap' in purposes, concerns and careers between managers and teachers (Bowe *et al.*, 1992).

The 'decomprehensivization' of secondary schooling

In the two decades preceding the Education Reform Act 1988, it has been possible to speak of a process of comprehensivization within school education in England. A comprehensive system of educational provision is based on the principles that it is socially and educationally advantageous for all children, whatever their ability, class or ethnic background, to be educated together in a 'common school' and in mixed-ability groups, and that all children should have access to a learning environment which enables them to realize their potential. Since the Warnock Report (1978), a central tenet of English comprehensivism has been that the majority of children with SEN are better achievers when integrated in mainstream schools and in mainstream classes. This is predicated on the argument that 'the higher the range of achievement and expectation within an educational community, the higher standards all children will reach' (Housden, 1993: 8). The available evidence suggests that comprehensivization is of particular benefit to working-class children. The school 'context' (or social class nature of the pupil composition) has been shown to be an important factor in affecting achievement (Coleman *et al.*, 1966: Bridge *et al.*, 1979). Data from Scotland suggest that

comprehensive reorganisation substantially reduced between-school SES [socio-economic status] segregation . . . This gave manual pupils access to more 'favourable' school contexts, and is probably one reason why levels of attainment rose faster for manual pupils up to the mid-1980s than for non-manual pupils.

(Echols *et al.*, 1990: 217)

However, England has never had a completely comprehensive system (comprehensivization was more thorough in Scotland): status hierarchies persisted throughout the so-called comprehensive era; only a minority of schools had fully comprehensive intakes; a few LEAs never undertook comprehensive re-organization; and middle-class families have always benefited disproportionately within this continuingly diverse educational provision (Mortimore and Blackstone, 1982). This situation, which is replicated in other areas of welfare, is used by supporters of public sector markets to bolster their arguments. Gray (1993: 104), for instance, claims: 'There is no persuasive ethical justification for the massive, over extended welfare states of most modern societies, which often involve perverse redistributions to the middle-classes.' Such 'perverse redistributions' have led a number of observers to question why those on the left are so opposed to the recent welfare reforms. We would argue, however, with respect to education, that although the pre-1988 English education system was far from perfectly comprehensive, many schools were able to maintain relatively mixed intakes and to develop, often in conjunction with LEAs, policies and strategies designed to promote equal opportunity for students on the basis of class, 'race', gender and ability. We share the view of Housden (1993: 13): 'However flawed the concept may originally have been, the comprehensive structure has created the conditions for the further development of inclusive strategies.'

Our evidence suggests that the processes of the English market seem to be halting and reversing such developments and contributing to a process of 'decomprehensivization'. As we have indicated, parents participate differently in the education market and for some children the costs of these differences are considerable. Across schools, we appear to be seeing an intensification of status hierarchies, provisional differentiation and segregation within the state system. Working-class children, and particularly children with SEN, are likely to be increasingly 'ghetto-ized' in underresourced and understaffed low-status schools. The effects of school 'context' on pupil achievement, together with the underresourcing and understaffing of such schools, are likely to significantly impair the learning achievements of the children attending them. Because ethnic-minority children are disproportionately represented amongst the economically disadvantaged sections of the population, they are likely also to be disproportionately represented in the underresourced and understaffed schools. The re-introduction of setting and the devalorisation of SEN means that within schools, segregation and provisional differentiation also seem to be occurring.

Conclusion

Effectively, the market system of education and the concomitant processes of decomprehensivization mean that resources are flowing from those children with greatest need to those with least need. Thus we are seeing a growing inequality of access to the quality of provision necessary for children to succeed educationally. This is perhaps not surprising given that the architects of the English market were not primarily committed to needs-based equity. However, our research also indicates that the English market fails the desert-based equity test, as we defined it in Chapter 1, because success in the marketplace is not primarily a function of family motivation but rather of parental skill, social and material advantages, the perceived raw-score potential of the child, and, to some extent, pure chance.

In many ways, the education markets we have been researching are peculiar and specific to metropolitan areas within England where parents have access, geographically, to a range of schools and where there is genuine competition between schools for children. However, we believe that there are lessons to be learned from our research, lessons which are of relevance across and beyond England. The class nature of the market as a mode of social engagement, and the advantages it thereby offers to the middle classes, are likely to be replicated whatever the particular market form adopted. Middle-class parents, we suggest, will always be most inclined to engage with the market and best skilled to exploit it to their children's advantage. The market is a perverse system of education income allocation in this respect, in that children are rewarded largely in proportion to the skill and interest of their parents. That some parents make choices on the basis of the class and 'racial' composition of schools is also likely to be a general characteristic of markets in socially and culturally diverse societies. That schools are increasingly oriented towards meeting the perceived demands of middle-class parents, however, may well be a more specific product of the English market. It is the outcome of a market where funding takes minimal account of pupils' needs, where there is a highly regulated curriculum and regime of testing which encourages segregation and provisional differentiation, where schools are made to feel they are going to be primarily judged on their raw examination scores, and where the devices of selection and exclusion are permitted as means of controlling pupil compositions.

Typically, advocates of choice in education respond to the English 'market-in-practice' as being a deformed version of their 'market-in-theory'. However, the market-in-theory is a utopian vision which is constructed outside of the political and financial realities of modern education systems. It ignores the class interests represented within the state. It rests on forms of regulation and funding provisions and distributions which lie well outside the financial limits currently being imposed upon public education. And it takes no account of the drive for political legitimation and control which are so central to the contemporary concerns of the state. The market-in-practice in England is a subtle and multi-facetted instrument. It rests on a rhetoric of school autonomy and parental freedom of choice but delivers a very effective means of surrogate control. It also provides a mechanism for driving down educational expenditures which draws upon a discourse of efficiency and which effectively uses the procedures of competitive formula funding to disguise cuts in public expenditure. Individual institutions are left with the freedom to manage their own contraction. Furthermore, the ideology of the market is introduced by, and introduces, a common *management mode of regulation* across the private and public sectors based on non-principled self interest. Management here is a 'transformational force' (Clarke and Newman, 1992) set over and against the values of welfare professionalism. Finally, the education market serves to further the ideological dissemination of the commodity form (Offe, 1984). The contradictions and 'planning' interventions in the English market-in-practice indeed reflect and represent generic political and economic problems faced by the state, as well as conflicting ideological positions within the Government.

Given the above, it still might be possible, with some imagination, to regulate an education market in ways which encourage a more equitable outcome on a needs-based definition of equity. By adopting needs-led funding, more educationally useful performance indicators and assessment procedures, and by completely removing from schools the right to control their own pupil compositions, it may well be possible to curb the iniquities associated with relatively uncontrolled choice and competition, for example by the recommendations made by Adler (1993) and Walford (1993). In a market system divested of provisional and intake differentials, however, it is highly questionable whether any demand for choice in education would be sustained. This is because, on the whole, parental desire for choice is a response to inequitable provision. But choice, however regulated, is not the *solution* to inequity. From a needs-based perspective, primacy needs to be given to establishing comprehensive pupil intakes, to allocating resources in ways which will facilitate the realization of children's learning potentials, and to making schools responsive to the values and cultures of the children that go to them. It is regulation, commitment and flair, not choice, that is necessary for the realization of these goals. As far as equity is concerned, choice is a dangerous irrelevance.

GLOSSARY OF TERMS*

General

CTC	City Technology College
DES	Department of Education and Science (UK Ministry of Education re-organized in 1994 as DFE)
DFE	Department for Education
EWO	Education Welfare Officer
GCSE	General Certificate of Secondary Education (public examination for 16-year olds)
GM (GMS)	Grant Maintained (status) (schools which, by vote of parents have 'opted out' of LEA control, are funded directly by DFE and have additional 'autonomies' as a result)
LEA	Local Education Authority
LMS	Local Management of Schools (system of devolved school budgets, where schools have control over all of their own expenditures)
NUT	National Union of Teachers
OFSTED	Office for Standards in Education
SEN	Special Educational Needs
SMT	Senior Management Team
TQM	Total Quality Management

* Names represent those of actual LEAs, schools and locations which have been altered to preserve anonymity.

Local Education Authorities

Brokerage	Large, middle-class county LEA to south of Westway
Burbley	Upper-middle-class county LEA to south of Riverway
Eldridge	Urban LEA north of Westway
Fanshaw	Urban LEA east of Westway
Fromley	Urban LEA north of Westway
Kensea	Inner-urban LEA north of Northwark
Mersley	LEA to south of Northwark, has secondary transfer age 13 years
Northwark	Case-study LEA
Riverway	Case-study LEA
Streetley	LEA to east of Northwark with poor reputation for its schools
Westway	Case-study LEA

Secondary schools

Arthur Lucas	Boys' comprehensive in Burbley LEA
Blenheim	Comprehensive in Riverway LEA
Cardinal Heenan	GM boys' Catholic school in Fanshaw
Brookside	Girls' comprehensive school merged to form Martineau school
Carbridge Technology College	In north Northwark. Formerly known as Carbridge Road School, which had a poor reputational history, it was redesignated as an LEA Technology College in 1993.
Corpus Christi	Ecumenical comprehensive, Riverway LEA
Crawford Park	Boys' comprehensive closed by Northwark LEA
Elizabeth Anderson	Girls' comprehensive closed by Northwark LEA
Fletcher	Case-study school, Riverway LEA
Flightpath	Case-study school, Westway LEA
Florence Nightingale	Girls' LEA foundation school in Kensea LEA
Goddard	Case-study school, Riverway LEA
Gorse	Comprehensive, Westway LEA, rival of Flightpath and Lymethorpe schools
Hutton	GM rival of Martineau and Northwark Park schools
Lockmere	Comprehensive school, Riverway LEA, rival of Overbury school

Lymethorpe	Case-study comprehensive school, Westway LEA
Martineau	Case-study girls' GM school, Northwark LEA
Milton	Case-study GM school, Northwark LEA
Nancy Astor Girls	Girls' comprehensive in Burbley LEA
Northwark Park	Case-study comprehensive school, Northwark LEA
Overbury	Case-study comprehensive school, Riverway LEA
Pankhurst	Case-study girls' comprehensive school, Riverway LEA
Parkside	Case-study comprehensive school, Westway LEA
Parsons	Case-study comprehensive school, Riverway LEA
Princess Elizabeth	LEA girls' foundation school in Kensea LEA
Ramsay Macdonald	LEA boys' school, Northwark LEA
Reverend Smith	LEA comprehensive in Brokerage LEA, rival of Lymethorpe school
Robin Hood	Boys' comprehensive closed by Northwark LEA
Sacred Heart	Girls' Catholic School in Mersley LEA
St Ignatious	Case-study Catholic comprehensive school, latterly GM
Suchard	Grammar school in Burbley LEA
The CTC	In Northwark, established 1991
Trumpton	Case-study GM school, Northwark LEA

Independent schools

Camberwick HS	Girls' school, Mersley
Green House	Prep school, Riverway
Harrod	Mixed school, Riverway
Jericho	Prep school, Riverway
Lady Bracknell	Girls' school, Riverway
Madeley High	Girls' school, Northwark
Trinity	Boys' school, Northwark

Primary schools

Angrave	Northwark LEA
Chinon	Riverway LEA
Grasshopper	Westway LEA

John Noakes	Northwark LEA
Ladybird	Westway LEA
Nelson	Riverway LEA
Randleside	Northwark LEA
St Bernadette	Northwark LEA
St Joseph's	Northwark LEA
Windsor	Riverway LEA
St Helena	Riverway LEA
Smith Street	Westway LEA

Geographical locations

Carbridge	Area in north Northwark
Lockmere	Area in Riverway
Misslethwaite	Area in north-east Westway, bordering on Riverway
Pendry	Area in north Riverway
Riseborough	Area in Northwark/Riverway borders
Tidewash	Area in Riverway
Walford	Outer-London industrial area
Westing	Area in south Northwark

REFERENCES

Adler, M. (1993). An alternative approach to parental choice. In *Briefings for the Paul Hamlyn Foundation National Commission on Education*. London: Heinemann.

Adler, M., Petch, A. and Tweedie, J. (1989). *Parental Choice and Educational Policy*. Edinburgh: Edinburgh University Press.

Angus, L. (1994). Sociological analysis and educational management: the social context of the self-managing school. *British Journal of Sociology of Education* 15(1): 79–92.

Ball, S. J. (1981). *Beachside Comprehensive: A Case Study of Secondary Schooling*. Cambridge: Cambridge University Press.

Ball, S. J. (1987). *The Micropolitics of the School: Towards a Theory of School Organisation*. London: Routledge.

Ball, S. J. (1990). *Politics and Policymaking in Education*. London: Routledge.

Ball, S. J., Bowe, R. and Gewirtz, S. (1994). Competitive schooling: values, ethics and cultural engineering. *Journal of Curriculum and Supervision* 9(4): 350–367.

Ball, S. J., Bowe, R. and Gewirtz, S. (1995). Circuits of schooling: a sociological exploration of parental choice of school in social class contexts. *Sociological Review* 43(1): 52–78.

Bartlett, W. (1992). *Quasi-Markets and Educational Reforms: A Case Study*. Bristol: School for Advanced Urban Studies, University of Bristol.

Bash, L. and Coulby, D. (1989). *The Education Reform Act: Competition and Control*, London: Cassell.

Baudrillard, J. (1983). *Simulations*. New York: Semiotext(e).

Bernstein, B. (1975). *Class, Codes and Control*. Volume 1. London: Routledge.

Blank, R. (1990). Educational effects of magnet high schools. In Witte, J. and

Clune, J. (eds) *Choice and Control in American Education, Volume 2: The Practice of Choice, Decentralization and School Restructuring*. Basingstoke: Falmer Press.

Bottery, M. (1992). *The Ethics of Educational Management*. London: Cassell.

Bottery, M. (1994). *Lessons for Schools? A Comparison of Business and Educational Management*. London: Cassell.

Boulton, P. and Coldron, J. (1989). *The Pattern and Process of Parental Choice*. Sheffield: Department of Education, Sheffield City Polytechnic.

Bourdieu, P. (1986). *Distinction: A Social Critique of the Judgement of Taste*. London: Routledge.

Bourdieu, P. and Passeron, J-C. (1990). *Reproduction*. London: Sage.

Bourdieu, P. and Wacquant L. (1992). *An Invitation to Reflexive Sociology*. Oxford: Polity Press.

Bourne, J., Bridges, L. and Searle, C. (1994). *Outcast England: How Schools Exclude Black Children*. London: Institute of Race Relations.

Bowe, R. (1995). *Globalising the Education Market*. ESRC Market Forces in Education Project Paper No.13.

Bowe, R. and Ball, S. J. with Gold, A. (1992). *Reforming Education and Changing Schools: Case Studies in Policy Sociology*. London: Routledge.

Bowe, R., Ball, S. J. and Gewirtz, S. (1994). Captured by the discourse? Issues and concerns in researching 'Parental Choice'. *British Journal of Sociology of Education* 15(1): 63–78.

Bowe, R., Ball, S. J. and Gewirtz, S. (1995). Market forces, inequality and the city. In Jones, H. and Lansley, J. (eds) *Social Policy and the City*. Aldershot: Avebury House Press.

Bridge, R. G., Judd, C. M. and Moock, P. R. (1979). *The determinants of educational outcomes: The impact of families, peers, teachers and schools*. Cambridge, MA: Ballinger.

Bush, T., Coleman, M. and Glover, D. (1993). *Managing Autonomous Schools: the Grant-Maintained Experience*. London: Paul Chapman.

Caldwell, B. and Spinks, J. (1988). *The Self-Managing School*. Lewes: Falmer.

Carlen, P., Gleeson, D. and Wardhaugh, J. (1992). *Truancy: the Politics of Contemporary Schooling*. Buckingham: Open University Press.

Carspecken, P. (1990). *Community Schooling and the Nature of Power: The Battle for Croxteth Comprehensive*. London: Routledge.

Chenoweth, T. (1987). Unanticipated consequences of schools of choice: some thoughts on the case of San Francisco. *Equality and Choice* 5(7).

Chubb, J. and Moe, T. (1990). *Politics, Markets and America's Schools*. Washington, DC: The Brookings Institution.

CIPFA (1993). *Education Statistics 1993–4 Estimates*. London: CIPFA.

Clarke, J. (1979). Capital and Culture. In Clarke, J., Critcher, C. and Johnson, R. (eds) *Working Class Culture*. London: Hutchinson.

Clarke, J. and Newman, J. (1992). 'Managing to Survive: Dilemmas of Changing Organisational Forms in the Public Sector'. Paper presented at Social Policy Association Conference, University of Nottingham, July.

Clarke, K. (1991). 'Education in a Classless Society.' Westminster Lecture to the Tory Reform Group, 12 June 1991.

Clarke, P. and Round, E. (1991). *The Good State Schools Guide.* London: Ebury Press.

Coldron, J. and Boulton, P. (1991). 'Happiness' as a criterion of parents' choice of school. *Journal of Education Policy* **6**(2): 169–178.

Coleman, J. S., Campbell, E. Q., Hobson, C. J., McPartland, J., Mood, A. M., Weinfeld, F. D., and York, R. I. (1966). *Equality of Educational Opportunity.* Washington, DC: U. S. Government Printing Office.

Commission for Racial Equality (1993). *Draft Circular on Admission Arrangements – Comments by CRE,* February. London: CRE.

Considine, M. (1988). The corporate management framework as administrative science; a critique. *Australian Journal of Public Administration* **37**(1): 4–18.

Coopers and Lybrand (1988). *The Local Management of Schools: A Report to the DES.* London: Coopers and Lybrand.

Cremin, L. A. (1979). *Public Education.* New York: Basic Books.

Cribb, A. (1995). A Turn for the Better? Philosophical Issues in Evaluating Health Care Reforms. In Seedhouse, D. (ed.) *Reforming Health Care.* Chichester: John Wiley and Sons.

Crump, S. J. (1994). *Public School Choice: A Pragmatist Perspective.* Sydney: Department of Social and Policy Studies in Education, University of Sydney.

Dale, R. (1994). National reform, economic crisis and 'New Right' theory: a New Zealand perspective. *Discourse* **14**(2): 17–29.

Dale, R. and Ozga, J. (1993). Two hemispheres – both New Right? In Lingard, R., Knight, J. and Porter, P. (eds) *Schooling Reform in Hard Times.* London: Falmer Press.

David, M., West, A. and Ribbens, J. (1994). *Mothers' Intuition: Choosing Secondary Schools.* London: Falmer Press.

Deem, R., Brehony, K. and Heath, S. (1994). Governors, schools and the miasma of the market.' *British Education Research Journal* **20**(4): 535–550.

DES (1991). *The Parent's Charter.* London: Department of Education and Science.

DFE (1993). *Report on LEA Recoupment Procedures.* London: Department for Education.

DFE (1994). *Our Children's Education: The Updated Parent's Charter.* London: Department for Education.

Domanico, R. (1989). *Model for Choice: A Report on Manhattan's District 4.* New York: Manhattan Institute for Policy Research.

Duncan, S. and Goodwin, M. (1988). *The Local State and Uneven Development.* Cambridge: Polity Press.

Echols, F. H. and Willms, J. D. (1993). *Scottish Parents and Reasons for School Choice.* Vancouver: Department of Social and Educational Studies, University of British Columbia.

Echols, F., McPherson, A. and Willms, J. D. (1990). Parental choice in Scotland. *Journal of Education Policy* **5**(3): 207–222.

Edwards, T. and Whitty, G. (1992). Parental choice and educational reform in Britain and the United States. *British Journal of Educational Studies* **40**(2): 101–117.

Edwards, T., Fitz, J. and Whitty, G. (1989). *The State and Private Education: An Evaluation of the Assisted Places Scheme*. Lewes: Falmer Press.

Espinola, V. (1992). *Decentralization of the Education System and the Introduction of Market Rules in the Regulation of Schooling: The Case of Chile*. Santiago: Centro de Investigación y Desarrollo de la Educación.

Featherstone, M. (1992). *Consumer Culture and Postmodernism*. London: Sage.

Fitz, J., Halpin, D. and Power, S. (1993). *Grant Maintained Schools: Education in the Market Place*. London: Kogan Page Educational Management Series.

Fliegel, S. (1990). Creative non-compliance. In Witte, J. and Clune, J. (eds) *Choice and Control in American Education*, Volume 2: *The Practice of Choice, Decentralization and School Restructuring*. Basingstoke: Falmer Press.

Flude, M. and Hammer, M. (eds.) (1990). *The Education Reform Act 1988*. Lewes: Falmer Press.

Gewirtz, S. (1994). Market discipline versus comprehensive education: a case study of a London comprehensive school struggling to survive in the education market place. *New Policy Contexts for Education*. Kallos, D. and Llindblad, S. (eds) Umeå: Pedagogiska Institutionen, Umeå Universitet.

Gewirtz, S., Ball, S. and Bowe, R. (1993a). Parents, privilege and the education market. *Research Papers in Education* **9**(1): 3–29.

Gewirtz, S., Ball, S. J. and Bowe, R. (1993b). Values and ethics in the marketplace: the case of Northwark Park. *International Journal of Sociology of Education* **3**(2): 233–254.

Giddens, A. (1984). *The Constitution of Society*. Oxford: Polity Press.

Glenn, C. (1990). Perestroika for American education. In Richards, W. and Firestone, C. (eds) *Rethinking Effective Schools*. Englewood Cliffs, NJ: Prentice Hall.

Goldring, E. B. and Shapira, R. (1993). Choice, empowerment and involvement: what satisfies parents? *Educational Evaluation and Policy Analysis* **15**(4): 396–409.

Gray, J. (1993). *Beyond the New Right: Markets, Government and the Common Environment*. London: Routledge.

Gray, L. (1991). *Marketing Education*. Buckingham: Open University Press.

Grieco, M. (1991). *Low Income Families and Inter-Household Dependency: The Implications for Policy and Planning*. Oxford: University of Oxford, Transport Studies Unit.

Grieco, M. and Pearson, M. (1991). *Spatial Mobility Begins at Home? Re-Thinking Inter-Household Organisation*. Oxford: University of Oxford, Transport Studies Unit.

Grieco, M., Jones, P. and Polack, P. (1991). *Time to Make the Connection*. Oxford: University of Oxford, Transport Studies Unit.

Halpin, D. and Troyna, B. (in press). The Politics of Education Policy Borrowing. *Comparative Education* **31**(3).

Hargreaves, D. (1967). *Social Relations in a Secondary School*. London: Routledge and Kegan Paul.

Harvey, D. (1989). *The Condition of Postmodernity*. Oxford: Basil Blackwell.

Hatcher, R. (1994). Market relations and the management of teachers. *British Journal of Sociology of Education* **15**(1): 41–62.

Hayek, F. (1980). *Individualism and Economic Order*. Chicago: University of Chicago Press.

Hershkoff, H. and Cohen, A.S. (1992). School choice and the lessons of Choctaw County. *Yale Law and Policy Review* **10**(1): 1–29.

Housden, P. (1993). *Bucking the Market: LEAs and Special Needs*. Stafford: Nasen.

Hunter, J. B. (1989). *Which School? A Study of Parents' Choice of Secondary School*. London: ILEA, Research and Statistics Branch.

Johnson, T. (1972). *Professions and Power*. London: Macmillan.

Keep, E. (1992). Schools in the marketplace? Some problems with private sector models. In Wallace, G. (ed.) *Local Management of Schools: Research and Experience*. Clevedon: Multilingual Matters.

Kirby, M. (1992a). *Generating Income*. Cambridge: Pearson.

Kirby, M. (1992b). *Promoting Your School*. Cambridge: Pearson.

Lacey, C. (1970). *Hightown Grammar: The School as a Social System*. Manchester: Manchester University Press.

Lareau, A. (1989). *Home Advantage: Social Class and Parental Intervention in Elementary Education*. Lewes: Falmer Press.

Lauder, H., Hughes, D., Waslander, S., Thrupp, M., McGlinn, J., Newton, S. and Dupuis, A. (1994). *The Creation of Market Competition for Education in New Zealand*. Wellington: Department of Education, Victoria University at Wellington.

Le Grand, J. and Bartlett, W. (eds) (1993). *Quasi-Markets and Social Policy*. Basingstoke: Macmillan.

Lee, T. (1992). Local management of schools and special education. In Booth, T., Swann, W., Masterson, M. and Potts, P. (eds) *Policies for Diversity in Education*. London: Routledge.

Levačić, R. (1992). The LEA and its schools: The decentralised organisation and the internal market. In Wallace, G. (ed.) *Local Management of Schools: Research and Experience*. Clevedon: Multilingual Matters.

Levin, H. M. (1990). The theory of choice applied to education. In Witte, J. and Clune, J. (eds) *Choice and Control in American Education*, Volume 1: *The Theory of Choice, Decentralization and School Restructuring*. Basingstoke: Falmer Press.

Mclaughlin, R. (1991). Can the information systems for the NHS internal market work? *Public Money and Management*, Autumn: 37–41.

McPherson, A. F. and Willms, J. D. (1987). Equalization and Improvement: some effects of comprehensive reorganization in Scotland. *Sociology* **21**(4): 509–59.

Mintzberg, H. (1983). *Structure in Fives: Designing Effective Organisations*. Englewood Cliffs, NJ: Prentice Hall.

Moore, D. and Davenport, S. (1990). Choice: the new improved sorting machine. In Boyd, W. L. and Halberg, H. J. (eds) *Choice in Education: Potential and Problems*. Berkeley, CA: McCutchan.

Mortimore, J. and Blackstone, T. (1982). *Disadvantage and Education*. London, Heinemann.

Murgatroyd, S. and Morgan, C. (1993). *Total Quality Management and the School*. Buckingham: Open University Press.

Offe, C. (1984). *Contradictions of the Welfare State*. London: Hutchinson.

Ozga, J. (1992). Essay review: education management. *British Journal of Sociology of Education* **13**(3): 279–280.

Ozga, J. (1995). 'Markets, Management and the Manufacture of Consent in Primary Schools.' Paper presented to the Second Comparative Education Policy Seminar: Sweden and the UK, School of Education, King's College London. April, 1995.

Pardey, D. (1991). *Marketing for Schools*. London: Kogan Page.

Parsons, C., Benns, L., Hailes, J. and Howlett, K. (1994). *Excluding Primary School Children*. London: Family Policy Studies Centre.

Peters, T. (1989). *Thriving on Chaos*. London: Pan.

Peters, T. and Waterman, R. (1982). *In Search of Excellence*. London: Harper Row.

Plant, R. (1992). Enterprise in its place: the moral limits of markets. In Heelas, P. and Morris, P. (eds) *The Values of the Enterprise Culture*. London: Routledge.

Power, S. (1992). Researching the Impact of Education Policy: difficulties and discontinuities. *Journal of Education Policy* **7**(5): 493–500.

Power, S. (1994). Review of Bowe, Ball and Gold 'Reforming Education and Changing Schools'. *Journal of Curriculum Studies* **26**(5): 569–71.

Power, S., Fitz, J. and Halpin, D. (1994). 'The Grant-Maintained Schools Policy: The English Experience of Self-Governance.' Paper presented to American Educational Research Association Annual Meeting, New Orleans, April 1994.

Riches, C. and Morgan, C. (1989). *Human Resource Management in Education*. Buckingham: Open University Press.

Saltman, R. B. and Von Otter, C. (1992). *Planned Markets and Public Competition*. Buckingham: Open University Press.

Sinclair, J., Ironside, M. and Seifert, R. (1993). 'Classroom Struggle? Market Oriented Education Reforms and their Impact on Teachers' Professional Autonomy, Labour Intensification and Resistance.' Paper presented to the 11th Annual International Labour Process Conference, Blackpool, 1 April 1993.

Slaughter, D. T. and Schnieder, B. L. (1986). *Newcomers: Blacks in Private Schools*. Evanston, IL: Northwestern University Press.

Smyth, J. (ed.) (1993). *A Socially Critical View of the Self-Managing School*. London: Falmer Press.

Spalding, B. (1993). Money talks louder than special needs code, *Times Educational Supplement*, 19 November 1993.

Stillman, A. and Maychell, K. (1986). *Choosing Schools: Parents, LEAs and the 1980 Education Act*. Windsor: NFER/Nelson.

Storey, J. (1992). *Developments in the Management of Human Resources*. Oxford: Blackwell.

Strauss, A. L. (1987). *Qualitative Analysis for Social Scientists*. New York: Cambridge University Press.

Strauss, A. and Corbin, J. (1990). *Basics of Qualitative Research: Grounded Theory Procedure and Techniques*. Newbury Park, CA: Sage.

Thomas, A. and Dennison, B. (1991). Parental or pupil choice – who really decides in urban schools? *Education Management and Administration* **19**(4): 243–251.

Thomas, J. (1991). *Doing Critical Ethnography*. Newbury, CA: Sage.

Tomlinson, S. (1987). Curriculum option choices in multi-ethnic schools. In Troyna, B. (ed.) *Racial Inequality in Education*. London: Tavistock.

Troyna, B. (1978). Race and streaming: a case study. *Educational Review*, **30**(1): 59–65.

Troyna, B., Hatcher, R. and Gewirtz, D. (1993). *Local Management of Schools and Racial Equality*. London: Commission for Racial Equality.

Vincent, C. (1993). *Parental Participation in Primary Education*. Coventry: Centre for Research in Ethnic Relations, University of Warwick.

Vincent, C., Evans, J., Lunt, I. and Young, P. (1993). *The Market Forces? The Effect of Local Management of Schools on Special Educational Needs Provision*. London: Department of Policy Studies, Institute of Education, University of London.

Wacquant, L. (1989). Towards a Reflexive Sociology. *Sociological Theory* **7**(1): 26–63.

Walford, G. (1993). 'Selection for secondary schooling'. In *Briefings for the Paul Hamlyn Foundation National Commission on Education*. London: Heinemann.

Warner, D. and Leonard, C. (1992). *The Income Generation Handbook*. Buckingham: Open University Press/SRHE

Warner, D. and Kelly, G. (eds) (1993). *Managing Educational Property*. Buckingham: Open University Press/SRHE.

Weimann, G. (1982). On the importance of marginality: one more step in the two-way flow of information. *American Sociological Review* **47**: 764–773.

West, A. and Varlaam, A. (1991). Choosing a secondary school: parents of junior school children. *Educational Research* **33**(1): 22–30.

Whiteley, R. C. (1991). *The Customer Driven Company – Moving from Talk to Action*. New York: Addison-Wesley.

Whitty, G., Edwards, T., and Gewirtz, S. (1993). *Specialisation and Choice in Urban Education: The City Technology College Experiment*. London: Routledge.

Willey, M. (1989). LMS: A rising sense of alarm. *British Journal of Special Education* **16**(4).

Williams, E. (1994). The Exclusion Zone. *Search* 21 Winter: 11–14.

Williamson, B. (1981). Class bias. In Warren-Piper, D. (ed.) *Is Higher Education Fair?* Guildford: Society into Research into Higher Education.

Willms, J. D. and Echols, F. (1992). Alert and inert clients: the Scottish experience of parental choice of schools. *Economics of Education Review* **11**(4): 339–350.

Woods, P. (1992). Empowerment through choice? Towards an understanding of parental choice and school responsiveness. *Education Management and Administration* **20**(4): 204–211.

Woods, P. (1993). Responding to the consumer: parental choice and school effectiveness. *School Effectiveness and School Improvement* **4**(3): 205–229.

INDEX

EDUCATION REFORM
A CRITICAL AND POST-STRUCTURAL APPROACH

Stephen J. Ball

This book builds upon Stephen J. Ball's previous work in the field of education policy analysis. Its subjects the ongoing reforms in UK education to a rigorous critical interrogation. It takes as its main concerns the introduction of market forces, managerialism and the national curriculum into the organization of schools and the work of teachers. The author argues that these reforms are combining to fundamentally reconstruct the work of teaching, to generate and ramify multiple inequalities and to destroy civil virtue in education. The effects of the market and management are not technical and neutral but are essentially political and moral. The reforms taking place in the UK are both a form of cultural and social engineering and an attempt to recreate a fantasy education based upon myths of national identity, consensus and glory. The analysis is founded within policy sociology and employs both ethnographic and post-structuralist methods.

Contents
Preface – Glossary – Post-structuralism, ethnography and the critical analysis of educational reform – What is policy? Texts, trajectories and toolboxes – Education, Majorism and the curriculum of the dead – Educational policy, power relations and teachers' work – Cost, culture and control: self-management and entrepreneurial schooling – 'New headship' and school leadership: new relationships and new tensions – Educational markets, choice and social class: the market as a class strategy in the UK and USA – Competitive schooling: values, ethnics and cultural engineering – References – Index.

176pp   0 335 19272 6 (Paperback)   0 335 19273 4 (Hardback)

'GOOD SCHOOL, BAD SCHOOL'
EVALUATING PERFORMANCE AND ENCOURAGING IMPROVEMENT

John Gray and Brian Wilcox

- How can one tell a 'good' school from a 'bad' one?
- How should schools be judged?
- How best might schools be improved?

Questions about the quality of schooling have dominated the political agenda for much of the past decade. As a direct result new policies have been introduced involving more performance indicators, league tables of exam results, more frequent inspection and the closure of 'failing' schools.

Studies of school effectiveness and school improvement have much to contribute to these questions. Drawing on the latest research, John Gray and Brian Wilcox take a fresh and critical look at some of the reforms. How can one ensure that a broader view of what education is about is retained in the face of narrow performance indicators? What contribution can value-added approaches make to ensuring that schools in disadvantaged areas are judged more fairly? How sound are inspection procedures? What happens after a school has been inspected? How much do schools actually improve over time? And what prospects are there for turning round 'failing' schools rather than simply closing them?

Contents

304pp   0 335 19489 3 (Paperback)   0 335 19490 7 (Hardback)

ACTIVE CITIZENSHIP AND THE GOVERNING OF SCHOOLS
Rosemary Deem, Kevin J. Brehony and Sue Heath

- Should school governors be seen as active citizens or state volunteers?
- Can recent educational reforms and changes in the status of school governing bodies be seen as part of a wider political process?

Are all the activities of school governance equally open to both men and women and to members of minority ethnic groups?

Active Citizenship and the Governing of Schools draws on recent research evidence and theories from sociology, political science, gender studies and organizational analysis to answer these and many other questions.

The book examines whether educational reforms are attributable to 'new right' ideologies or to broader notions of 'new managerialism', before looking critically at concepts of active citizenship, what constitutes lay administration of schools, and the knowledge resources drawn upon by lay school governors. Careful attention is paid to issues of class, gender and ethnicity, and the voices of both governors and teachers are heard throughout.

The book will be relevant to anyone concerned with critical public policy, the governance and management of schools and/or educational reform, including school governors, teachers and headteachers, policy makers and politicians. All three authors are experienced school governors.

Contents
School governance in the context of educational reform – Public policy, the New Right and 'new managerialism' – Active citizenship and school government – Lay administration and knowledge in the governance of schools – Governing schools: some organizational challenges – School governance, decision making and cultures of autonomy – Governors, power and political processes – School governors: citizens or state volunteers? – References – Index.

208pp   0 335 19183 5 (Paperback)   0 335 19184 3 (Hardback)